Getting Started with Unity 2018
Third Edition

A Beginner's Guide to 2D and 3D game development
with Unity

Dr. Edward Lavieri

BIRMINGHAM - MUMBAI

Getting Started with Unity 2018

Third Edition

Commissioning Editor: Kunal Chaudhari
Acquisition Editor: Larissa Pinto
Content Development Editor: Mohammed Yusuf Imaratwale
Technical Editor: Shweta Jadhav
Copy Editor: Safis Editing
Project Coordinator: Hardik Bhinde
Proofreader: Safis Editing
Indexer: Partik Shirodkar
Graphics: Jason Monterio
Production Coordinator: Shantanu Zagade

First published: August 2013
Second edition: May 2015
Third edition: March 2018

Production reference: 1160318

Published by Packt Publishing Ltd.
Livery Place
35 Livery Street
Birmingham
B3 2PB, UK.

ISBN 978-1-78883-010-2

www.packtpub.com

To Veronica Brentwood for being an inspiration

– Dr. Edward Lavieri

`mapt.io`

Mapt is an online digital library that gives you full access to over 5,000 books and videos, as well as industry leading tools to help you plan your personal development and advance your career. For more information, please visit our website.

Why subscribe?

- Spend less time learning and more time coding with practical eBooks and Videos from over 4,000 industry professionals

- Improve your learning with Skill Plans built especially for you

- Get a free eBook or video every month

- Mapt is fully searchable

- Copy and paste, print, and bookmark content

PacktPub.com

Did you know that Packt offers eBook versions of every book published, with PDF and ePub files available? You can upgrade to the eBook version at `www.PacktPub.com` and as a print book customer, you are entitled to a discount on the eBook copy. Get in touch with us at `service@packtpub.com` for more details.

At `www.PacktPub.com`, you can also read a collection of free technical articles, sign up for a range of free newsletters, and receive exclusive discounts and offers on Packt books and eBooks.

Contributors

About the author

Dr. Edward Lavieri, is a veteran game designer and developer with a strong academic background. He earned a Doctorate in Computer Science from Colorado Technical University. He has taught and been a curriculum developer since 2002. In 2008, he started a software design and development studio, focusing on educational games. He currently serves as the Founder and Creative Director of that studio. Edward authored several books on adaptive learning, Java, Unity, AWS Lumberyard, and LiveCode.

Thank you to Packt Publishing for your continual support and belief in me. There are so many great people at Packt that I worked with on this project, including, Larissa, Yusuf, the reviewers, technical editors, proofreaders, the indexer, and the marketing team. It is a pleasure to have worked with such an amazing team.

About the reviewers

Andreas Oehlke is a professional full-stack software engineer. He holds a bachelor's degree in computer science and loves to experiment with software and hardware. His trademark has always been his enthusiasm and affinity for electronics and computers. His hobbies include game development, building embedded systems, sports, and making music. He currently works full-time as a senior software engineer for a German financial institution. He has also worked as a consultant and game developer in San Francisco, CA. He is also the author of the book *Learning LibGDX Game Development*.

Ludovico Cellentani is a senior engine programmer at King AB, and he has been working as a professional game programmer for almost 20 years. During this time, he has worked on a number of games released on various platforms, spanning PC, consoles, and mobile.

During the past 6 years, he has worked on a considerable number of games, VR experiences, and gamification projects released for PC, mobile, and custom-built computer installations, all powered by the Unity game engine.

He is currently living with his wife and son in Stockholm, Sweden.

Packt is searching for authors like you

If you're interested in becoming an author for Packt, please visit `authors.packtpub.com` and apply today. We have worked with thousands of developers and tech professionals, just like you, to help them share their insight with the global tech community. You can make a general application, apply for a specific hot topic that we are recruiting an author for, or submit your own idea.

Table of Contents

Preface   1

Chapter 1: Downloading and Installing Unity   7

  Game engine overview   8

    Game engines for specific game genres   9

      First-person shooters (FPS)   9

      Third-person games   10

      Other game genres   12

    Available 3D game engines   12

      CryENGINE   12

      Lumberyard   13

      Microsoft's XNA Game Studio   13

      Unreal game engine   14

  Unity – past, present, and future   15

    Version 1.0 - 2005   15

    Version 2.0 - 2007   16

    Version 3.0 - 2010   17

    Version 4.0 - 2012   17

    Version 5.0 - 2015   18

    Version 2017 - 2017   18

    Version 2018 – 2018   19

  The case for Unity   20

    Unity features   20

      Editor   21

      Graphics   21

    Unity community   22

  System requirements   22

    Development system requirements   23

    Playback system requirements   24

  Downloading Unity   25

  Installing Unity   25

  Summary   28

Chapter 2: The Unity Interface   29
  Screen real estate   30
  Menu   31
    Unity   32
    File   33
    Edit   33
    Assets   35
    GameObject   36
    Component   37
    Window   38
    Help   41
  Scene view   42
  Game view   43
  Project window   45
  Hierarchy window   47
  Inspector window   48
  Toolbar   49
    Transform tools   50
    Gizmo Toggles   52
    Cloud and Account Buttons   53
    Layers and Layouts   53
  Layouts   54
  Summary   60
Chapter 3: Designing the Game   61
  Game concept   61
    Game idea   62
    Input controls   63
    Winning and losing   64
  Game characters   64
    Cucumber Man   65
    Cucumber Beetle   66
  Gameplay   68
    Game world layout   68
    Starting condition   70
    Point system   71

Heads-Up Display   72
The difficulty balance   74
Difficulty balance questions   74
Implementation plan   76
Project organization   77
Custom assets   78
Standard assets   80
Organization   80
Summary   81
Chapter 4: Creating Our Terrain   83
Creating the terrain   83
Working with height maps   84
Importing the terrain   84
Shaping the terrain   86
Smoothing our terrain   86
Creating our spawn points   88
Painting the terrain   90
Adding water   92
Saving your work   95
Adding vegetation   95
Summary   100
Chapter 5: Lights, Cameras, and Shadows   101
Working with cameras   102
Understanding camera projections   105
Orientating your frustum   105
Creating a Skybox   106
Using multiple cameras   108
Working with lighting   109
Directional lighting   110
Point lighting   111
Spot lighting   112
Area lighting   113
Implementing reflection probes   114
Understanding shadows   116

Summary	117
Chapter 6: Creating and Importing 3D Objects for Our Game	119
Understanding assets and GameObjects	120
Asset packages	121
Understanding GameObjects	122
Creating 3D objects in Unity	124
Using prefabs	126
Using additional 3D objects	128
Using the Unity Asset Store	128
Hands-on with the Unity Asset Store	130
Incorporating custom assets in our game	131
Working with imported assets	133
Planting Cherry Trees	134
Planting Cucumber Patches	137
Summary	140
Chapter 7: Implementing Our Player Character	141
Working with Unity's standard asset package	142
Importing the game character	144
Configuring a player controller	145
Fine-tuning our character	148
Fine-tuning the motor controls	148
Fine-tuning scale	151
Fine-tuning the Capsule Collider	153
Changing and refining input controls	154
Animating our player character	157
Reviewing the player controller script	157
Reviewing the Animator component	160
Previewing the animations	163
Terraforming the terrain for our Cucumber Man	164
Summary	164
Chapter 8: Implementing Our Non-Player Characters	165
Understanding the non-player characters	166
Importing the non-player characters into our game	167
Animating our non-player characters	168

Incorporating the non-player characters into our game   169
Working with the Animation Controller   171
Terraforming the terrain for our Cucumber Beetles   178
Designating a sandbox area   178
Planting additional cherry trees   179
Creating spawning sites   180
Adding cucumber patches to our terrain   181
Creating a cucumber patch area in the sandbox   182
Planting cucumber patches   183
Adding cucumbers to our terrain   185
Scripting our non-player characters   188
Getting organized   188
Beetle patrol   189
Beetle finds and eats cucumber   193
Beetle attacks player on the ground   195
Beetle stands to attack   196
Summary   201
Chapter 9: Adding a Heads-Up Display   203
Designing our Heads-Up Display   204
Working with a canvas   205
Adding the canvas   205
Adding the health bar UI components   206
Creating the Lives Remaining UI components   209
Adding the scoring UI components   210
Adding the cherry UI components   211
Adding the cucumber and Cucumber Beetle UI components   213
Creating a mini-map   215
Scripting for dynamic content   217
Scripting the cucumber count   218
Scripting the beetle count   219
Summary   220
Chapter 10: Scripting Our Points System   221
Collecting cherries from trees   221
Detecting collisions of Cucumber Man and cherry trees   222

Simulating the collection of cherries 223
Updating the inventory and HUD with cherry count 225
Adding the cherry-throwing capability 227
Creating a spot for the cherry 227
Writing a CherryControl script 229
Adding points based on cherry collection and combat hits 231
Creating a points manager script 231
Adding points for each cherry picked 232
Adding points for hitting a beetle with a cherry 234
Summary 235

Chapter 11: Scripting Victory and Defeat 237
Designing victory and defeat conditions 238
Updating the player's health 239
Scripting the health bar 239
Decrementing health 242
Implementing victory 243
Implementing defeat 246
Scripting defeat based on no cucumbers remaining 246
Scripting defeat for no lives remaining 247
Updating the HUD with lives remaining 248
Scripting the player character's respawning 249
Summary 252

Chapter 12: Adding Audio and Visual Effects to Our Game 253
Discovering Unity's audio system 254
Unity audio basics 254
Unity's Audio Mixer 255
Planning our game's audio 257
Implementing our game's audio 258
Importing audio assets 259
Implementing the Cucumber Beetle audio 260
Implementing the Cucumber Man audio 263
Introduction to Unity's lights and shadows 267
Adding light sources 268
Directional light 268

Point light   269
Spot light   270
Area light   270
Shadows   271
Discovering Unity's special effects   271
Particle System   272
Trail Renderer   274
Adding visual effects to our game   275
Adding a Point light to our cherry trees   275
Add a special effect using the Particle System   276
Summary   278
Chapter 13: Optimizing Our Game for Deployment   279
Using the Profiler window   280
Getting more out of the Profilers   282
Optimizing scripts   283
Optimized code example   284
Optimizing graphics rendering   285
Occlusion culling   285
Lighting   286
Mesh renderer   286
Additional optimizations   286
Level of detail   286
Static colliders   287
Creating builds   287
Understanding the Unity build process   287
Build settings   288
PC, Mac, and Linux standalone   289
iOS   290
tvOS   291
Android   292
HTML 5/WebGL   292
Facebook   293
Xbox One   294
PlayStation 4 and PlayStation Vita   294
Player Settings   294
Summary   296

Chapter 14: Virtual Reality   297

  Welcome to virtual reality   298

    Development tools   299

      Oculus   299

      GearVR   299

      OpenVR   300

      PlayStation VR   300

  Enabling virtual reality in Unity   300

    Requisite SDKs   301

    Configuring your Unity project   302

    Recommendations from Unity technologies   303

  Starter content   304

    Oculus VR   304

      Oculus Sample Framework   304

      Oculus Stereo Shading Re-Projection Sample   305

      Oculus Integration   306

    Vive software   307

      Vive Stereo Rendering Toolkit   307

      Vive Input Utility   307

      Vive Media Decoder   308

    NVIDIA   308

      NVIDIA VRWorks   308

      NVIDIA VR Samples   309

    Unity Technologies   310

  Summary   310

Other Books You May Enjoy   311

Index   315

Preface

With the pervasiveness of games and the use of gamification in nearly every industry, the desire to discover how to use state-of-the-art development software has never been so great. There is an increasing number of software tools available to help developers create amazing games for consoles, the web, desktop computers, and mobile devices. Game engines are among the most powerful of these tools available. The Unity 3D game engine is one of the elite game engines. It has been used to create popular 2D and 3D games by large game studios and indie developers. With a free version available, and the newest release of Unity, the time has never been better to start using Unity.

Getting Started with Unity 2018, Third Edition covers one of the most popular game engines available. This book will guide you through the entire process of creating a 3D game, from downloading the Unity game engine to publishing your game. You will enjoy the coverage of some exciting topics in this book, including player-controlled characters and animation. Whether you are just getting started as a game developer or have experience with Unity or other game engines, this book will provide you with a guided tour of developing games with Unity 2018. With clear explanations, tips, and ample screenshots, you will be provided with detailed steps to develop your game.

This book takes a practice hands-on approach to learning Unity 2018. As you progress through each chapter, you will build a 3D interactive game called Cucumber Beetle. As you create the game, you'll learn the key features of Unity 2018, including creating a game environment, animating characters, scripting, and more. All meshes, models, textures, animations, and other assets are available on the book's website.

By the time you complete the lessons in this book, you'll have the confidence to start using Unity 2018 to create your own games.

Who this book is for

This book is written for people new to Unity or those who have some experience with a version prior to Unity 2018. If you want to take a look at Unity 2018, get a refresher, or if you just want to see how games can be developed with a top game engine, this book is for you.

What this book covers

Chapter 1, *Downloading and Installing Unity*, gives an overview of game engines, followed by a deep look at Unity's beginnings, where the game engine is today, and how it progressed to being one of the top game engines in use today. Unity's capabilities and features are highlighted, and instructions are provided for downloading and installing it.

Chapter 2, *The Unity Interface*, examines Unity's primary views, windows, layouts, and the toolbar. The interface components covered in this chapter are the ones used most often.

Chapter 3, *Designing the Game*, covers the design of the book's featured game—Cucumber Beetle. The game design includes gameplay, game mechanics, the player character, the non-player characters, game assets, animations, and more. Screen mock-ups and narratives are used to document the game's design.

Chapter 4, *Creating Our Terrain*, features the creation and customization of game terrain. Shaping tools are introduced, and water and vegetation features are added to the game environment.

Chapter 5, *Lights, Cameras, and Shadows*, explores cameras and lighting in Unity. The chapter starts with a look at cameras to include perspectives, frustums, and Skyboxes. The use of multiple cameras to include mini-maps is covered. Different types of lighting, reflection probes, and shadows are also explored.

Chapter 6, *Creating and Importing 3D Objects for Our Game*, focuses on making the game environment more robust, and trees and other objects are added to the game scene. This chapter also examines the steps necessary to create 3D objects using Unity's native modeling tools. Assets are added to the game from the Unity Asset Store and from 3D assets prepared specifically for the Cucumber Beetle game.

Chapter 7, *Implementing Our Player Character*, incorporates the game's player character—the Cucumber Man. The character is imported, and the controls and animations are reviewed. By the end of the chapter, the game will be ready for testing in the game mode.

Chapter 8, *Implementing Our Non-Player Characters*, explains the non-player characters—the Cucumber Beetles. The beetles' 11 animations are examined and changes are made to the non-player character's animation controller. In addition, scripts will be written to control the non-player characters. Also, in this chapter, cucumber patches, cucumbers, and cherries are added to the game world.

Chapter 9, *Adding a Heads-Up Display*, covers the design and development of, and how to incorporate, a Heads-Up Display (HUD) in the game. A canvas is used to create text and graphics that provide visual indicators of points, health, and additional information to help the player maintain situational awareness during game play. A mini-map is also implemented.

Chapter 10, *Scripting Our Points System*, looks at the design, scripting, and implementation of the game's point system. This includes providing frame-by-frame updates to key onscreen components of the game's HUD.

Chapter 11, *Scripting Victory and Defeat*, dives into the design and scripting of the game's victory and defeat conditions. Scripts will be updated to manage the Cucumber Man's health, provide frame-by-frame onscreen updates, and ensure that a player life is lost when the health runs out. Character lives and respawning are also covered.

Chapter 12, *Adding Audio and Visual Effects to Our Game*, demonstrates the plan and implementation of audio and visual effects in the game to help enhance overall game play. Specifically, audio is added to the key events in the combat system and several special effects, using Unity's particle system, are added to the game.

Chapter 13, *Optimizing Our Game for Deployment*, discusses optimization and deployment. The steps required to diagnose Unity games for performance problems are explored, in addition to how to optimize scripts and graphic rendering. The Unity build process is explained along with how to create a standalone player and how to deploy games for multiple platforms.

Chapter 14, *Virtual Reality*, examines Unity's capabilities with regard to virtual reality. An introduction to Virtual Reality is provided, including the hardware requirements. you will learn how to create a Virtual Reality game using the Unity game engine.

To get the most out of this book

You do not need to have experience of programming, working with game engines, or knowledge of Unity to benefit from this book. No assumptions have been made regarding knowledge or experience.

The only software requirement is downloading and installing the Unity game engine. Those steps are detailed in the book, so no software is required before you start reading.

Download the example code files

You can download the example code files for this book from your account at
`www.packtpub.com`. If you purchased this book elsewhere, you can visit
`www.packtpub.com/support` and register to have the files emailed directly to you.

You can download the code files by following these steps:

1. Log in or register at `www.packtpub.com`.
2. Select the SUPPORT tab.
3. Click on Code Downloads & Errata.
4. Enter the name of the book in the Search box and follow the onscreen instructions.

Once the file is downloaded, please make sure that you unzip or extract the folder using the latest version of:

- WinRAR/7-Zip for Windows
- Zipeg/iZip/UnRarX for Mac
- 7-Zip/PeaZip for Linux

The code bundle for the book is also hosted on GitHub at `https://github.com/PacktPublishing/Getting-Started-with-Unity-2018-Third-Edition`. In case there's an update to the code, it will be updated on existing GitHub repository.

We also have other code bundles from our rich catalog of books and videos available at `https://github.com/PacktPublishing/`. Check them out!

Download the color images

We also provide a PDF file that has color images of the screenshots/diagrams used in this book. You can download it here: `http://www.packtpub.com/sites/default/files/downloads/GettingStartedwithUnity2018ThirdEdition_ColorImages.pdf`.

Conventions used

There are a number of text conventions used throughout this book.

`CodeInText`: Indicates code words in text, database table names, folder names, filenames, file extensions, pathnames, dummy URLs, user input, and Twitter handles. Here is an example: "Ensure the `Skybox` folder is selected in the **Project** panel"

A block of code is set as follows:

```
public AudioSource audioSource;
public AudioClip eating;
public AudioClip attack;
public AudioClip die;
```

Bold: Indicates a new term, an important word, or words that you see onscreen. For example, words in menus or dialog boxes appear in the text like this. Here is an example: "Select Fill option from the **HUD_canvas**."

 Warnings or important notes appear like this.

 Tips and tricks appear like this.

Get in touch

Feedback from our readers is always welcome.

General feedback: Email `feedback@packtpub.com` and mention the book title in the subject of your message. If you have questions about any aspect of this book, please email us at `questions@packtpub.com`.

Errata: Although we have taken every care to ensure the accuracy of our content, mistakes do happen. If you have found a mistake in this book, we would be grateful if you would report this to us. Please visit `www.packtpub.com/submit-errata`, selecting your book, clicking on the Errata Submission Form link, and entering the details.

Piracy: If you come across any illegal copies of our works in any form on the Internet, we would be grateful if you would provide us with the location address or website name. Please contact us at `copyright@packtpub.com` with a link to the material.

If you are interested in becoming an author: If there is a topic that you have expertise in and you are interested in either writing or contributing to a book, please visit `authors.packtpub.com`.

Reviews

Please leave a review. Once you have read and used this book, why not leave a review on the site that you purchased it from? Potential readers can then see and use your unbiased opinion to make purchase decisions, we at Packt can understand what you think about our products, and our authors can see your feedback on their book. Thank you!

For more information about Packt, please visit `packtpub.com`.

1

Downloading and Installing Unity

In this chapter, you will learn about game engines and look at four different types before focusing on Unity. Once that foundation is set, we will start taking a deep look at Unity's beginnings, where the game engine is today, and how it has progressed to being one of the top game engines in use today. We will highlight Unity's capabilities and features. We will then review the system requirements for developing Unity as well as running, Unity games. Finally, we will download and install Unity.

Our topics for this chapter are:

- Game engine overview
- Unity—past, present, and future
- The case for Unity
- System requirements
- Downloading Unity
- Installing Unity

Game engine overview

A game engine can be defined as a set of tools that provide the functionality you need to develop and deploy video games. There is no single industry-accepted definition for game engines. That is largely due to the varied nature of them and their uses. Typically, game engines have at least the following set of features:

- 2D and/or 3D graphic design tools
- Animation
- Asset management—the ability to create and import game assets
- Audio support
- Cross-platform deployment—games can be made for multiple platforms (such as desktop, mobile, and console)
- Graphical user interfaces
- Networking—support for multiplayer games
- Physics
- Scripting support in one or more languages

The basic concept of game engines is that they provide a powerful set of tools to handle much of the grunt work of game development, allowing developers to focus on game aesthetics and gameplay. In the early days of video games, each game was coded from scratch without a game engine's libraries or capabilities. Instead of reinventing the wheel for each game, game engines started to emerge, making it easier for game studios to churn out games.

Game engines are not general-purpose software suites that can create any game imaginable. They are highly specialized and, although very flexible, are intended for a specific range of game genres. For example, the Ego Game Technology Engine by Codemasters is used primarily for creating racing games; Pyrogenesis, by Wildfire Games, is used for creating **real-time-strategy** (**RTS**) games; the Silent Storm Engine, by Nival Interactive, is used predominately for turn-base tactics games; and ONScripter, by Naomi Takahashi, is used for creating visual novels and first-person adventure games.

Game engines for specific game genres

There are a plethora of game engines available; many of them are free, some are open source, and others are proprietary. Selecting the right game engine for your game project is a critical pre-development step. Not every game engine will work for your game, and no single game engine will work for every game. Fortunately, we have a lot of options available to us.

When deciding on which game engine to use for a given game project, consider the typical characterization of games in the primary genre that your game is a part of.

 We use the phrase *primary genre* because many modern games blur the genre lines and incorporate characteristics of two or more genres. This genre blurring can result in new and innovative games.

First-person shooters (FPS)

This game genre has a long list of successful titles; here are some of them:

- Battlefield
- Bioshock
- Borderlands
- Call of Duty
- Destiny
- Doom
- HalfLife
- Halo
- Left4Dead
- Overwatch
- Rainbow Six

FPS games are created with the intent of immersing the player in the game world. They are playing as a character and, to obtain the desired level of immersion, animations, audio, and graphics quality are critically important. Special attention is given to the character's arms and weapons:

These games are typically characterized by the following:

- Large 3D segmented game worlds (indoors and outdoors)
- Character travels primarily on foot
- Some vehicle usage
- Standard camera and aiming controls
- Realistic animations
- Large and realistic inventory of hand-held objects (weaponry)
- **Non-player characters** (**NPCs**) with realistic artificial intelligence
- Single and multi-player modes

Third-person games

Third-person games are games where the player character is nearly or completely visible in the game scene. This genre includes **third-person shooters** (**TPS**) and third-person action/adventure. That means that a considerable effort needs to be focused on a character's appearance and animations. These games are based on the third-person character perspective as illustrated here:

Here are some of the more successful and popular third-person games:

- Dead Space
- Gears of War
- Grand Theft Auto
- Prince of Persia
- Rainbow Six
- Resident Evil
- SOCOM
- Splinter Cell
- Uncharted

These games are typically characterized by the following, in addition to the characteristics listed in the previous section for FPS games:

- Emphasis on the player character
- Camera that follows the player
- Player-controlled character motion sequences
- Full-bodied animations
- Character and camera rotation

Other game genres

There are a large number of other game genres, such as shooters, platformers, vehicle games, fighting, strategy, war, simulation, and puzzle. The difficulty in identifying a particular game's genre lies in the multiple ways in which game genres are classified. For example, you can have a TPS game that is also a **massively multiplayer online game** (**MMOG**) and, because it has a large number of puzzles, it can be added to the puzzle genre.

This is not something to be terribly concerned about. It is important to be able to identify what the key components of your game will be so that you can select the best available game engine for your project.

Available 3D game engines

In this section, we will briefly review selected leading game engines to give you a sense of what is available and what their capabilities are.

Because the Unity game engine is featured later in this chapter and used throughout this book, it is not covered in this section.

CryENGINE

CryENGINE is developed by Crytek. Interestingly, this game engine was initially created to produce a game demo for Nvidia, a **graphics processing unit** (**GPU**) manufacturer and because of that demo's great success, the game (Far Cry) was taken into full production and is now a commercial success. The game engine itself is also very successful.

The engine is freely available along with the full source code. There are no financial obligations for commercial use of CryENGINE such as royalties. This engine is capable of high-quality visuals and excellent performance, and you can develop games for the following platforms:

- Linux PC
- Oculus Rift
- Playstation 4
- Windows PC
- Xbox One

For further information on CryENGINE, I recommend *Mastering CryENGINE* by Packt Publishing: `https://www.packtpub.com/game-development/mastering-cryengine`.

Lumberyard

Lumberyard is part of the **Amazon Web Services (AWS)** platform and, at the time of this book's publication, is still in beta. This is a free AAA game engine based on CryENGINE. Lumberyard's unique selling point is that no other game engine offers deep integration with Amazon Web Services and Twitch.

 AAA, pronounced "triple-A," games are those with extremely large production and marketing budgets.

With this engine, you can develop for the following platforms:

- Android
- HTC Vive
- iOS
- Oculus Rift
- OSVR
- PC
- PlayStation 4
- PlayStation VR
- Xbox One

For further information on AWS Lumberyard, I recommend *Learning AWS Lumberyard Game Development* by Packt Publishing: `https://www.packtpub.com/game-development/learning-aws-lumberyard-game-development`.

Microsoft's XNA Game Studio

Microsoft's XNA Game Studio is a set of tools based on Microsoft's .NET framework. It is freely available. There are some redistribution restrictions that you will want to review if you plan to use this tool.

With XNA, you can develop for the following platforms:

- Windows PC
- Windows Phone
- Xbox 360

For further information on XNA, I recommend *Microsoft XNA 4.0 Game Development Cookbook* by Packt Publishing: `https://www.packtpub.com/game-development/microsoft-xna-40-game-development-cookbook`.

Unreal game engine

The Unreal game engine, by Epic Games, started as a **first-person shooter** (**FPS**) game nearly 20 years ago. Since that time, the Unreal game engine has significantly evolved and is now a freely-available AAA game engine. You can develop games with Unreal using C++ or Blueprints, a visual scripting system.

Unreal comes with several templates that make getting started very easy. These are:

- 2D File Scroller
- First Person
- Flying
- Puzzle
- Rolling
- Side Scroller
- Third Person
- Top Down
- Twin Stick Shooter
- Vehicle
- Vehicle Advanced

With Unreal, you can develop for the following platforms:

- Android
- Daydream
- HTML 5
- iOS
- Linux

- macOS
- Nintendo Switch
- Oculus Rift
- PlayStation 4
- PlayStation VR
- Samsung Gear VR
- Steam
- Viveport
- Windows PC
- Xbox One

For further information on Unreal, I recommend *Unreal Engine: Game Development from A to Z* by Packt Publishing: `https://www.packtpub.com/game-development/unreal-engine-game-development-z`.

Unity – past, present, and future

The Unity game engine was created by David Helgason, Nicolas Francis, and Joachim Ante in Copenhagen, Denmark, in 2004. They created the game engine to develop games, but ended up focusing on the game engine. Here is a brief look at its release history.

If you encounter a term or feature in this section that you are not familiar with, don't worry, we will cover them in subsequent sections and chapters.

Version 1.0 - 2005

This initial release could be used to develop projects for the macOS X operating system. The major features of Unity 1.0 included:

- Some documentation
- Transform script interface
- Alpha-mapped shaders
- Color-coded console warnings and errors
- Fully-sandboxed web player

Version 1.1 supported Microsoft Windows and web browsers as distribution platforms. It also included support for C/C++ external plugins.

Version 2.0 - 2007

Version 2.0 had several impressive features, including better support for projects made for the Windows platform. This release also improved the web player compatibility across platforms.

Engine updates included better graphic processing performance with the support of Microsoft's DirectX and OpenGL. The terrain engine was also introduced in this release, as was the ability for real-time soft shadows and networking.

The Unity Asset Server was also introduced in Version 2.0. This is an asset and version control system for teams working on Unity projects.

The major features of Unity 2.0 included:

- Terrain engine
- Video playback
- DirectX 9.0 renderer
- Networked multiplayer games
- Real-time dynamic shadows
- Game GUIs
- Web player streaming and compression
- Unity Asset Server
- Physics enhancements
- Scripting enhancements
- Water feature

After this, there were incremental releases. Most notably, Version 2.5 was released in 2009 and included cross-platform support so the Unity game engine could run on both Mac and Windows computers.

Version 3.0 - 2010

The release of Version 3.0 included a large number of new features and enhancements, as well as a large number of bug fixes in the editor, rendering, iOS-related, physics, scripting, and networking.

The major features of Unity 3.0 included:

- Support for Android OS
- Improved standard asset packages
- Improved editor
- New graphics features
- Asset pipeline improvements
- Audio improvements
- Physics improvements
- Documentation for scripting features

Version 3.5 represented a tremendous update and was released in 2011. It included support for Flash deployment. Additional key updates included:

- Shuriken particle system
- Built-in pathfinding
- Upgraded occlusion culling
- New level of detail
- Linear space lighting

Version 4.0 - 2012

Version 4.0 was released in 2012 and enabled game developers to create stunning gameplay and animations. The primary updates to the game engine for this release were:

- A new animation system called Mecanim
- Real-time shadows (for all platforms)
- Support for DirectX 11 rendering
- Updated the Shuriken particle system, including support for world collision

- Added new deployment platforms:
  - Linux
  - Adobe Flash
- Support for cross-platform dynamic fonts

Version 5.0 - 2015

Unity 5.0 launched with a free personal edition. This edition was provided to anyone with less than $100,000 in revenue or funding. No royalties were assessed either, making this a great way to get into the game industry without the initial expense of game engine technology. With the free version, published games included a non-customizable splash screen.

Key features in version 5.0 were:

- Performance improvements to 3D physics
- Animation system updates
- WebGL preview
- Visual fidelity enhancements with HDR reflection probes
- An audio mixer
- Real-time global illumination
- Physically-based standard shader

Version 2017 - 2017

In 2017, Unity Technologies announced that they would shift the version of the Unity game engine from an incremental number to the year of release. So the major release in 2017 was version 2017, and, since then, all minor releases in that year followed semantic versioning.

 Semantic versioning is a formal software versioning convention that uses a three-part version identification schema: major.minor.patch.

The actual first release of 2017 was as 2017.1 in July, 2017. Here are some of the major features introduced with Unity 2017:

- Timeline—a visual tool for creating cinematic content
- Cinemachine—an advanced camera system
- Post-processing—functionality where you can apply filters, controls, and more
- Unity Teams—a new cloud-based collaborative service
- Improved graphics and platform support
- Particle system improvements
- Progressive Lightmapper improvements
- 2D improvements
- Animation improvements
- Real-time shadow improvements

Version 2018 – 2018

The release of Unity 2018 is anticipated in – 2018">the spring of 2018. There will be some exciting enhancements to the game engine, especially with the stated focus of graphics.

Here are the highlights of the changes expected for Unity 2018:

- **Scriptable Rendering Pipelines (SRP)**: A new SRP API will be available, giving us finite control of the rendering pipeline via C# scripting. Unity 2018 will include two rendering pipelines (Lightweight and HD) that can be used, replicated, or modified.
- Upgraded post-processing stack: A new version of the post-processing stack includes automatic volume blending, and enhanced controls for custom effects.
- Shader graph: A visual interface for creating shaders.
- Integrated IDE: MonoDevelop will no longer be shipped with Unity as the integrated development environment for scripting. Windows users will receive Visual Studio 2017, and Mac users will receive Visual Studio for Mac. Visual Studio is a much more robust development environment.
- C# job system: This system will empower developers to create safer multithreaded code with performance gains.

The case for Unity

With so many game engine options available for both 2D and 3D game development, you might wonder why you should select Unity. The first release in 2005 introduced us to an excellent game engine that has been continually improved upon over the last decade with new features, support, and enhancements. With each new release, developers are presented with more functionality to help them develop stunning games.

Unity Technologies, the creators of Unity, is a well-established company dedicated to continual improvement of the game engine. As new processing technologies and platforms arise, Unity support will not be far behind. As with all Unity features, excellent official documentation accompanies all new functionality and features.

Being able to use a free version of the game engine without having to pay royalties is a game changer. Individuals, hobbyists, and small studios can make games using the same powerful game engine as large studios. In addition, the robust feature set and Unity community are additional factors that make Unity the right choice for your game development projects.

Unity features

In this section, we will list the core features of the Unity game engine. We will explore them in detail in subsequent chapters. Unity can be used to develop applications for the following devices, which span consoles, desktops, mobile, AR, TV, VR, and the web:

- Android/Android TV
- Daydream
- Facebook Gameroom
- Fire OS
- Gear VR
- Google Cardboard
- iOS/tvOS
- Linux
- macOS
- Microsoft Hololens
- Nintendo 3DS/Nintendo Switch
- Oculus Rift
- PlayStation 4/PlayStation Vita/PlayStation VR

- Samsung SMART TV
- Steam OS/Steam VR
- Tizen
- WebGL
- Wii Universe (no longer supported in Unity 2018)
- Windows/Windows Phone/Windows Store Apps
- Xbox One

Editor

Unity's Editor is the main game engine interface, where you will spend most of your time. Here are the key features of the Unity Editor:

- Can be used on both Macs and Windows PCs
- 2D and 3D scene design tools
- Instant play mode
- Powerful animation tools
- Timeline tool for creating cinematic sequences
- Cinemachine tool for smart cameras
- **Artificial Intelligence (AI)** pathfinding tools
- Extensible—there are ample available plugins available
- Particle system
- Supports C# and JavaScript
- Supports single and multi-player games
- Includes collaborative tools

Graphics

The graphics capabilities of the Unity game engine are impressive. We have the ability to create game objects natively in the game engine using geometry, meshes, textures, and materials. We can also use high-quality graphics imported from external, specialized software tools including Maya, 3DS Max, and Blender. Advanced lighting and shadow controls as well as the level of detail feature adds an important touch of realism to our games.

Key graphic features include:

- Real-time rendering
- Global illumination
- Physically-based shading
- Native graphics API for faster rendering
- Multiple lighting techniques

Unity community

Unity has one of the most vibrant communities. Community members share content and help answer questions regarding developing with Unity. The community is heralded by Unity Technologies. In addition to official tutorials, you can find a host of blogs, tutorials, and videos to help you get started with Unity development, as well as learn how to accomplish specific operations with your game.

The Unity Asset Store includes free and for-fee assets from Unity Technologies and the Unity community. Available assets include models, art, animations, scripts, and tools. The Asset Store has an intuitive interface making finding what you need easy. We will explore the Asset Store in Chapter 6, *Creating and Importing 3D Objects for Our Game*.

Unity hosts periodic live events that allow you to learn about Unity directly from Unity Technologies and connect with fellow designers and developers. Unity Unite events are hosted in America, Asia, and Europe each year. You can learn about past and future Unite events here: https://unite.unity.com/.

System requirements

System requirements has two parts. The first refers to what hardware and software you need in order to use Unity for game development. The second refers to the hardware and software you need to run a game developed in Unity. While these requirements might change, the requirements, as of Unity 2017, are detailed in the next two sections.

Development system requirements

You can use a Mac or a Windows computer for Unity development. The Mac must have macOS X 10.9 or later. For Windows computers, you must have Windows 7 SP1+, Windows 8, or Windows 10.

Windows XP and Windows Vista are not officially supported.

The **Graphics Processing Unit (GPU)** on your development computer must have DX9 (shader model 3.0) or DX11 with feature level 9.3 capabilities.

There are additional requirements that are specific to what distribution platforms you are targeting. Please refer to the following table for further information.

If you are developing for...	You must have...	
Android	• Android SDK • Java Development Kit	
iOS	• macOS X 10.9.4 or higher • Xcode 7.0 or higher	
WebGL	One of the following: • macOS X 10.9+ • Windows 7 SP1+ (64-bit)	
Windows Store	Windows 8.1 (64-bit) and one of the following as applicable:	
	IL2CPP (used for compiling .NET assemblies)	Visual Studio with C++ compiler feature
	Universal Windows Platform (UWP)	Visual Studio 2015 or later Windows 10 SDK
	Windows 8.1/Windows Phone 8.1	Visual Studio 2013 or later Windows 8.1 SDK

Playback system requirements

There are not a lot of requirements for users playing Unity games on devices you developed for. Typically, having an up-to-date device, in terms of hardware and operating system, will result in the optimal playing experience.

The basic requirements are detailed as follows:

Device/Platform	Requirements
Android	<ul><li>ARMv7 (Cortex) CPU with NEON support or Atom CPU</li><li>OpenGL ES 2.0 or later</li><li>OS 4.1 or later</li></ul>
Desktop	CPU • Must support SSE2 instruction set Graphics card options • DX9 (shader model 3.0) • DX11 with feature level 9.3 capabilities Operating system options • macOS X 10.9+ • SteamOS+ • Ubuntu 12.04+ • Windows XP SP2+
iOS	iOS 7.0 or higher
WebGL	A recent version of one of the following browsers • Chrome • Edge • Firefox • Safari
Windows Phone	Windows Phone 8.1 or later

Downloading Unity

Getting your hands on Unity is relatively straightforward. Start by visiting the Unity site at `https://unity3d.com`. In the top-right corner, as shown here, you will see a link to **Get Unity**:

That link takes you to the `https://store.unity.com` page where you can click on the **Try Personal** link as part of the **Personal** plan option.

You will be taken to the **Download Unity Personal** page. You should review the information on that page to be sure that you qualify for the Personal Plan.

 Depending on your system, you might be prompted to select a Windows or macOS X button. If presented with this choice, select the appropriate operating system for your computer.

Once you acknowledge your eligibility, the **Download Installer** button will be enabled.

The installer downloads very quickly. It is just an installer and not the game engine itself. We will review the installation process in the next section.

Installing Unity

In the previous section, you downloaded the Unity Installer. Locate that file, likely in your `downloads` folder, and launch the program.

For the remaining steps, and throughout this book, we will use Unity running on macOS. The steps and processes for installing and using Unity are the same for both systems; the interfaces might vary slightly in appearance.

Once you launch the Download Assistant, your computer might present you with a security prompt:

Once you accept the security warning, and after clicking the **Open** button, you will see the **Introduction** pane. Click the **Continue** button.

Next, you will see the **Software License Agreement** pane (not shown here). You can read, print, and save the Software License Agreement. Click the **Continue** button to proceed. This will result in a popup asking you if you consent to the terms of the software license agreement. If you do agree, click the **Agree** button.

The next step is the **Unity component selection screen**. By default, all components will be selected. You will see how much space is required for these components to be installed on your computer and how much space you have left. You can disable components you know you will not need right away and install them later. Alternatively, you can install all components if space is not an issue:

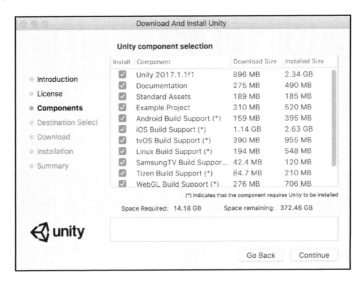

In order to follow along with this book's tutorials, you will need to, at a minimum, select the following components:

- **Unity 2017.1** (or later version that is presented in the interface)
- **Standard Assets**

In addition, the following components are highly recommended:

- **Documentation**
- **Example Project**

Next, you will select an installation destination and click the **Continue** button.

The **Download Assistant** will start downloading the components you previously identified (not shown here). If you have a slow internet connection, this could take a while.

This is a good time to create your free Unity ID. If you still have Unity open in your browser, you will see the person icon in the top-right of their page. If you do not see that icon, you can revisit `https://unity3d.com`. When you click on the icon, you will see a new interface with a **Create a Unity ID** button. Click that button and fill out the registration form:

You will need your account to use the Unity Asset Store, even for obtaining free content.

Once all components have been downloaded and installed, you will be notified by the Download Assistant.

When you first launch Unity, you will need to select a license. Unity is now successfully installed on your computer and you are ready to use it.

Summary

In this chapter, we explored game engines and looked at four different game engines to support our foundational knowledge about game engines. We also looked at the history of Unity and how it evolved from one release to the next. In addition, we discovered Unity's key capabilities and features. Unity's system requirements for developing Unity games was covered, as were the system requirements for running them. Finally, we downloaded and installed Unity.

In Chapter 2, *The Unity Interface*, we will provide details on the Unity Editor's User Interface. You will learn about the various views, windows, layouts, and transform tools.

2
The Unity Interface

In Chapter 1, *Downloading and Installing Unity*, we explored game engines and took a quick look at four alternative game engines to help us appreciate Unity. We looked at the history of Unity and how it evolved from one release to the next. In addition, we discovered Unity's key capabilities and features. We covered Unity's system requirements for developing Unity games and the system requirements for running them. Finally, we downloaded and installed Unity.

In this chapter, we will examine Unity's primary views and windows; we will also cover layouts and the toolbar. The interface components covered in this chapter are the ones used most often. Additional interface components will be covered in subsequent chapters as new functionality and tools are introduced.

Specifically, we will cover the following components:

- Screen Real Estate
- Menu
- Scene view
- Game view
- Project window
- Hierarchy window
- Inspector window
- Toolbar
- Layouts

 Unity can be run on Windows PCs and Macs. The screen images used in this chapter and throughout the book are from Unity running on a Mac. There might be slight interface differences between the screenshots provided and you see when Unity is running on a Windows PC.

Screen real estate

When we first launch Unity, we might be intimidated by all the areas, tabs, menus, and buttons on the interface. Unity is a complex game engine with a lot of functionality, so we should expect more components for us to interact with. If we break the interface down into separate components, we can examine each one independently to gain a thorough understanding of the entire interface.

As you can see here, we have identified six primary areas of the interface. We will examine each of these in subsequent sections. As you will quickly learn, this interface is customizable. The following screenshot shows the default configuration of the Unity user interface.

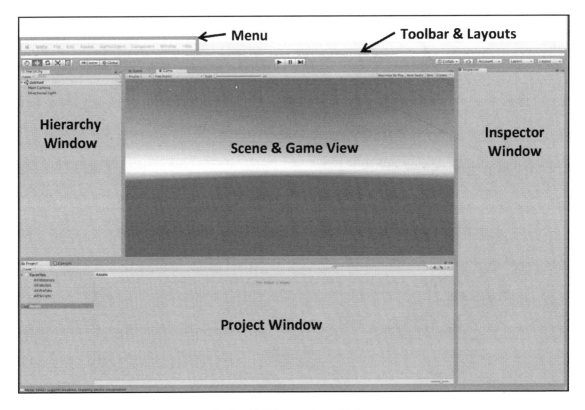

Overview of the Unity game engine user interface.

In the next sections, we will cover each of the following components indicated by the preceding screenshot:

- Menu
- Scene view
- Game view
- Project window
- Hierarchy window
- Inspector window
- Toolbar
- Layouts

 Unity 2017 was the latest release when this book was published, so the screenshots reflect the Unity 2017 interfaces. Unity 2018 was available in beta so interface differences are provided in information boxes throughout the chapter.

Menu

The Unity editor's main menu bar, as depicted here, consists of eight pull-down options. We will briefly review each menu option in this section. Additional details will be provided in subsequent chapters, as we start developing our *Cucumber Beetle* game:

Unity's menus are contextual. This means that only menu items pertinent to the currently selected object will be enabled. Other non-applicable menu items will appear as gray instead of black and not be selectable.

 Starting with Unity 2018, an additional top menu is **Mobile Input**. This menu item allows you to toggle mobile input on and off.

Unity

The **Unity** menu item, shown here, gives us access to information about Unity, our software license, display options, module information, and access to preferences:

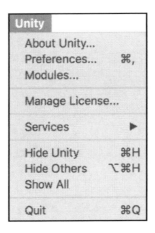

Accessing the **Unity | About Unity...** menu option gives you access to the version of the engine you are running. There is additional information as well, but you would probably only use this menu option to check your Unity version.

The **Unity | Preferences...** option brings up the Unity Preferences dialog window. That interface has seven side tabs: **General**, **External Tools**, **Colors**, **Keys**, **GI Cache**, **2D**, and **Cache Server**. You are encouraged to become familiar with them as you gain experience in Unity. We will use the **External Tools** tab in Chapter 13, *Optimizing Our Game for Deployment*.

The **Unity | Modules** option provides you with a list of playback engines that are running as well as any Unity extensions.

You can quit the Unity game engine by selecting the **Unity | Quit** menu option.

In Unity 2018, the **Unity** menu item is not present. The functionality will be moved to the **Help** menu.

File

Unity's **File** menu includes access to your game's scenes and projects. We will use these features throughout our game development process. As you can see in the following screenshot, we also have access to the **Build Settings....** We will explore this functionality in Chapter 13, *Optimizing Our Game for Deployment*.

Edit

The **Edit** menu has similar functionality to standard editors, not just game engines. For example, the standard **Cut**, **Copy**, **Paste**, **Delete**, **Undo**, and **Redo** options are there. Moreover, the short keys are aligned with the software industry standard.

As you can see from the following screenshot, there is additional functionality accessible here. There are **play**, **pause**, and **step** commands. We can also sign in and out of our Unity account:

The **Edit** | **Project Settings** option gives us access to **Input**, **Tags and Layers**, **Audio**, **Time**, **Player**, **Physics**, **Physics 2D**, **Quality**, **Graphics**, **Network**, **Editor**, and **Script Execution Order**. In most cases, selecting one of these options opens or focuses keyboard control to the specific functionality.

Assets

We will use the **Assets** menu functions extensively throughout this book, starting with Chapter 4, *Creating Our Terrain*. Assets are representations of things that we can use in our game. Examples include audio files, art files, and 3D models. There are several types of assets that can be used in Unity. As you can see from the following screenshot, we are able to create, import, and export assets:

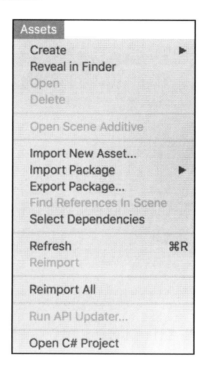

You will become increasingly familiar with this collection of functionality as you progress through the book and start developing your game.

GameObject

The **GameObject** menu provides us with the ability to create and manipulate GameObjects. In Unity, GameObjects are things we use in our game such as lights, cameras, 3D objects, trees, characters, cars, and so much more. As you can see here, we can create an empty **GameObject** as well as an empty child **GameObject**:

We will have extensive hands-on dealings with the **GameObject** menu items throughout this book. At this point, it is important that you know this is where you go to create GameObjects as well as perform some manipulations on them.

Component

In the last section, we mentioned that GameObjects are just *things*. They actually only become meaningful when we add components to them. Components are an important concept in Unity, and we will be working with them a lot as we progress with our game's development. It is the components that implement functionality for our GameObjects.

The following screenshot shows the various categories of components. This is one method for creating components in Unity:

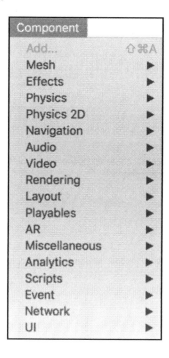

Window

The **Window** menu option provides access to a lot of extra features. As you can see here, there is a **Minimize** option that will minimize the main Unity editor window. The **Zoom** option toggles full screen and zoomed view:

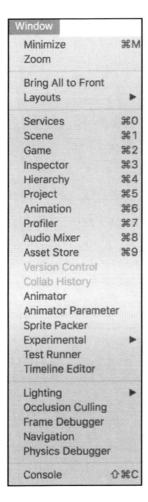

The **Layouts** option provides access to various editor layouts, to save or delete a layout. Layouts will be covered in greater depth later in this chapter.

The following table provides a brief description for the remaining options available via the **Window** menu item. You will gain hands-on experience with these windows as you progress through this book:

Window Option	Description
Services	Access to integrated services: **Ads, Analytics, Cloud Build, Collaborate, Performance Reporting, In-App Purchasing,** and **Multiplayer.**
Scene	Brings focus to the **Scene** view. Opens the window if not already open. Additional details are provided later in this chapter.
Game	Brings focus to the **Game** view. Opens the window if not already open. Additional details are provided later in this chapter.
Inspector	Brings focus to the **Inspector** window. Opens the window if not already open. Additional details are provided later in this chapter.
Hierarchy	Brings focus to the **Hierarchy** window. Opens the window if not already open. Additional details are provided later in this chapter.
Project	Brings focus to the **Project** window. Opens the window if not already open. Additional details are provided later in this chapter.
Animation	Brings focus to the **Animation** window. Opens the window if not already open. Additional details are provided in `Chapter 7`, *Implementing Our Player Character*.
Profiler	Brings focus to the **Profiler** window. Opens the window if not already open. Additional details are provided in `Chapter 13`, *Optimizing Our Game for Deployment*.
Audio Mixer	Brings focus to the **Audio Mixer** window. Opens the window if not already open.
Asset Store	Brings focus to the **Asset Store** window. Opens the window if not already open.
Version Control	Unity provides functionality for most popular version control systems.
Collab History	If you are using an integrated collaboration tool, you can access the history of changes to your project here.
Animator	Brings focus to the **Animator** window. Opens the window if not already open.
Animator Parameter	Brings focus to the **Animator Parameter** window. Opens the window if not already open.

Sprite Packer	Brings focus to the **Sprite Packer** window. Opens the window if not already open. In order to use this feature, you will need to enable **Legacy Sprite Packing** in **Project Settings**.
Experimental	Brings focus to the **Experimental** window. Opens the window if not already open. By default, the **Look Dev** experimental feature is available. Additional experimental features can be found in the Unity **Asset Store**.
Test Runner	Brings focus to the **Experimental** window. Opens the window if not already open. This is a tool that runs tests on your code both in edit and play modes. Builds can also be tested.
Timeline Editor	Brings focus to the **Timeline Editor** window. Opens the window if not already open. This is a contextual menu item.
Lighting	Access to the **Lighting** window and the **Light Explorer** window. Lights will be covered in `Chapter 5`, *Lights, Cameras, and Shadows*.
Occlusion Culling	This feature allows you to select and edit how objects are drawn. With occlusion culling, only the objects within the current camera's visual range, and not obscured by other objects, are rendered.
Frame Debugger	This feature allows you to step through a game, one frame at a time, so you can see the draw calls on a given frame.
Navigation	Unity's navigation system allows us to implement artificial intelligence with regards to non-player character movement. We will cover this concept in `Chapter 8`, *Implementing Our Non-Player Characters*.
Physics Debugger	Brings focus to the **Physics Debugger** window. Opens the window if not already open. Here we can toggle several physics-related components to help debug physics in our games.
Console	Brings focus to the **Console** window. Opens the window if not already open. The **Console** window shows warnings and errors. You can also output data here during gameplay, which is a common internal testing approach.

Some windows will open as tabs. You can drag and drop windows to make it a tab. You can also drag a tab to an open space to make it its own window.

Help

As indicated by the following screenshot, you can access Unity's documentation and scripting manual using the **Help** menu selection:

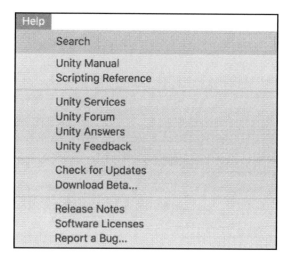

Additional functionality available via the **Help** menu is as follows:

Help Content	Description
Unity Services	This menu option takes you to a Unity page that serves as a gateway to information about integrated Unity services.
Unity Forum	This menu option takes you to the Unity forums site, which features several different Unity forums and includes a search feature.
Unity Answers	This menu option takes you to the **Unity Answers** web page. Here you can ask new questions about Unity development and search previous questions and answers.
Unity Feedback	Search previous feedback or enter your own feedback directly to Unity.
Check for Updates	This helps ensure you have the most recent version of the Unity game engine.
Download Beta...	This directs you to a web page featuring the Unity beta program.
Release Notes	This is a quick web-link to the current version of Unity's release notes.

Software Licenses	This provides you with the legal information regarding the software components used by Unity.
Report a Bug...	This brings up the Unity bug reporter, allowing you to enter a bug report.

Additional **Help** menu options in Unity 2018 will be:

- **About Unity**
- **Manage Licenses**
- **Reset Packages to Default**
- **Troubleshoot Issues**

Scene view

Referring to the first screenshot in this chapter, the **Scene** view is typically in the center of the Unity editor and might be tabled alongside the **Game** view tab.

The **Scene** view is where you will spend most of your time working on your game. You will build and manipulate your game levels here. Some of the actions you will take in this view are adding and modifying game characters, lights, cameras, and other objects related to your game.

As shown in the following screenshot, the **Scene** view has a set of controls lining the top of the interface. This is referred to as the control bar:

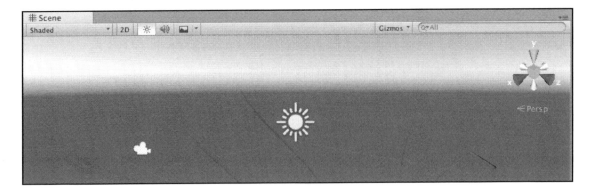

An overview of these controls follows:

Icon	Control	Description
Shaded ▾	Render Mode	Various drawing options that impact how things are seen in **Scene** view.
2D	2D/3D	This is a toggle between 2D and 3D views.
☀	Lighting	Toggles lights on/off.
◀))	Audio	Toggles audio on/off.
▣ ▾	Effects	This control contains toggles for **Skybox**, **Fog**, **Flares**, **Animated Materials**, and **Image Effects**.
Gizmos ▾	**Gizmos**	This control provides a large number of options for how some objects are displayed.
Q▾All	Search	This powerful search feature enables you to filter objects in the **Scene** view.

Game view

The **Game** view allows you to preview your game while you work on it in the editor. You do not manipulate your game in this view, but you can preview it.

You can also play your game. To launch **Game** mode, you click the play button located in the top center of the toolbar:

You can make changes to your game while you are in **Game** mode. Any changes you make while in **Game** mode are temporary. Once you get out of **Game** mode, those changes will be automatically undone.

As shown in the following screenshot, the **Game** view has a set of controls lining the top of the interface. This is referred to as the control bar:

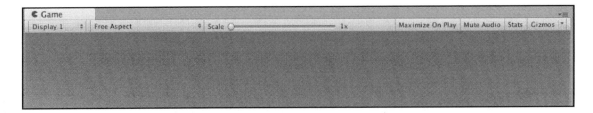

The following table includes each of the components of the aforementioned control bar. The image, name of control, and description are provided for each component:

Icon	Control	Description
Display 1 ⇕	**Display**	If you have multiple cameras in your scene, you can change the view to a specific camera.
Free Aspect ⇕	**Aspect**	Available aspect ratios are: • **Low Resolution Aspect Ratios** • **Free Aspect** • **5:4** • **4:3** • **3:2** • **16:10** • **16:9** • **Standalone (1024x768)**
Scale ◯━━━━ 1x	**Scale Slider**	This slider allows you to zoom in to a specific area for a more detailed view.

Maximize On Play		**Maximize On Play**	This control is a toggle that lets you maximize the **Game** view to the full size of your editor when in **Game** mode.
Mute Audio		**Mute Audio**	This toggle allows you to mute the game's audio when in **Game** mode.
Stats		**Stats**	This control toggles the statistics overlay on/off.
Gizmos ▾		**Gizmos**	This powerful search feature enables you to filter objects in the **Game** view.

Project window

The **Project** window is one that you will use frequently and provides quick access to objects in your project. As you can see here, the **Project** window is organized in a hierarchical view on the left. Selecting a folder on the left reveals the contents in the panel on the right.

That panel displays breadcrumbs on top and has a slider in the bottom-right corner to control the size of the icons:

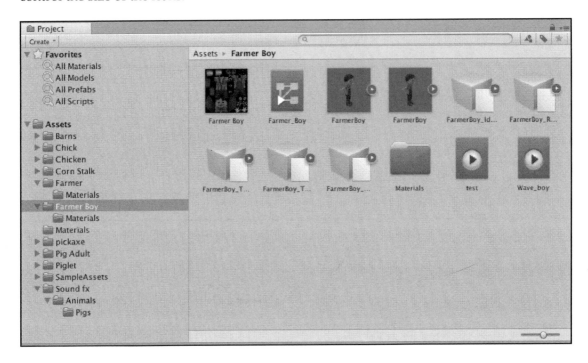

The **Create** drop-down menu in the top-left section of the **Project** window gives you quick access to creating a game asset in the current folder.

To the right of the **Create** drop-down menu is a search bar followed by three icons. The first two icons are Search by Type and Search by Label, respectively. The third icon allows you to save your search.

 The contents of the **Project** window provided in this section are representative and not part of this book's game.

Hierarchy window

The **Hierarchy** window lists all GameObjects in the current scene. This is different than what is displayed in the **Project** window because a game project contains one or more scenes, and not every object in a project is in a scene. As you can see in the following screenshot, some items in the **Hierarchy** window have a triangle on the left. Clicking a triangle will expand the contents, showing child objects. Parenting, or subordinating GameObjects with one another, is important and something that you will gain exposure to as you start adding GameObjects to your game:

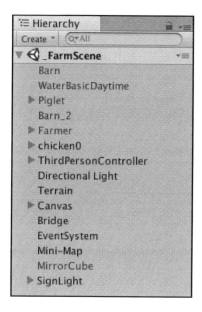

The **Create** drop-down menu in the top-left section of the **Hierarchy** window gives you quick access to creating game assets.

To the right of the **Create** drop-down menu is a search bar. Below the search bar and to the right is a menu icon. Clicking that icon reveals the following list of options:

As you can see from the menu above, it is contextual so not all items will be enabled all the time.

Inspector window

The **Inspector** window is where we can inspect our GameObjects. You will remember that GameObjects are composed of more than one component, and those components are what make the GameObjects worth having in our games.

This example screenshot shows a **ThirdPersonController** GameObject with 11 components. The gray triangles to the left of each component allow you to expand the component and make any desired changes to that component's properties:

When you select a GameObject in **Scene** view, the **Hierarchy** window, or the **Project** window, the **Inspector** window will display the selected GameObject's components and properties. Each component has a different set of properties.

At the bottom of the **Inspector** window, when a GameObject has been selected, you will see the **Add Component** button. Clicking this button allows you to add a component to the current GameObject.

Toolbar

Unity's toolbar, depicted here, is located at the very top of the editor's interface. It spans the entire width of the window, and spacing is dependent on the current width.

The toolbar can be, theoretically, organized into the following categories: **Transform Tools**, **Gizmo Toggles**, Play Buttons, Cloud and **Account** Buttons, and **Layers** and **Layouts**. We covered the Play Buttons in the *Game view* section; the remaining toolbar categories are detailed as follows.

Transform tools

The transform tools are a set of five fundamental tools for manipulating GameObjects in the **Scene** view. Each tool is represented by an icon:

The first button is the Hand tool or View tool. When this tool is selected, our cursor in the **Scene** view turns to a hand. This lets us know which mode we are in. With this tool selected, we can scroll with our mouse to zoom in and out of the scene. If you click on the left mouse button, you are able to pan around the scene. With the right mouse button clicked, you are able to look around, based on the current position of your cursor.

If you hold down the *Alt* key on a PC or *Option* key on a Mac and click on the left mouse button, you can orbit around the current area. Pressing that same key and the right mouse button allows you to zoom in and out of the scene.

The second button is the Translate tool and is in the shape of a quad arrow. When an object is selected, click on the translate tool; the object will have three gizmos, one for each axis. Clicking and dragging any of these gizmos moves the object along the respective axes, as shown in the following screenshot:

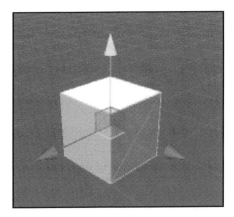

Cube with Transform Translate Tool

The third transform tool is the Rotate tool, which looks like two rotating arrows. This tool allows us to rotate an object along any axis (x, y, or z). Instead of line and arrow gizmos, this tool is instantiated with three colored rings, one for each axis. Clicking a ring and dragging it rotates the object along that axis, as shown in the following screenshot:

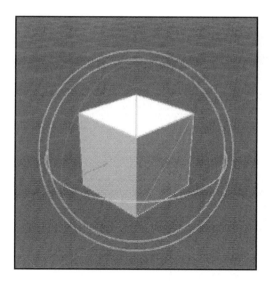

Cube with Transform Rotate Tool

The fourth transform tool is the Scale tool, which is represented with line and block gizmos. Like the other transform tools, there is one gizmo for each axis. Clicking and dragging one of these gizmos increases or decreases the object along the selected axis. For example, you can make a cube wider, narrower, taller, or shorter. If you want to maintain aspect ratio, you can click on the center square instead of the red, blue, or green square. Now, when you click and drag, your object will grow or shrink in perfect aspect ratio, as shown in the following screenshot:

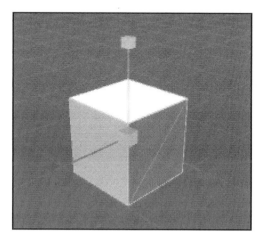

Cube with Transform Scale Tool

The final transform tool is the Rect tool and is represented by a rectangle with intersecting points. The Rect tool can be used to move, resize, and rotate an object in the **Scene** view. So, this is a versatile tool that also has corresponding properties that you can edit directly using the **Inspector** view. Take a look at the following screenshot:

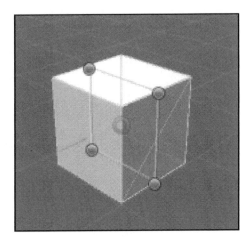

Cube with Transform Rect Tool

Unity 2018 will introduce a sixth transform tool that will permit the moving, rotating, and scaling of selected objects.

Gizmo Toggles

As shown here, there are two **Gizmo Toggles** on the toolbar, called **Transform Gizmo Toggles**:

Transform Gizmo Toggles: Center and Global

The first is a toggle between **Center** and **Pivot**. The second toggle is between **Global** and **Local**.

Cloud and Account Buttons

There are three buttons in this category, as shown here:

Toolbar: Collab, Cloud and Action buttons

The first button is the **Collab**, or Collaboration, button. If you are using an integrated collaboration tool, you can access the history of changes to your project here.

The second button is the **Cloud** button. This simply opens the Unity services window.

The third button is the **Account** button. This is a drop-down button that allows you to access your Unity account.

Layers and Layouts

The final section of buttons on the toolbar consists of the **Layers** drop-down and the **Layout** drop-down buttons. These buttons are illustrated beneath and are located in the far-right end of the toolbar:

Toolbar: Layers and Layout Dropdown Buttons

Selecting the **Layers** drop-down button allows you to select what layers you want to view, not view, and which ones you want to lock. Also, as you can see here, you have access to edit layers:

Editing layers consists of creating user-defined layers that you can reorder and rename.

The **Layout** drop-down reveals the set of options:

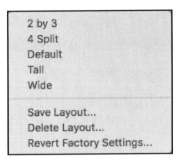

Layouts are covered in the next section.

Layouts

One of the wonderful things about working with Unity is that you can customize the way the user interface is laid out. You can use one of the predefined layouts of **2 by 3**, **4 Split**, **Tall**, or **Wide**, or you can create your own. Layouts refer to how the various views in Unity are arranged on the screen.

To change a layout, we simply click on the **Layout** button that is located in the far top-right corner of the Unity interface. Let's look at each layout to see the differences.

The first layout is the **2 by 3** layout. This layout provides a nice arrangement with the **Scene** and **Game** views on the left, the **Hierarchy** and **Project** views in the middle and a full **Inspector** view on the right, as shown in the following screenshot:

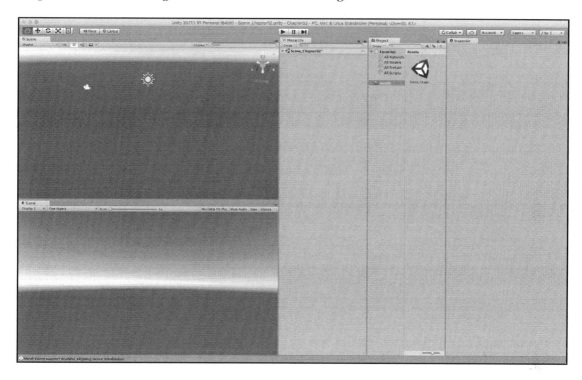

The **4 Split** layout provides four different views of the same scene, as shown in the following screenshot. This is a good way to review how lighting and shading is implemented in your game. We'll talk about lighting and shading later in the book. The **4 Split** layout is shown here:

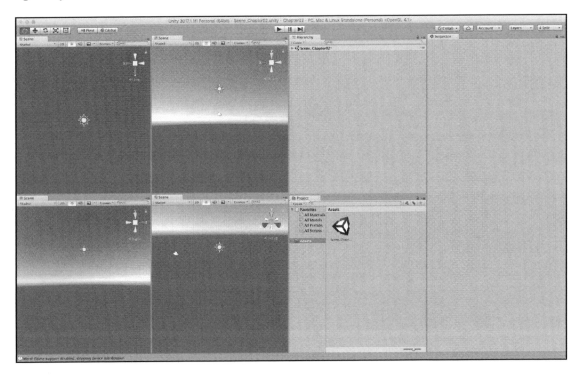

The **Tall** layout provides a tall, but not wide, view of the **Scene** view with other views located on the right, as shown in the following screenshot:

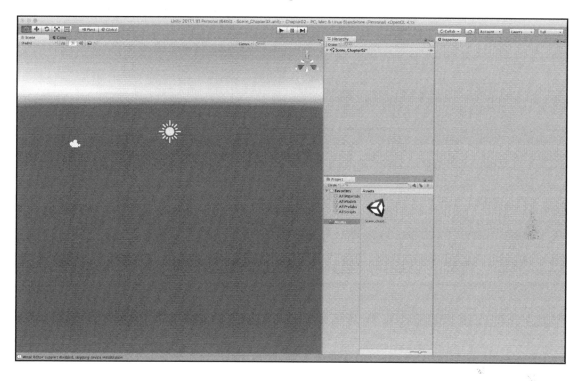

The **Wide** layout provides a wide view of the **Scene** view, with other views located on the bottom and on the right, as shown in the following screenshot:

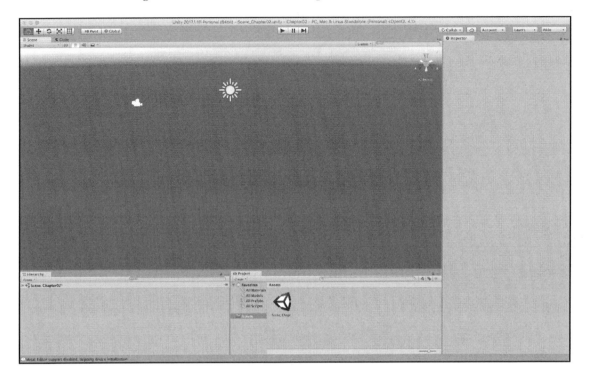

The **Default** layout is a variation of the **Wide** layout. The difference is that with the **Default** layout, the **Hierarchy** view is on the left, as shown in the following screenshot:

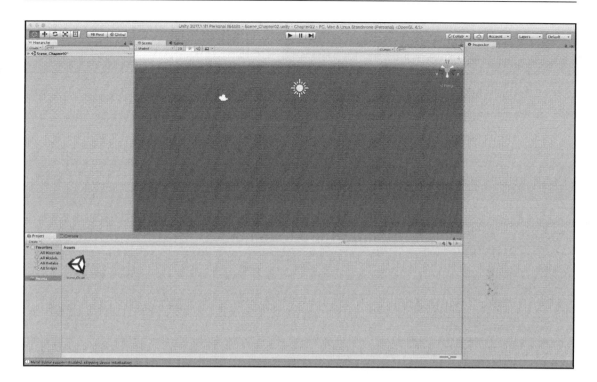

You can switch between layouts any time you want, without it impacting your game. Most Unity developers do not work in just one layout. Different layouts provide different benefits and are appropriate for different tasks. You can also modify any layout by dragging any of the borders of a view or window. If you want to save a layout, make any changes to the current layout, then select the **Layout** button and select **Save Layout**. You will be prompted for a name.

Summary

In this chapter, we examined the primary components of the Unity user interface. This included the **Scene** and **Game** views. We also looked at the **Project, Hierarchy,** and **Inspector** windows. We then reviewed the various layouts as well as the toolbar. Lastly, we established that additional interface components will be covered in subsequent chapters as new functionality and tools are introduced.

In the next chapter, we will start designing our *3D Cucumber Beetle* game. This design will inform our development of the game throughout the rest of the book.

3
Designing the Game

In Chapter 2, *The Unity Interface*, we examined Unity's user interface and paid specific attention to the most commonly used components that include: menus, **Scene** view, **Game** view, **Project** window, **Hierarchy** window, **Inspector** window, Toolbar, and **Layouts**. Becoming familiar with Unity's interface gives us the confidence to move forward with the game engine and to explore additional interface components as we introduce new functionality necessary to create our game.

In this chapter we will design our game, *Cucumber Beetle*, so that we can create a development plan. Our game design will include all the functionality we want in our game, the player character, the non-player characters, game assets, animations, and more. We will use screen mock-ups, as well as narrative, to document our game's design. We will look at related concepts regarding using Unity for our game along the way.

Specifically, we will examine the following concepts in this chapter:

- Game concept
- Game characters
- Gameplay
- The difficulty balance
- Project organization

Game concept

Why design our game, why not just start developing it? This question spawns from the excitement of developing games, especially with the Unity game engine. All games start with an idea. That idea is translated into a design, and that design is the basis for development and, eventually, the final game.

A game's design is like a blueprint for a house. You would not consider building a house without a blueprint, and it is an equally bad idea to develop a game without designing it first. The reason for this is to save time and frustration. For larger projects, time wasted also means unnecessary funds were expended. Imagine that you employed a project team of twelve developers, animators, and artists. If you shared your game idea, would they have enough to go on? Would they do great things, but not have a cohesive set of components for your game? All we are doing with our game design is documenting as much as we can in the beginning so that the development process is purposeful. Without question, you will continually modify your game's design during development, so having a strong base to start from is critical to your success.

Our game design will serve as the foundation for the look of our game, what the player's objectives are, what the gameplay will be, supporting user actions, animations, audio, artificial intelligence, and victory conditions. That is a lot to think about, and underscores the importance of translating the game idea into a game design.

Throughout the book we will be covering a range of components, however, in this section, we will cover those which are listed beneath:

- Game idea
- Input controls
- Winning and losing

Game idea

The basic concept of our *Cucumber Beetle* game is that it will be a 3D game featuring a Cucumber Man as the player character. The character must protect the cucumber patches, fighting off Cucumber Beetles. These beetles are intent on destroying the cucumber patches and anyone that gets in their way, including our Cucumber Man.

The Cucumber Man will harvest cherries from cherry trees and throw them at the Cucumber Beetles. This will be the only form of defense our Cucumber Man has against the Cucumber Beetles, except for running away.

Input controls

It is important to consider how players will interact with our game. The player will control the Cucumber Man using the standard set of controls. Players have an expectation that the industry norms for user controls will be implemented in games. So our default set of user input control, as shown here, will consist of the keyboard and mouse:

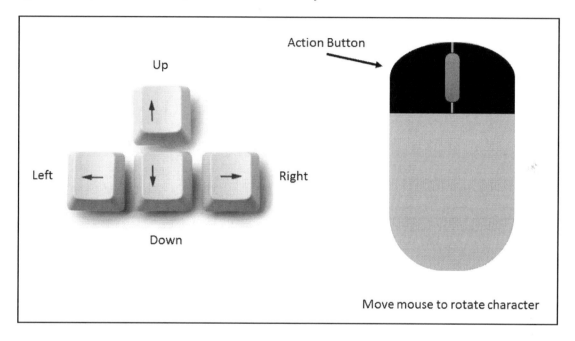

We will configure and program our game so that user input from the keyboard matches the key and action pairings in the following table:

Keyboard input	Action
Up arrow	Move forward/up
Down arrow	Move back/down
Left arrow	Move left
Right arrow	Move right
W	Move forward/up
S	Move back/down
A	Move left

D	Move right
Space bar	Jump

The mouse will also be a significant source of user input. We will implement two components using the mouse as indicated in the following table:

Mouse input	**Action**
Mouse movement	Rotate character
Left button	Throw cherry

The left mouse button will be our action button. We will need to ensure cherries are thrown only when the player has one or more cherries remaining.

Winning and losing

Our winning condition will be when all the Cucumber Beetles have been eliminated. There will be two different ways the player can lose the game. The first losing condition is when all the cucumbers have been eaten by the Cucumber Beetles. The second losing condition is if the player runs out of lives.

By this short description, you can tell there will be several things to keep track of, including the following:

- Number of Cucumber Beetles
- Number of cucumbers
- Number of Cucumber Man lives

Game characters

Our game will use several game objects, but only two game characters. The first game character is the Cucumber Man, and will be controlled by the player. The second game character is the Cucumber Beetle. This is a non-player character that is controlled by artificial intelligence. Let's look more closely at both of these characters.

Cucumber Man

The player will play our game as the Cucumber Man, our game's protagonist. This is a character that we will import for use in our game. It was created using Maya, a professional 3D modeling and animation software suite, and Photoshop. Here is a look at our Cucumber Man:

So, what can the Cucumber Man player character do? We already know we will be able to move him throughout our game environment using a combination of keyboard and mouse inputs. We also know that the space bar will cause him to jump and that the left mouse button, our action button, will cause him to shoot cherries.

 Because the Cucumber Man is controlled by the human player, it is referred to as the **Player Character**.

We will implement the following animations for the Cucumber Man:

- **Idle**: This will play when the character is not being moved by the player.
- **Walk**: This is the animation that will play when the player causes the Cucumber Man to walk, regardless of direction.

- **Run**: This animation is similar to the walk animation. It is faster and covers distances quickly.
- **Jump**: We will implement a jump whenever the space bar is pressed.
- **Die**: Should our character be overcome by the Cucumber Beetles, we will play this animation.
- **Throw**: This is the animation that will cause the Cucumber Man to throw a cherry.

The other action our Cucumber Man can make is to collect cherries. We will implement this with an auto-collection system. Whenever the Cucumber Man is touching a cherry tree, we will increment the number of cherries he has by one.

We will implement the Cucumber Man in `Chapter 7`, *Implementing Our Player Character*.

Cucumber Beetle

Our game's antagonist will be the Cucumber Beetle. We will control how many of them we want in our game and where they are placed. We will also control their behaviors through artificial intelligence. The Cucumber Beetle character was created using Maya and Photoshop, the same software pair used to create the Cucumber Man. Here is a look at our Cucumber Beetle:

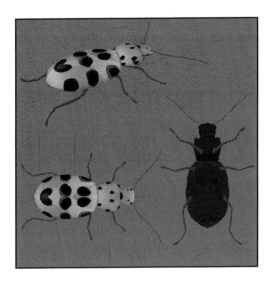

The Cucumber Beetles will search for and consume cucumbers. We will determine how long it takes a cucumber to be consumed. As you can see in the preceding illustration, there are images for the cucumber beetle in its normal state, with all six legs on the ground, and standing up. The stand-up position will be used when it is attacking the Cucumber Man.

 Because the Cucumber Beetle is controlled by artificial intelligence and not a human player, it is referred to as the **Non-Player Character**.

We will implement the following animations for the Cucumber Beetles:

- While on the ground:
    - **Idle**: This will play when the cucumber beetle is not searching, eating, or attacking.
    - **Ground Walk**: This is the animation that will play when the cucumber beetle is walking.
    - **Eating**: This animation will play when the cucumber beetle has located a cucumber and is eating it. Beetles are smaller than cucumbers, so it takes more than one bite.
    - **Ground Attack**: The cucumber beetle will attack the Cucumber Man with its feelers.
    - **Stand then Idle**: This animation takes the cucumber beetle from being on the ground to standing up and remaining idle.
    - **Ground Death**: This animation will play when the Cucumber Man defeats a cucumber beetle in its on-ground position.
- While standing:
    - **Walk**: We will give our Cucumber Beetles the ability to walk on their back two legs
    - **Run**: The Cucumber Beetles will be able to run towards the Cucumber Man on its back two legs
    - **Standing Attack**: When standing, the Cucumber Beetles will be able to attack the Cucumber Man with its top four legs
    - **Standing Death**: This animation will play when the Cucumber Man defeats a Cucumber Beetle in its standing position

We will require careful planning and scripting to create the desired Cucumber Beetle behaviors. The number and placement of the Cucumber Beetles are decisions we will need to make.

We will implement the Cucumber Beetles in `Chapter 8`, *Implementing Our Non-Player Characters*.

Gameplay

The game will start with the player in the center of the game world. The Cucumber Man, controlled by the player, will need to defend the cucumber patches from the Cucumber Beetles. To fend off the Cucumber Beetles, the Cucumber Man will need to collect cherries from nearby cherry trees. The goal is to defeat all the Cucumber Beetles before the cucumbers in the cucumber patches are all gone.

Let's look at how we will make all this happen. The following game play components are covered in this section:

- Game world layout
- Starting condition
- Point system
- Heads-Up Display

Game world layout

Will will create our game world in `Chapter 4`, *Creating Our Terrain*, and then add cameras and lighting effects in `Chapter 5`, *Lights, Cameras, and Shadows*. We will create a basic outdoor environment that consists of a large island surrounded by water. The water will be for aesthetics and boundary purposes. We will not make use of the water; after all, cucumbers cannot swim.

Here is a mock-up of the shape our game world will take:

Top-Down View

Water

Spawn Point

Spawn Point

Cherry Trees

Cherry Trees

Spawn Point

Cherry Trees

Spawn Point

Spawn Point

Cherry Trees

Water

There are four basic things illustrated in the preceding mock-up:

- **Water**: This will just be used for our game world border.
- **Spawn Points**: There are five spawn points, and we can randomly spawn our player character to one after losing a life.
- **Cherry Trees**: We will place four sizeable clumps of cherry trees in the game world.
- **Cucumber Patches**: These are not labeled in the mock-up, but are represented by the green scribbled areas. This represents the rough approximation of where the vast cucumber patches will be planted or, in our Unity terminology, placed.

The only item not represented in our mock-up is the placement of the Cucumber Beetles. We will place the beetles somewhat randomly through scripting. We will do that in `Chapter 8`, *Implementing Our Non-Player Characters*.

Starting condition

When our game is first launched, we will have several starting conditions set. Here is a list of those conditions:

- Cucumber Man spawn point
- Number and placement of Cucumber Beetles
- Number of cherries held by Cucumber Man
- Number and placement of cucumbers

Let's look at each of these starting conditions.

The first starting condition is where to spawn the Cucumber Man. As you saw in our earlier mock-up, there will be five possible spawn points in the game. We will write a script to spawn the player in a random spot each time. While there are only five spots, it does add enough randomness into the game to make this a fun and challenging component.

The number and placement of Cucumber Beetles is the second starting condition. This is an important pair of decisions to make. If we decide poorly, the game is likely to be too easy or too hard and, in both of these situations, the game would not be challenging enough to make it fun to play. We will look at this issue in greater detail in the section titled *The difficulty balance* later in this chapter.

The number of cherries held by the Cucumber Man is our third starting condition. The Cucumber Man will start with zero cherries and, each time he is respawned, he will also have zero cherries. So, if the Cucumber Man has 319 cherries and is defeated by one or more Cucumber Beetles, the Cucumber Man will respawn with zero cherries, losing the 319 cherries he had.

Our fourth and final starting condition is the number and placement of cucumbers. This is an important set of considerations, and is tied to the placement and number of Cucumber Beetles. We will examine the possibilities and the likely outcomes of our decisions regarding this issue in the section titled *The difficulty balance* later in this chapter.

Point system

So far, we have established that we would track several components in the game. These are listed here along with the variable name that we will use in our scripts:

- Number of Cucumber Beetles:
  - `numberOfCucumberBeetles`
- Number of cucumbers:
  - `numberOfCucumbers`
- Number of Cucumber Man lives:
  - `livesLeft`

Based on what we decided earlier regarding the end-of-game condition, we can apply the following mathematical checks to determine if the game has ended and what the outcome is. Each end-of-game condition is listed in the following table along with the outcome:

Condition number	End-of-game condition	Outcome
1	`numberOfCucumbers == 0`	Cucumber Beetles Win
2	`numberOfCucumberBeetles == 0`	Cucumber Man Wins
3	`livesLeft == 0`	Cucumber Beetles Win

In order to implement the three end-of-game conditions, we know we have to track the number of beetles, cucumbers, and lives. This is not optional. Where we do have flexibility is with what we display to the user. We will make that decision in the next section, *Heads-Up Display*.

Since we are tracking key information that involves numbers, it makes it easy for us to implement a point system. We could, for example, give the player 50 points each time a Cucumber Beetle is exterminated. We could also take away points each time a Cucumber Beetle takes a bite out of the Cucumber Man.

The point system that we will implement in our *Cucumber Beetle* game will consist of two types of events, those that result in points being added and those resulting in points being subtracted. Here is a table with the details of our point system:

In-game event	Points
Start of Game	+ 1,500
Cucumber Man Picks Cherry	+ 5
Cucumber Man Hits Cucumber Beetle with Cherry on the Ground	+ 10
Cucumber Man Exterminates Cucumber Beetle on the Ground	+ 25
Cucumber Man Hits Standing Cucumber Beetle with Cherry	+ 50
Cucumber Man Exterminates Standing Cucumber Beetle	+100
Cucumber Man Loses Life	- 500

As you can see from the preceding table, we will start our player with 1,500 points and subtract 500 each time a life is lost. This will ensure we do not have a negative point total, and is one less thing for us to check in our scripts. This also gives players a bonus for each life they save.

Heads-Up Display

We have decided to keep track of information during gameplay that has value beyond calculating points and the end of game. The player will want to see this information as it tends to provide motivation and adds to the fun of the game. So, we will create a Heads-Up Display for the player, and dynamically update the data in the game.

A **Heads-Up Display (HUD)** is a visual layer of information that is always present on the screen.

Here is a mock-up of what our **Heads-Up Display** will look like in our *Cucumber Beetle* game:

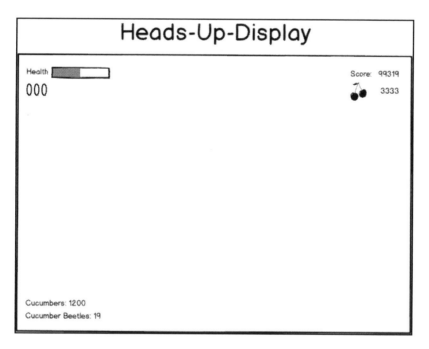

As you can see, there are six components to our HUD. Each of these are explained in detail:

- **Health**: This will consist of a text label and a health meter.
- **Lives**: The icons underneath the **Health** text label signify how many lives remain. We will not add a label to this as its function will be clear to the player. We will use an image of the Cucumber Man as the icon.
- **Score**: The score will be presented in the top-right-hand corner of the screen.
- **Cherries**: We will show the number of cherries directly beneath the score.
- **Cucumbers**: The bottom left-hand-corner of the HUD contains two components. The first component is the number of cucumbers left in the game.
- **Cucumber Beetles**: The number of Cucumber Beetles currently left in the game will be displayed in the bottom-left-hand corner of the HUD, below the number of cucumbers.

The difficulty balance

There are a lot of considerations to make when determining how difficult your game should be. If it is too difficult, players will lose interest, and if the game is too easy, it might not appeal to your intended audience. Some games include difficulty levels for users to select from. Other games have multiple levels, each with an increasing level of difficulty. There are several questions that we must contend with in order to achieve our desired difficulty balance.

In this section, we will first look at the difficulty balance questions, followed by our implementation plan.

Difficulty balance questions

There are a lot of questions about our game that we need to consider in our game design. A review of the questions in this section will help us gain an appreciation for the issues that even a simple game such as ours must contend with to achieve the desired difficulty balance.

This first set of questions are related to the overall implementation of difficulty in our game:

- Should we have different levels of difficulty, selectable by the player?
    - How many different difficulty levels should there be?
    - What will the difficulty levels be called?
    - What specifically will be different with each difficulty level?
- Should we have multiple game levels, each with an increased amount of difficulty?
    - How many different game levels should there be?
    - What will the game levels be called?
    - What specifically will be different with each game level?

Consider the following questions regarding the Cucumber Beetles in our game:

- How many Cucumber Beetles should there be?
- How passive or aggressive should the Cucumber Beetles be?
- At what distance should a cucumber beetle become aware of the Cucumber Man?
- How effective should the Cucumber Beetles be in finding cucumbers?

- How much damage should a Cucumber Beetle inflict on the Cucumber Man with each attack?
- How much damage can a Cucumber Beetle endure before it dies?
- Should Cucumber Beetles communicate and help each other in coordinated attacks?

This next set of questions refers to our playable character, the Cucumber Man:

- How many lives should the character have?
- How much damage will the character take from a single cucumber beetle attack?
- How much damage can the character endure before they die?
- Should the character be able to outrun Cucumber Beetles?
- Should there be a maximum number of cherries held by the character? If so, how many?
- Where should the player spawn? In a safe area?
- When the character loses a life, should they respawn without their cherries?
- When the character respawns, should full health be restored?

We also have cucumbers and cherries to account for in our game. Here are a couple of questions for each of those game assets that we will implement in our game.

Cucumbers:

- How many bites should it take for a cucumber beetle to consume a cucumber?
- How many cucumbers should there be in the game?
- Where should the cucumbers be located in the game environment?

Cherries:

- At what pace should the player be able to gather cherries?
- What will be the maximum number of cherries the Cucumber Man can have?
- How much damage will the cherries inflict on the Cucumber Beetles?
- How many cherries will be available in the game?

As you can see, there are several questions that we need to answer as part of our design. Some of the questions may seem redundant as they relate to more than one component in the game.

Implementation plan

Based on the questions posed in the last section, we must come up with some answers. So, let's do that here. This set of answers will serve as the implementation plan for our difficulty balance.

Our first set of decisions focuses on the overall game concept. Here are those decisions:

- Implement one game level.
- Provide the user with three game difficulty settings. Setting names are provided here:
  - I'm a Baby Cucumber (Easiest)
  - I Can Handle This (Moderate)
  - Bring It! (Most difficult)

Now that we've decided to create three game levels, we must determine how they will be different. This is easily managed by using a matrix. As we fill in the matrix, we will be able to document answers to most of the previously listed questions. Here is what we will refer to as the *Difficulty Implementation Matrix*:

Component	I'm a Baby Cucumber	I Can Handle This	Bring It!
Number of Cucumber Beetles	X	X * 2	X * 5
Damage from Cucumber Beetles (to Cucumber Man)	-5 health points per second	-10 health points per second	-20 health points per second
Damage from Cucumber Beetles (to Cucumbers)	-5 points per second	-7 points per second	- 9 points per second
Cucumber Beatle Starting Health	X	X * 2	X * 5
Cucumber Man Starting Health	X	X * .75	X * .5
Cucumber Starting Health	300	400	500
Number of Cucumbers	X	X * .75	X * .5

Cherry Gathering Rate	1 cherry per second	1 cherry every 2 seconds	1 cherry every 3 seconds
Maximum Number of Cherries Held by Cucumber Man	99	75	50
Damage from Cherry (to Cucumber Beetles)	X	X * .75	X *.50

There will also be a set of decisions that will not change based on the user-selected difficulty level. Here is a list of those decisions:

- The aggressiveness of the Cucumber Beetles will not change. We will script them so that if they are aware of the Cucumber Man, they will attack him.
- We will establish a pretty small vision area for the Cucumber Beetles making it easy for the Cucumber Man to sneak past them and perhaps, more importantly, outrun them.
- Cucumber Beetles will be able to easily find cucumbers.
- Cucumber Beetles will not communicate with one another. So, there will be no coordinated attacks. This does not mean that more than one Cucumber Beetle can't attack the Cucumber Man at the same time. All Cucumber Beetles' within range of the Cucumber Man will attack.
- The Cucumber Man will start with three lives.
- We will not limit the number of cherries a player can collect, but they will all be lost as part of the respawn process.
- Respawning will be randomized between the five respawn points previously identified in the game's mock-up.
- The Cucumber Man will start with full health after a respawn.
- The cucumbers will be placed randomly in the game within the cucumber patches.
- The number of cherry trees and cherries will not vary with different difficulty levels.

Project organization

Our project will consist of a lot of assets. So far we have identified and detailed our planned use of the Cucumber Man, our player characters, and the Cucumber Beetles, our non-player character. We will also use cherry trees, cherries, and cucumber patches. Let's briefly look at those in the next section, *Custom assets*.

Custom assets

Several custom assets have been created using Maya and Photoshop for use in our game. The first set of assets are two forms of cucumber patches, both shown in the following image:

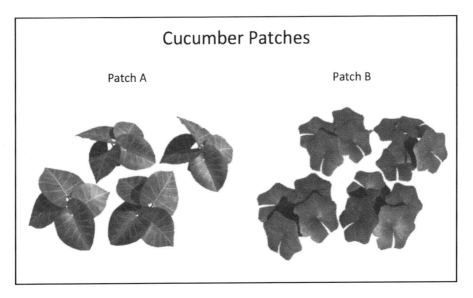

We will use these cucumber patches to cover large sections of our game environment, as identified earlier in this chapter. We have two different patch formations to help create an authentic and non-repetitive look to the game environment. We will also rotate the patches to add variability to the overall visual appearance of the ground covering.

A custom cucumber will also be provided in our game. While there might be hundreds of them in the game, we will use one base cucumber, pictured here, and replicate it throughout the game environment. We can modify the size and rotation to ensure we have what will appear to be a lot of unique cucumbers:

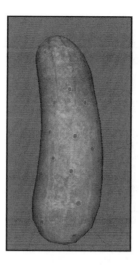

Our next custom asset is a cherry tree. Our base tree is shown here and has a unique form. We can alter the size and rotation of this tree to create the visual of a bunch of unique trees. Certainly this is not an authentic cherry tree, but it will be suitable for our purposes:

Although our cherry trees have cherries on them, they are all part of the tree and not separate objects. So, our player character can collect cherries from the cherry trees, but there will be no visual indication that the cherries have been picked. We will update our HUD to provide that indication. For throwing cherries at Cucumber Beetles, we will use the cherry shown in the following image:

Standard assets

In addition to the custom assets created for this game, we will use many of Unity's standard assets including textures, materials, and 3D objects. We will start using textures and materials in Chapter 4, *Creating Our Terrain*. We will create our own 3D assets using Unity's native tools, as well as importing additional ones in Chapter 6, *Creating and Importing 3D Object for Our Game*.

Organization

If we do not have a plan to be organized, our project can quickly get out of hand. Unity has great search support for project components, but we would rather be able to quickly navigate to our assets. Here is the basic structure that we will make as we start creating our game:

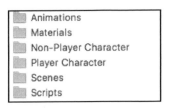

Summary

In this chapter, we fully designed our game, *Cucumber Beetle*, and we plan to use our design to drive our development efforts. Our game design includes functionality, the player character, the non-player characters, game assets, animations, and more. We used screen mock-ups to help document our game's design. In addition, we planned our game's difficulty balance to help ensure the game is appropriately difficult based on user selection.

In the next chapter, you will learn how to create the game's terrain. You will gain exposure to shaping tools and terrain painting. You will also learn how to add vegetation and water to our terrain. By the end of the next chapter, you will have created the game world for the *Cucumber Beetle* game.

4
Creating Our Terrain

In the last chapter, we designed our game so that we have a plan for our development efforts. We designed all the game's functionality, how to use the player character, what role the non-player character will have, what assets we will use, and what animations we will use in the game. We also mocked-up the main game screen as well as our heads-up display. In addition to this, we made key decisions on our game's difficulty balance. With the design work complete, we are ready to start creating our game.

In this chapter, we will create our game's terrain and perform several actions to customize the terrain based on our design mock-up in Chapter 3, *Designing the Game*. We will use shaping tools and add water and vegetation features to complete our game environment.

Specifically, we will cover the following topics in this chapter:

- Creating the terrain
- Shaping the terrain
- Painting the terrain
- Adding water
- Adding vegetation

Creating the terrain

Unity terrain is essentially the ground in your game environment; it is your landscape. Unity has several tools that we can use to create, shape, and customize the terrain. We will use those tools later in this chapter.

For our game, we will use a terrain that was created from a height map and then edited in Photoshop. If you are interested in learning how to accomplish this, read the *Importing the terrain* section. Otherwise, you can skip this brief section and resume with the section on importing the terrain.

Working with height maps

You will find a lot of free height maps with a simple internet search. Once you have the one you want, perform the following steps:

This subsection is not required and only provided for informational purposes. The game's terrain file will be provided along with instructions on how to incorporate it in our game.

1. Open PhotoShop and select **File** | **New**. Use the following settings:

Component	Setting
Width	512 pixels
Height	512 pixels
Resolution	72 pixels
Color mode	Grayscale 8bit

2. Drag the height map you downloaded into the new Photoshop image.
3. Make any necessary placement adjustments and commit the transform.
4. Select **Image** | **Auto Tone**. Make any brightness and contrast adjustments you feel are necessary.
5. Save the file as a Photoshop Raw file.

Importing the terrain

Before we import our terrain, we need to set up a new Unity 3D project. To do that, follow these steps:

1. Launch Unity.
2. Click the **New** icon.

3. Enter a project name and select **3D**.

4. Click the **Create project** button.

5. Using the top menu, select **GameObject | 3D Object | Terrain**. This creates a default terrain, called `terrain`.

6. With the terrain selected, click the settings cog icon under **Terrain** in the **Inspector** panel:

7. Change the **Terrain Height** to 200.

8. Still in the **Inspector** panel, scroll down until you see the **Import Raw...** button. Click that button and navigate to the Photoshop Raw file you created in the previous section. Alternatively, you can download the `terrain.raw` file from the publisher's companion site:

9. Select **Mac** for the **Byte Order** in the **Import Heightmap** dialog window and click the **Import** button. It is important to use this option, even if you are on a computer running Windows:

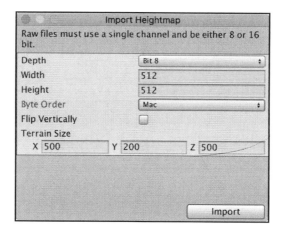

Once you click the **Import** button, watch the lower right-hand corner of the Unity interface. The import process can take several minutes. Watching that section of the interface will indicate your progress. See the example here. Be patient:

7/11 Light Transport | 2 jobs

Once the import process is complete, your terrain will reflect the imported height map. As you can see here, it will have some pointed peaks and edges. We will work on those in the next section:

Shaping the terrain

In this section, we will take several actions to shape our terrain. We will start with smoothing, and then create our five spawn points.

Smoothing our terrain

As we identified in the previous section, our terrain currently has some bumpy edges and pointed peaks. We will use the smoothing tool, which is available in the **Terrain** section of the **Inspector** panel. As you can see here, it is the third icon from the left:

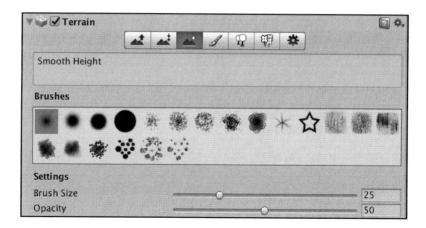

When the smoothing tool is selected, you are presented with different brush types and sizes. Once you make those selections, simply use the left-button of the mouse to smooth the terrain.

The following screenshot shows the results of the terrain after significant smoothing has been applied:

If you are following along with these steps in Unity, your results will vary and that is okay. The exact terrain construction is not required in order to follow along with the remaining steps in this and other chapters.

Creating our spawn points

Our game design called for five spawn points: one in the center, and one each in four corners. Our game environment is not a perfect square, so we will create a spawn point in the center of our terrain and four additional spawn points throughout the terrain.

We are not scripting the spawning yet; that will take place in `Chapter 11`, *Scripting Victory and Defeat*. For now, we will simply create the areas using terrain-shaping tools. Specifically, we will use the **Paint Height** tool. As you can see here, it is the second icon in the **Terrain** section of the **Inspector** panel:

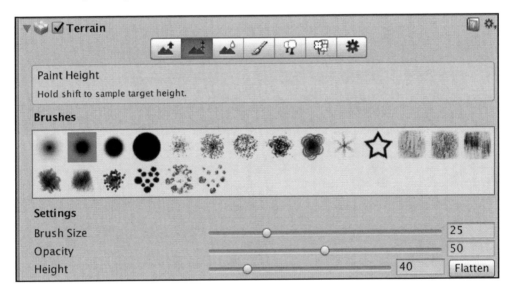

Selecting the a **Brush Size** of 25, we simply click and paint the five areas where we want the spawn points to be. We will use the one in the center as the default starting point at the beginning of the game, and then randomly select one of the five for spawning in-game.

When making the spawn points, we want them to be elevated, but not too high. The following screenshot shows the five spawn points located throughout the terrain:

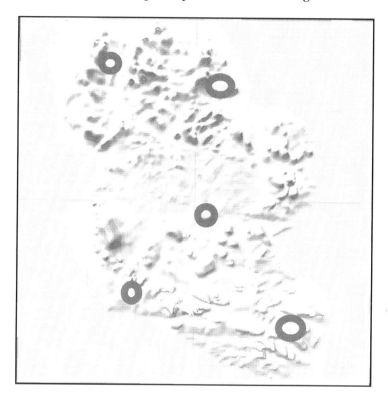

Painting the terrain

We are now ready to give our terrain some color. We will start by covering the entire terrain with a grass texture. To accomplish this, ensure the **Terrain** is selected in the **Hierarchy** panel. Then, in the **Inspector** panel, select the **Paint Texture** tool. As you can see here, that is the fourth icon in the **Terrain** section of the **Inspector** panel:

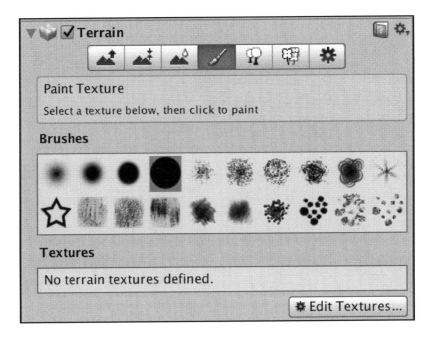

As you can see, we do not have any textures defined. We actually do not have any appropriate textures in our project yet, so let's take care of that with a few simple steps:

1. In the **Project** panel, click the `Assets` folder.
2. In the right section, right-click and select **Create | Folder**. Name the folder `Textures`.
3. Download the `grass_starter_texture.jpg` file from the publisher's companion site.
4. Drag the `grass_starter_texture.jpg` file from your filesystem to the `Textures` folder you created in step 1.

Now that you have a grass texture in your Unity project, let's apply it to our terrain. Here are the steps:

1. Select **Terrain** in the **Hierarchy** panel.
2. In the **Inspector** panel, click the **Edit Textures** button, and then **Add Texture**. This will reveal the **Add Terrain Texture** dialog window, depicted here:

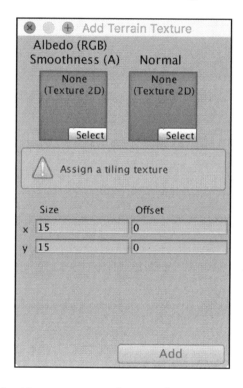

3. Click the left **Select** button to reveal a set of textures.
4. Double-click the `grass_starter_texture`.
5. Change both the **x** and **y**, **Size** from 15 to 2.
6. Click the **Add** button.

You will see that your terrain is now covered with grass. When you zoom in, you can see the quality of the grass increases.

In the next section, we will add water to our terrain.

Adding water

Our next step is to add the water surrounding our island. We do not intend to swim in the water or have objects in it, so we can get by with a simple approach. We will refine our water in Chapter 6, *Creating and Importing 3D Objects for Our Game*.

Perform the following steps to create a material and a water plane, and then apply the material to the plane:

1. In the **Project** panel, click the Assets folder.
2. In the right section, right-click and select **Create | Folder**. Name the folder Materials.
3. Double-click the Materials folder you just created.
4. Right-click in the Materials folder and select **Create | Material**. Name the material temp_water.
5. With the temp_water material selected, click the white color box to the left of the eye dropper icon in the **Inspector** panel:

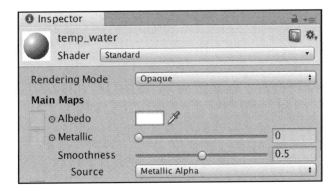

6. In the **Color** dialog window, select a blue color for your water and close the dialog window. You should now see your color selection indicated in both the **Project** panel and the **Inspector** panel:

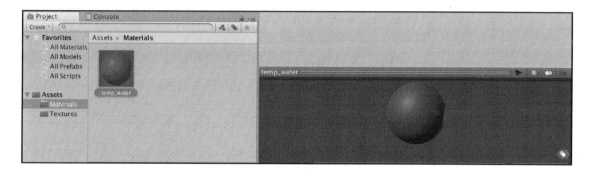

Now that we have our material ready, let's create a GameObject to simulate our water. Follow these steps:

1. Select **GameObject** | **3D Object** | **Plane** from the top menu.
2. Using the transform tools, increase the size of the plane to match the size of the entire game world.
3. Raise or lower the plane until it looks similar to this:

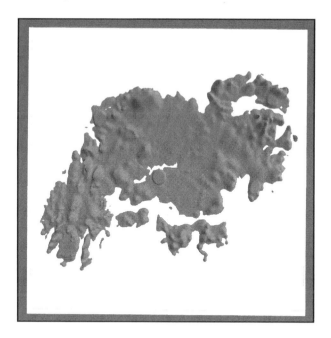

4. With the plane selected, click the small circle to the right of `Default-Material` in the **Mesh Renderer** section of the **Inspector** panel. The following screenshot shows that section:

5. You should now see the **Select Material** dialog window. Select the `temp_water` texture you created and close the dialog window.

6. In the **Hierarchy** panel, right-click the **Pane** object and rename it `WaterPane`. This will help us stay organized and enable us to identify our game objects.

Your game environment should now look something similar to this:

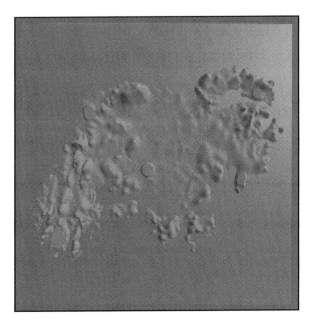

Saving your work

This is a good time to save your work. In order to remain organized, let's create a `Scenes` folder under `Assets`. Here are the steps to accomplish that:

1. In the **Project** panel, click the `Assets` folder.
2. In the right-hand section, right-click and select **Create | Folder**. Name the folder `Scenes`.

Now you are ready to save your work. From the top menu, select **File | Save** Project. You can use the **File | Save Scenes** or **File | Save Scene As...** option to save your scene. Also, when you exit without having saved your scene, you will be prompted for a name. Save your scene using any of those options, give your scene the name of `Main` and ensure it is saved in the `Assets | Scenes` folder.

Adding vegetation

So far, our game environment only consists of a land mass covered in grass, surrounded by water. As you will remember from `Chapter 3`, *Designing the Game*, we plan to incorporate the following game objects related to the terrain:

- Cherry trees
- Cucumber patches
- Cucumbers

We will add those game objects in `Chapter 6`, *Creating and Importing 3D Objects for Our Game*. For now, we can add some regular trees to start filling in our game environment.

Instead of simply importing trees that others have made, we will go through the steps to create our own trees. Follow these steps to create your first 3D tree in Unity from scratch:

1. Select **GameObject | 3D Object | Tree** from the top menu. This will create a new tree and place it in your game world at **Transform** 0, 0, 0.

 Double-clicking an object in the **Hierarchy** panel will focus it in the center of the **Scene** view. It will also provide a zoomed-in view of the object.

2. Using the transform tools, increase the Y axis so the tree is above your water line. It will only consist of a single branch:

With the **Tree** selected, we turn our focus to the **Tree** window in the **Inspector** panel. The following diagram indicates the various buttons that we will be using to continue creating our tree:

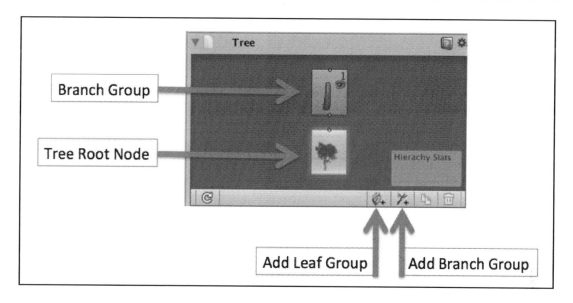

3. Select the Branch Group icon in the **Tree** window. Next, click the Add Branch Group button. You will see a branch has been added to the main Branch, which serves as a tree trunk. As you can see here, there is a **Length** setting that you can adjust in the **Inspector** panel:

There are three additional tools that can help you make unique trees. The buttons, illustrated as follows, are Move Branch, Rotate Branch, and Free Hand:

4. Continue to create branches on your tree trunk until it looks the way you want it to. Remember, you can individually move, resize, and rotate branches. You can also add branches to branches. When you add a new branch, it is added to the currently selected branch.

When you first create a new branch, it is best to change the size before moving it. Once you relocate the branch, you might lose the ability to make certain adjustments.

When you are done adding and configuring branches, your tree will look quite unique. An example is provided in the following screenshot:

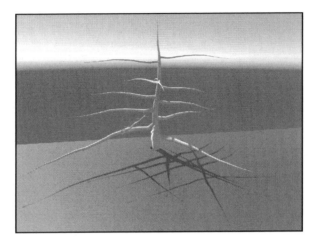

As you can see, there is one tree trunk and several branches. We can see, in the **Tree** window, the hierarchy of branches:

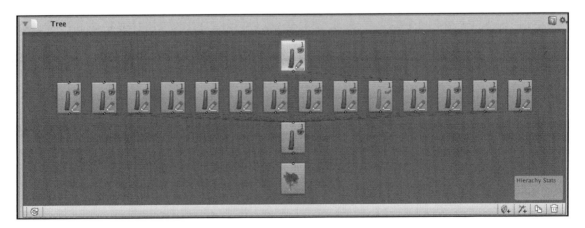

Your next step is to add leaves to your tree.

5. Click on the branch you want to apply leaves to and click the Add Leaf Group button.

6. In the **Distribution** section of the **Inspector** panel, change the **Frequency** to select how many leaves you want on that branch. This image shows the **Frequency** slider interface:

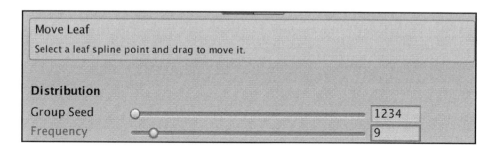

7. Continue adding leaves to the branches until you have your desired look. When you are done, your tree will look like it has paper for leaves:

As you can see, there is one tree trunk with several branches and leaf groups. We can see this in the **Tree** window:

The next step would be to apply materials to the branches and leaves. Since we do not have any of those materials in our game project yet, we will leave the tree as it is. Learning how to create unique trees can contribute to unique gaming environments. There are several quality trees available from Unity Technologies, as well as other content creators. We will explore some of those trees, and actually incorporate them into our game, in Chapter 6, *Creating and Importing 3D Objects for Our Game*.

8. In the **Hierarchy** panel, rename the Tree to Tree_Special.
9. Using the transform tools, relocate the tree on dry land. It is not important where you put it, as long as it is on dry land and not on a spawn point.
10. With Tree_Special selected, change the **Scale** from 1, 1, 1 to 3, 3, 3. That will make our tree more prominent in our game world.
11. Do not forget to save your Unity project.

Summary

In this chapter, we created our game's terrain and made several customizations to the terrain based on our design mock-up in Chapter 3, *Designing the Game*. We used shaping tools, painted the terrain, added water, and even created our own tree from scratch. In addition, we created a material and imported a texture file.

In Chapter 5, *Lights, Cameras, and Shadows*, we will explore the different types of lighting and cameras available in Unity. We will use lights and cameras in our *Cucumber Beetle* game to achieve appropriate light and shadow effects for the game.

5
Lights, Cameras, and Shadows

In the previous chapter, we created our game's terrain and made several customizations to the terrain, based on our design mock-up in Chapter 3, *Designing the Game*. We used shaping tools, painted the terrain, and added water. We even created our own tree from scratch. In addition, we created a material and imported a texture file.

In this chapter, we will explore cameras and lighting in Unity. We will start with a look at cameras to include perspectives, frustums, and Skyboxes. Next, we will learn a few uses of multiple cameras to include mini-maps. We will also cover the different types of lighting, explore reflection probes, and conclude with a look at shadows.

Specifically, we will cover the following concepts:

- Working with cameras
- Using multiple cameras
- Working with lighting
- Implementing reflection probes
- Understanding shadows

If you want to use the same Unity project featured in this chapter, you can download the Starting-Chapter-05.zip file from the publisher's companion site. Once you download the file, decompress it and then open the project in Unity. It contains the completed work from the previous chapters.

Working with cameras

Cameras render scenes so that the user can view them. Think about the hidden complexity in that statement. Our games are 3D, but people playing our games view them on 2D displays such as a televisions, computer monitors, or mobile devices. Fortunately for us, Unity makes implementing cameras easy work.

Cameras are GameObjects and can be edited using transform tools in the **Scene** view as well as in the **Inspector** panel. Every scene must have at least one camera. In fact, when a new scene is created, Unity creates a camera named **Main Camera**. As you will see later in this chapter, a scene can have multiple cameras.

In the **Scene** view, cameras are indicated with a white camera silhouette, as shown in the following screenshot:

When we click our **Main Camera** in the **Hierarchy** panel, we are provided with a **Camera Preview** in the **Scene** view. This gives us a preview of what the camera sees as if it were in game mode. We will change this in Chapter 7, *Implementing Our Player Character*. We also have access to several parameters via the **Inspector** panel. The **Camera** component in the **Inspector** panel is shown here:

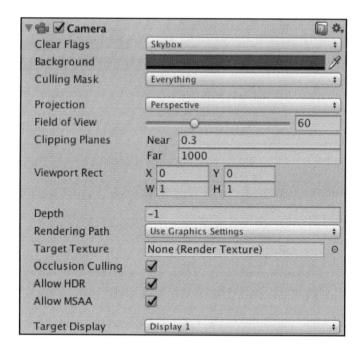

Let's look at each of these parameters with relation to our *Cucumber Beetle* game:

- The **Clear Flags** parameter lets you switch between **Skybox**, **Solid Color**, **Depth Only**, and **Don't Clear**. The selection here informs Unity which parts of the screen to clear. We will leave this setting as **Skybox**. You will learn more about Skyboxes later in this chapter.

- The **Background** parameter is used to set the default background fill (color) of your game world. This will only be visible after all game objects have been rendered and if there is no Skybox. Our *Cucumber Beetle* game will have a Skybox, so this parameter can be left with the default color.

- The **Culling Mask** parameter allows you to select and deselect the layers you want the camera to render. The default selection options are **Nothing**, **Everything**, **Default**, **TransparentFX**, **Ignore Raycast**, **Water**, and **UI**. For our game, we will select **Everything**. If you are not sure which layer a game object is associated with, select it and look at the **Layer** parameter in the top section of the Inspector panel. There you will see the assigned layer. You can easily change the layer as well as create your own unique layers. This gives you finite rendering control.

- The **Projection** parameter allows you to select which **projection**, **perspective** or **orthographic**, you want for your camera. We will cover both of those projections later in this chapter. When *perspective* projection is selected, we are given access to the **Field of View** parameter. This is for the width of the camera's angle of view. The value range is 1-179°. You can use the slider to change the values and see the results in the **Camera Preview** window. When **orthographic** projection is selected, an additional **Size** parameter is available. This refers to the viewport size. For our game, we will select perspective projection with the **Field of View** set to 60.

- The **Clipping Planes** parameters include **Near** and **Far**. These settings set the closest and furthest points, relative to the camera, that rendering will happen at. For now, we will leave the default settings of 0.3 and 1000 for the **Near** and **Far** parameters, respectively.

- The **Viewport Rect** parameter has four components – **X**, **Y**, **W**, and **H** – that determine where the camera will be drawn on the screen. As you would expect, the **X** and **Y** components refer to horizontal and vertical positions, and the **W** and **H** components refer to width and height. You can experiment with these values and see the changes in the **Camera Preview**. For our game, we will leave the default settings.

- The **Depth** parameter is used when we implement more than one camera. We can set a value here to determine the camera's priority in relation to others. Larger values indicate a higher priority. The default setting is sufficient for our game.

- The **Rendering Path** parameter defines what rendering methods our camera will use. The options are **Use Graphics Settings**, **Forward**, **Deferred**, **Legacy Vertex Lit**, and **Legacy Deferred (light prepass)**. We will use the **Use Graphics Settings** option for our game, which also uses the default setting.

- The **Target Texture** parameter is not something we will use in our game. When a render texture is set, the camera is not able to render to the screen.

- The **Occlusion Culling** parameter is a powerful setting. If enabled, Unity will not render objects that are occluded, or not seen by the camera. An example would be objects inside a building. If the camera can currently only see the external walls of the building, then none of the objects inside those walls can be seen. So, it makes sense to not render those. We only want to render what is absolutely necessary to help ensure our game has smooth gameplay and no lag. We will leave this as enabled for our game.

- The **Allow HDR** parameter is a checkbox that toggles a camera's **High Dynamic Range** (HDR) rendering. We will leave the default setting of enabled for our game.

- The **Allow MSAA** parameter is a toggle that determines whether our camera will use a **Multisample Anti-Aliasing (MSAA)** render target. MSAA is a computer graphics optimization technique and we want this enabled for our game.

Understanding camera projections

There are two camera projections used in Unity: **perspective** and **orthographic**. With perspective projection, the camera renders a scene based on the camera angle, as it exists in the scene. Using this projection, the further away an object is from the camera, the smaller it will be displayed. This mimics how we see things in the real world. Because of the desire to produce realistic games, or games that approximate the realworld, perspective projection is the most commonly used in modern games. It is also what we will use in our *Cucumber Beetle* game.

The other projection is orthographic. An orthographic perspective camera renders a scene uniformly without any perspective. This means that objects further away will not be displayed smaller than objects closer to the camera. This type of camera is commonly used for top-down games and is the default camera projection used in 2D and Unity's UI system.

We will use perspective projection for our *Cucumber Beetle* game.

Orientating your frustum

When a camera is selected in the **Hierarchy** view, its frustum is visible in the **Scene** view. A frustum is a geometric shape that looks like a pyramid that has had its top cut off, as illustrated here:

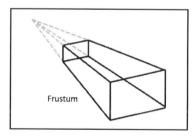

The near, or top, plane is parallel to its base. The base is also referred to as the far plane. The frustum's shape represents the viable region of your game. Only objects in that region are rendered. Using the camera object in **Scene** view, we can change our camera's frustum shape.

Creating a Skybox

When we create game worlds, we typically create the ground, buildings, characters, trees, and other game objects. What about the sky? By default, there will be a textured blue sky in your Unity game projects. That sky is sufficient for testing but does not add to an immersive gaming experience. We want a bit more realism, such as clouds, and that can be accomplished by creating a Skybox.

A Skybox is a six-sided cube visible to the player beyond all other objects. So, when a player looks beyond your objects, what they see is your Skybox. As we said, Skyboxes are six-sided cubes, which means you will need six separate images that can essentially be clamped to each other to form the cube.

The following screenshot shows the **Default Skybox** that Unity projects start with as well as the completed **Custom Skybox** you will create in this section:

 To follow along, you will need the six images located in the Chapter5-Skybox.zip file on the publisher's companion site.

Perform the following steps to create a Skybox:

1. In the **Project** panel, create a Skybox subfolder in the Assets folder. We will use this folder to store our textures and materials for the Skybox.

2. Drag the provided six Skybox images, or your own, into the new `Skybox` folder.

3. Ensure the `Skybox` folder is selected in the `Project` panel.

4. From the top menu, select **Assets | Create | Material**. In the **Project** panel, name the material `Skybox`.

5. With the **Skybox** material selected, turn your attention to the **Inspector** panel.

6. Select the **Shader** drop-down menu and select **SkyBox | 6 Sided**.

7. Use the **Select** button for each of the six images and navigate to the images you added in step 2. Be sure to match the appropriate texture to the appropriate cube face. For example, the `SkyBox_Front` texture matches the `Front[+Z]` cube face on the **Skybox Material**.

8. In order to assign our new Skybox to our scene, select **Window | Lighting | Settings** from the top menu. This will bring up the **Lighting** settings dialog window.

9. In the **Lighting** settings dialog window, click on the small circle to the right of the **Skybox Material** input field. Then, close the selection window and the **Lighting** window. Refer to the following screenshot:

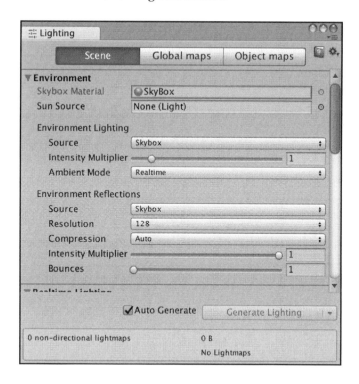

You will now be able to see your Skybox in the **Scene** view. When you click on the **Camera** in the **Hierarchy** panel, you will also see the Skybox as it will appear from the camera's perspective.

Be sure to save your scene and your project.

Using multiple cameras

Our Unity games must have a least one camera, but we are not limited to using just one. As you will see in Chapter 7, *Implementing Our Player Character*, we will attach our main camera, or primary camera, to our player character. It will be as if the camera is following the character around the game environment. This will become the eyes of our character. We will play the game through our character's view.

A common use of a second camera is to create a mini-map that can be seen in a small window on top of the game display. These mini-maps can be made to toggle on and off or be permanent/fixed display components. Implementations might consist of a fog-of-war display, a radar showing enemies, or a global top-down view of the map for orientation purposes. You are only limited by your imagination. In Chapter 9, *Adding a Heads-Up Display*, we will create a mini-map as a radar showing where beetles are in relation to the Cucumber Man's current position.

Another use of multiple cameras is to provide the player with the ability to switch between third-person and first-person views. You will remember from Chapter 1, *Downloading and Installing Unity*, that the first-person view puts the player's arms in view, while in the third-person view, the player's entire body is visible. We can use two cameras in the appropriate positions to support viewing from either camera. In a game, you might make this a toggle—say, with the C keyboard key—that switches from one camera to the other. Depending on what is happening in the game, the player might enjoy this ability.

Some single-player games feature multiple playable characters. Giving the player the ability to switch between these characters gives them greater control over the game strategy. To achieve this, we would need to have cameras attached to each playable character and then give the player the ability to swap characters. We would do this through scripting. This is a pretty advanced implementation of multiple characters.

Another use of multiple cameras is adding specialty views in a game. These specialty views might include looking through a door's peep-hole, looking through binoculars at the top of a skyscraper, or even looking through a periscope. We can attach cameras to objects and change their viewing parameters to create unique camera use in our games. We are only limited by our own game designs and imagination.

We can also use cameras as cameras. That's right! We can use the camera game object to simulate actual in-game cameras. One example is implementing security cameras in a prison-escape game.

Working with lighting

In the previous sections, we explored the uses of cameras for Unity games. Just like in the real world, cameras need lights to show us objects. In Unity games, we use multiple lights to illuminate the game environment.

In Unity, we have both dynamic lighting techniques as well as light baking options for better performance. We can add numerous light sources throughout our scenes and selectively enable or disable an object's ability to cast or receive shadows. This level of specificity gives us tremendous opportunity to create realistic game scenes.

Perhaps the secret behind Unity's ability to so realistically render light and shadows is that Unity models the actual behavior of lights and shadows. Real-time global illumination gives us the ability to instantiate multiple lights in each scene, each with the ability to directly or indirectly impact objects in the scene that are within range of the light sources.

 Indirect light refers to lights bouncing off objects and reflecting on other objects.

We can also add and manipulate ambient light in our game scenes. This is often done with Skyboxes, a tri-colored gradient, or even a single color. Each new scene in Unity has default ambient lighting, which we can control by editing the values in the the **Lighting** window. In that window, you have access to the following settings:

- **Environment**
- **Real-time Lighting**
- **Mixed Lighting**
- **Lightmapping Settings**
- **Other Settings**
- **Debug Settings**

No changes to these are required for our game at this time. We have already set the environmental lighting to our Skybox. In `Chapter 12`, *Adding Audio and Visual Effects to Our Game*, we will look at **Fog**, which is available under the **Other Settings** section of the **Lighting** window.

When we create our scenes in Unity, we have three options for lighting. We can use real-time dynamic light, use the baked lighting approach, or use a mixture of the two. Our games perform more efficiently with baked lighting, compared to real-time dynamic lighting, so if performance is a concern, try using baked lighting where you can.

In addition to ambient lighting, there are four types of light: directional, point, spot, and area. We will look at each of these in the following sections.

Directional lighting

When we create a new scene in Unity, a directional light is automatically created for us. This emphasizes the importance of directional lights. This type of light provides illumination in a specific direction. Using transform tools, we have full control over the direction of these lights.

An example of directional lighting is generating sunlight in our scenes. Although the light from directional lights is similar to that of the sun, there is no actual sun-like object that the light comes from. As shown in the following screenshot, **Directional Lights**, when selected, indicate the direction of its illumination with yellow rays:

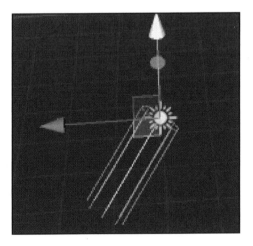

One of the great aspects of using directional lighting is that illumination strength is not dependent on an object's distance from the **Directional Light** object. This type of lighting defines the direction of the light, and distance has no impact on the illumination.

With a **Directional Light** selected, you have access to several parameters in the **Inspector** panel. In addition to the **Transform** section, there is a **Light** section where you can change several settings to include the light color and intensity. The remaining parameters are worth exploring and no changes are required to complete our game.

To add additional directional lights, you would select, from the top menu, **GameObject | Light | Directional Light**.

For the *Cucumber Beetle* game, we will keep the default **Directional Light**. You can use the transform tools to modify the location, rotation, and light direction.

Point lighting

Point lights get their name from the fact that they are lights sources emanating from a specific point. These light objects, as indicated in the following diagram, emit light in all directions:

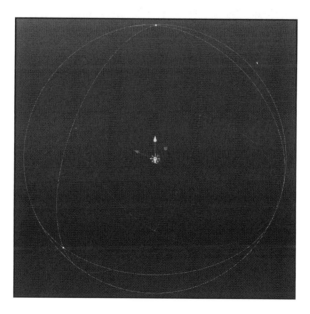

These lights are typically used to simulate fireballs or light bulbs. They can also be used to simulate some magic or special lighting effects. As you can see in the following screenshot, point lights have several properties that affect how they impact the game environment:

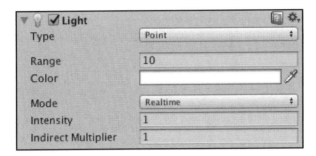

The **Range** is the distance between the center of the light to the outside arc of the light. We can also change the **Color** and **Intensity** to produce the results we desire.

To create a point light, we select **GameObject | Light | Directional Light** from the top menu.

Spot lighting

Spot lights are another type of lighting in Unity. They are meant to provide lighting on a specific spots. Common examples are flashlights and vehicle headlights. As you can see from the following screenshot, the light originates from the source in an outward cone shape:

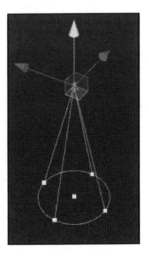

In the **Inspector** panel, we can change the **Range**, **Spot Angle**, **Color** and **Intensity**. **Range**, in this context, refers to the distance between the light source and the furthest point in the cone. The **Spot Angle** is the angle of the outward exterior edge of the cone shape. The **Spot Angle** range is 1-179°. The larger the value is, the larger the cone face will be.

To create a spotlight, we select **GameObject** | **Light** | **Spot Light** from the top menu.

Area lighting

To use an **area light**, we define a rectangle using the transform tools or the **Inspector** panel. Area lights emit light from one side of their rectangle. The following screenshot shows what an area light object looks like in the Unity editor:

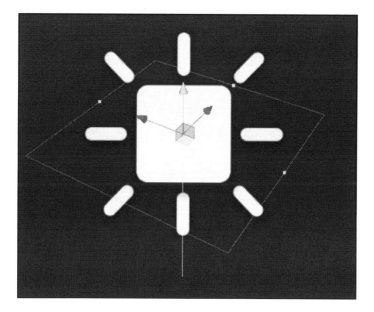

Area lights are unique from the other types of light as they can only be baked. This means that real-time rendering will not take place during gameplay. The reason for this is to conduct all the processing regarding area lights prior to gameplay. This processing, if accomplished in real time in a game, would likely result in sufficient lag.

As you can see in the following screenshot, the **Type** is set as **Area (baked only)** and cannot be changed:

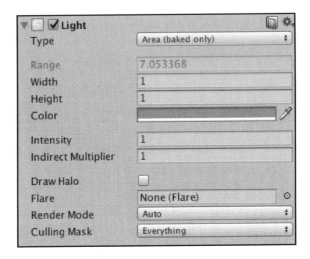

Area lights can be used instead of point lights when baked lighting is okay and you desire software shadows.

To create an area light, we select **GameObject | Light | Area Light** from the top menu.

Implementing reflection probes

Reflection probes capture a 360° spherical view of their surroundings. In this sense, it is somewhat like a camera. That captured image is used by nearby objects that have reflective materials.

To create a reflection probe, we select **GameObject | Light | Reflection Probe** from the top menu.

As you can see from the following screenshot, the reflection probe is a sphere and has captured the view of its surroundings. When objects are placed in close proximity to the reflection probe, the reflections will be visible on the object:

A review of a reflection probe in the **Inspector** panel, shown as follows, reveals several settings that we can change to affect how the probe works and how it impacts our game environment:

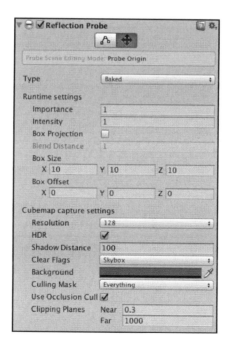

The following list of properties highlights the ones you are most likely to change in the Unity games you create:

- **Type**: You can select **Baked**, **Custom**, or **Realtime**. Remember, we can improve game performance if we bake our lighting whenever possible.
- **Importance**: When there are multiple rendering probes in the area, you can set the importance of each of them. The higher the value, the greater the importance.
- **Intensity**: The lowest value is zero. You can experiment with the results of changing this setting.
- **Resolution**: You can select **16, 32, 64, 128, 256, 512, 1024**, or **2048** for the resolution of the captured image reflection.

Understanding shadows

As indicated earlier in this chapter, our game scenes can have numerous light sources, and we can enable or disable an object's ability to cast or receive shadows. We have shadows in the real world and it is important to consider, for our Unity games, what objects cast shadows and what objects receive shadows.

The following screenshot shows the **Mesh Renderer** component of an object in the **Inspector** panel. Let's review the key settings of this component:

- **Light Probes**: It can be set to **Blend Probes, Use Proxy Volume**, or **Off**. You will most likely use the default **Blend Probes** for simple Unity games.
- **Reflection Probes**: This setting can be turned off or set to **Blend Probes, Blend Probes And Skybox**, or **Simple**.
- **Cast Shadows**: This setting can be set to **On, Off, Two-Sided**, or **Shadows Only**. The default is **On**, so you should disable this for all objects that do not need to cast shadows.
- **Receive Shadows**: This setting is a toggle that tells Unity whether you want that object to receive shadows or not. As you would expect, this takes extra processing to display during the game. So, if you do not need an object to receive shadows, deselect this for greater performance.

Summary

In this chapter, we explored cameras and lighting. We started with a look at cameras that included perspectives, frustums, and Skyboxes. Next, we learned possible uses of multiple cameras in Unity games. We also covered the different types of lighting, explored reflection probes, and concluded with a look at shadows.

In the next chapter, we will create 3D objects using Unity's native toolset. We will also import several objects into our game to complete our game environment, including the tree we made in Chapter 4, *Creating Our Terrain*.

6
Creating and Importing 3D Objects for Our Game

In the last chapter, we explored cameras and lighting. We started by looking at cameras, as well as the concepts of perspectives, frustums, and skyboxes. Next, we learned the possible uses of multiple cameras in Unity games. We also covered the different types of lighting, explored reflection probes, and concluded with a look at shadows.

We are ready to start making our game environment more robust. We will do that by adding trees and other objects to our scene. In this chapter, we will create 3D objects using Unity's native modeling tools. We will also import and use assets from two sources. Our first source will be the Unity Asset Store where we will download free-to-use assets for our game. We will also import 3D assets prepared specifically for our *Cucumber Beetle* game. As we obtain the assets, we will incorporate them into the game project and watch our game start to take shape.

We will cover the following concepts in this chapter:

- Understanding assets and GameObjects
- Creating 3D objects in Unity
- Using the Unity Asset Store
- Incorporating custom assets in our game
- Working with imported assets

 If you want to use the same Unity project featured in this chapter, you can download the `Starting-Chapter-06.zip` file from the publisher's companion site. Once you download the file, decompress it, and then open the project in Unity. It contains the completed work from the previous chapters.

Understanding assets and GameObjects

Assets are defined as useful or valuable things. In Unity, assets are things you will use in our game in conjunction with GameObjects. We'll discuss GameObjects later in this section. There are three basic categories of asset based on their source: Unity, user created, and third party. The Unity game engine comes with free assets and offers a library of premium (not free) assets. User-created assets are those that you create yourself. We will create our own assets later in this chapter. The final asset type is third party, meaning that someone other than you or Unity created it.

When we select the **Assets** drop-down menu, as shown in the following screenshot, we have several options available to us. You will become familiar with the **Create**, **Import New Asset**, and **Import Package** options in this chapter:

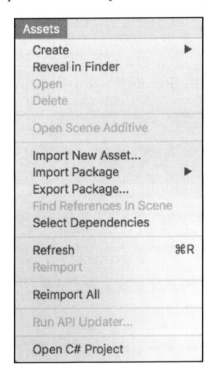

Regardless of the asset source, Unity, user-created, and third-party, assets can be of several types. As you can see in the following screenshot, these asset types include scripts, scenes, prefabs, materials, animations and more:

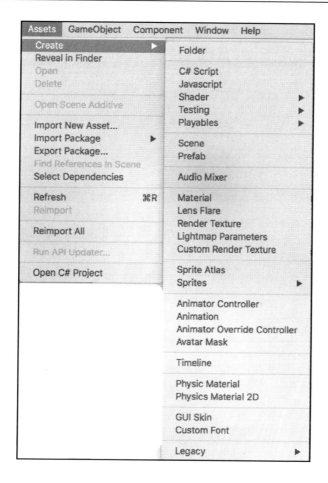

Asset packages

Asset packages are bundles of assets grouped together. We can create packages to share our assets with others, or to save them for use in another game or Unity application. We can even create asset bundles to sell in Unity's Asset Store.

To create an `asset` package, you simply select all the assets you want in the package using the **Project** panel. Then you have two options. Your first option is to right-click and select **Export Package**. The second option is to select **Assets** | **Export Package** from the top menu. Both options result in the same outcome.

In addition to the ability to export packages from Unity, we can also import `asset` packages into our Unity games. To import an `asset` package, we simply select the **Assets |** **Import Package** menu option. That reveals the options shown in the following screenshot:

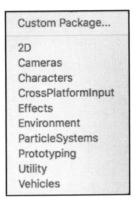

When importing `asset` packages, we can select from one of the standard asset packages listed: **2D**, **Cameras**, **Characters**, **CrossPlatformInput**, **Effects**, **Environment**, **ParticleSystems**, **Prototyping**, **Utility**, and **Vehicles**. We can also import a custom package from our computer's filesystem.

When a package is selected, Unity will decompress the package and then display the package contents to you. We will perform this operation later in this chapter.

Understanding GameObjects

GameObjects are things we use in our game, such as 2D objects, 3D objects, audio, cameras, lights, user interfaces, and visual effects. GameObjects have properties, which vary based on their type, and components. Components can consist of things such as scripts, animations, and more. You will learn a lot about GameObjects and how to work with them as we continue to work on our game.

GameObjects are composed of components. As you can see in the following screenshot of the **Inspector** panel, our game's **Main Camera** has four components: **Transform**, **Camera**, **GUI Layer**, **Flare Layer**, and **Audio Listener**:

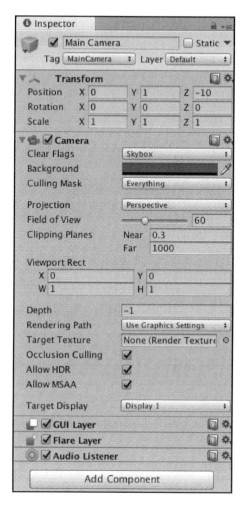

At the bottom of the **Inspector** panel is the **Add Component** button. That button gives us access to Unity's components using the following categories:

- **Mesh**
- **Effects**
- **Physics**
- **Physics 2D**
- **Navigation**
- **Audio**
- **Video**

- **Rendering**
- **Layout**
- **Playables**
- **AR**
- **Miscellaneous**
- **Analytics**
- **Scripts**
- **Event**
- **Network**
- **UI**
- **New Script**

Creating 3D objects in Unity

As mentioned in the previous section, GameObjects can include 3D objects with properties and components. In this section, we will create a 3D object to represent a blood droplet that we can use when the Cucumber Man is battling with a Cucumber Beetle. Before we create the object, let's create a material so that our blood droplet can have a realistic red color. Follow these steps to create the material:

1. In the **Project** panel, click **Materials**, and then right-click in the folder and select **Create | Material**
2. Name the new material **red**
3. With the new material selected, click the color box in the **Main Maps** section of the **Inspector** panel
4. In the color selector window that pops-up, select a red color and then close the selection box

Your new material, when viewed in the **Inspector** panel, should look similar to the following screenshot:

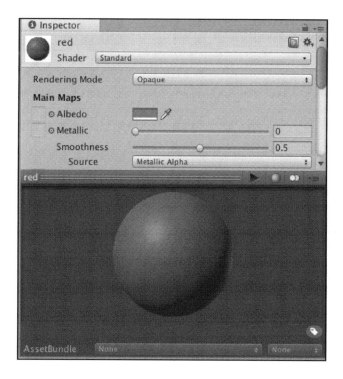

Next, let's create the sphere:

1. From the top menu, select **GameObject | 3D Object | Sphere**.

2. Use the transform tools to position the new sphere so that you can see it in the **Scene** view.

3. Use the **Transform** section of the **Inspector** panel to increase the **Scale** to **5** for the **X**, **Y**, and **Z Scale** parameters. This will help make the sphere larger and easier to work with.

4. Next, we will assign the red material to the sphere. With the sphere selected in the **Hierarchy** panel and the `Materials` folder selected in the project panel, drag the **red** material from the `Materials` folder to the **Inspector** panel **Mesh Renderer** component, in the **Materials | Element 0** parameter.

You will now see that the sphere in the **Scene** view is red.

If we intend on using this sphere to simulate blood droplets, we might need several dozen of them. We will explore our options in the next section.

Using prefabs

In the previous section, you created a sphere to simulate a blood droplet. You also created a red material and applied it to your sphere. In the game, we might want to simulate a great battle and have multiple blood droplets visible at once. In Unity, we can make as many copies of our master as we want. For example, let's assume we have 100 spheres, all copied from our master. What happens when we want to alter them, perhaps changing the size or material? It would be a laborious task to edit each one.

An alternative is to use a prefab. In Unity, a prefab is an asset type that serves as a shell for a GameObject along with properties and components. The sphere we created is a GameObject, and, as you can see in the following screenshot, our sphere has several components and properties:

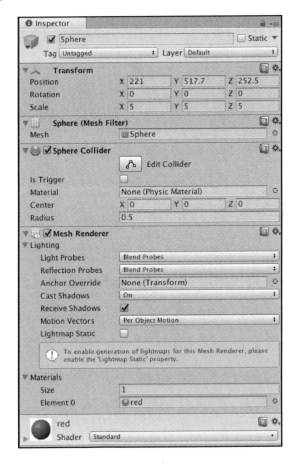

So, let's create a prefab to hold our sphere. Follow these steps:

1. In the **Project** panel, select the `Prefabs` folder.
2. Right-click on the `Prefabs` folder and select **Create | Prefab**. Alternatively, you could have selected, from the top menu, **Assets | Create | Prefab**.
3. Name the prefab `bloodDroplet`. You will notice that there are no components or properties visible in the **Inspector** panel for the new prefab.
4. Next, drag the `Sphere` GameObject from the **Hierarchy** panel to the new `bloodDroplet` prefab in the **Project** panel. Now, when you view the prefab in the **Inspector** panel, you can see the components and properties that our sphere had.
5. We no longer need the original sphere, so delete that in the **Hierarchy** panel.

Now that we have a `bloodDroplet` prefab, we can drag it into our scene as many times as we want. We can also add them to our scene using scripts.

To experience the power of prefabs in Unity, try the following:

1. Select the `bloodDroplet` prefab in the **Project** panel.
2. Drag several copies of the `bloodDroplet` prefab into your scene.
3. In the **Inspector** panel, change the color. You will notice that all the `bloodDroplets` in your scene were changed based on the change you made to the prefab.
4. Return the color of the prefab to the red material.
5. Delete any `bloodDroplets` from your scene. This is most easily done in the **Hierarchy** panel.

Deleting the `bloodDroplets` from your scene does not remove all `bloodDroplets` from your game. Because we have the `bloodDroplet` prefab, we can add `bloodDroplets` to our scene at any time.

Using additional 3D objects

In the previous section, you created a sphere. Unity also allows us to natively create other 3D objects: cubes, capsules, cylinders, planes, quads, rag dolls, terrain, trees, wind zones, and 3D text. The basic shapes—cube, sphere, capsule, cylinder, plane, and quad—may not be what you need for your game, and we certainly do not need them for our *Cucumber Beetle* game. These 3D objects are great for testing components and scripts in Unity projects. We can delete them even more easily than we can create them, so they make great and expendable testing assets. We can use them in our games to experiment with before we spend any time on final graphics.

Using the Unity Asset Store

Unity operates a store called the Unity Asset Store. There are a great number of assets available to Unity developers. The store is accessible directly on the web at `http://assetstore.unity3d.com`. You can also open a window within Unity to display the Asset Store. This is done by selecting **Window | Asset Store**.

Regardless of how you connect to the Unity Asset Store, you will see a hierarchical category listing in the top-right-hand corner of the store. As you can see in the following screenshot, there are eleven asset categories:

Clicking on the triangular icons to the left of each category reveals subcategories. Some categories have multiple subcategories, which helps you find what you are looking for quickly. You can also use the Asset Store's search functionality.

When you click on a category, its contents will be viewable. Clicking on a specific asset will display several characteristics of that asset. These characteristics include the following:

- Title
- Publisher
- Rating
- Price
- **Add to Cart** button, or, in the case of free assets, a **Download** button
- Version of Unity required
- Release date
- Description
- Package contents
- File size
- Version number (of the asset)
- Images
- Videos (not always available)
- Link to publisher's website
- User reviews

There are a couple of things to consider regarding obtaining assets from the Unity Asset Store. First, you will want to make sure you have the requisite rights to use the asset as you plan to. For example, if you do not have commercial use rights, you will not want to use that particular asset in your commercial game.

Another thing to consider before selecting assets from the Asset Store is how large the files are. Fortunately, this information is part of the metadata displayed when you preview an asset.

In the next section, we will visit the Unity Asset Store, select an asset, and add that asset to our game project.

Hands-on with the Unity Asset Store

In this section, we will go through the necessary steps to acquire assets from the Unity Asset Store. Follow these steps:

1. Using the top menu, select **Window** | **Asset Store**.
2. In the search box, enter `Unity Particle Pack` and hit your keyboard's return button.
3. In the results, find the **Unity Particle Pack** item by Unity Technologies. It will be a free asset package. Select that package by clicking on the title.
4. With the **Unity Particle Pack** displayed in the Asset Store, click the **Download** button.
5. You will be prompted to accept the **License Agreement**. Click the **Accept** button if you agree with the terms. This will start the download process.
6. When the download completes, the **Import** button will appear. Click that button.
7. You will now see the **Import Unity Package** dialog window. By default, all assets in the package will be selected. Click the **Import** button at the bottom of the interface. The import progress will be displayed in a pop-up window and will automatically close when the process completes.
8. When the import process completes, close the Asset Store by right-clicking the tab and selecting **Close** tab.

As you can see from the following screenshot, there will be a new `EffectExamples` folder under **Assets** in your **Project** panel:

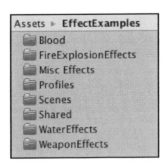

We now have a nice set of special effects we can use in our game. We will incorporate some of them in `Chapter 12`, *Adding Audio and Visual Effects to Our Game.*

Incorporating custom assets in our game

So far in this chapter, we have created our own game asset and downloaded an asset package from the Unity Asset Store. In this section, we will download assets from the publisher's companion website for use in our game.

Go through the following steps to obtain the asset packages that were created specifically for our *Cucumber Beetle* game:

1. Navigate to the publisher's website and download the following files:
   - CherriesAndTree.unitypackage
   - CucumberAndPatches.unitypackage

2. From the top menu, select **Assets** | **Import Package** | **Custom Package** and navigate to the CherriesAndTree.unitypackage file. Click the **Open** button.

3. As shown in the following screenshot, the **Import Unity Package** dialog window will have the necessary files for our Cherry Tree and the cherries. Click the **Import** button:

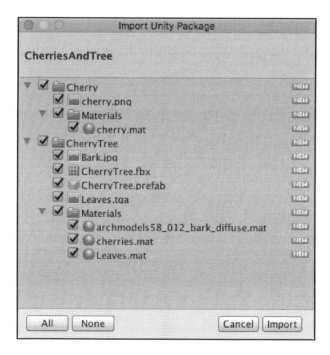

Next, we will import the cucumber and two Cucumber Patches. These are contained in the `CucumberAndPatches.unitypackage` asset package. Follow the preceding steps to import this asset package into your game.

As you can see in the following screenshot, there are several files in this asset package relating to the cucumber and both Cucumber Patches:

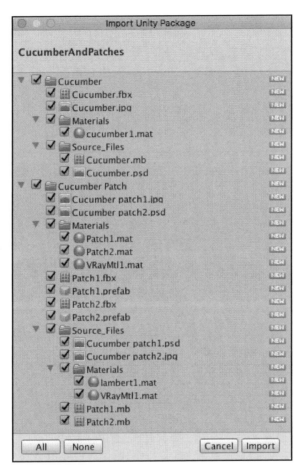

 In Chapter 7, *Implementing Our Player Character*, and Chapter 8, *Implementing Our Non-Player Character*, you will download additional asset packages.

Working with imported assets

In the previous section, you added the following listed assets to your game:

- Cherry
- Cherry Tree
- Cucumber
- Cucumber Patches

We will incorporate the cherry and cucumber assets in Chapter 10, *Scripting Our Points System*. In this section, we will plant our Cherry Trees and Cucumber Patches.

As you will recall from Chapter 3, *Designing the Game*, we created spawn points in four corners and the center of our game environment. We also selected four areas in which to plant our Cherry Trees. Now that we have actual terrain, we can be more specific with our design. Look at the following diagram to determine where to plant our Cherry Trees and Cucumber Patches:

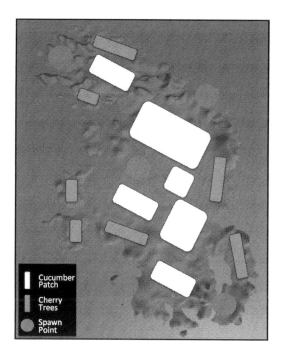

We will refer to this diagram in the next two sections as we plant our Cherry Trees and Cucumber Patches.

Planting Cherry Trees

In `Chapter 4`, *Creating Our Terrain,* we created a tree to demonstrate how to create one from scratch. Since we downloaded a Cherry Tree in the last section, we no longer need our experimental tree. In the hierarchy panel, delete the three we previously created. Next, delete any tree assets and tree-related texture folders in the project panel. This will help us stay organized and minimize the size of our Unity game project.

Basic trees in Unity can be painted on a terrain. To accomplish this, you start by orienting the scene view so that you have a top-down view of your terrain. Then, in the **Hierarchy** panel, select your terrain. You then use the **Place Trees** button in the **Terrain** component of the **Inspector** panel to paint the trees on your terrain.

Because our Cherry Trees are special and contain multiple meshes, we cannot use the terrain painting tool. Instead, we will make multiple copies of our Cherry Tree prefab and place them where we want them to be in our game world using the previously provided diagram as a reference.

We have a few preparatory steps to take prior to planting our Cherry Trees. Follow these steps to prepare the prefab:

1. In the **Project** panel, right-click on the `Prefabs` folder and select **Create | Prefab**. Name the prefab `CherryTreeCollider`.
2. In the **Project** panel, drag the `CherryTree.prefab` that you imported in the previous section into the **Scene** view. It doesn't matter where.
3. In the **Hierarchy** panel, select the Cherry Tree you just added to the **Scene** view.
4. In the **Inspector** panel, click the **Is Trigger** checkbox in the **Box Collider** component.
5. Still in the **Inspector** panel, click the **Add Component** button and then select **Physics | Box Collider**. We will use this collider to help us determine when the Cucumber Man is collecting cherries from a Cherry Tree.
6. Next, we will edit the collider to ensure it encapsulates the entire tree. In the **Box Collider** area of the **Inspector** panel, click the **Edit Collider** button.

As you can see from the following screenshot, the collider is at the base of the
`Cherry Tree` **prefab**:

7. Using the the squares of the box collider in the **Scene** view, enlarge the collider so
that it encompasses the majority of the Cherry Tree. It does not need to include
the tree trunk. An example configuration is shown in the following screenshot:

8. In the **Project** panel, ensure that the Prefabs folder is selected.

9. Drag the Cherry Tree from the **Hierarchy** panel to the CherryTreeCollider prefab in the Prefabs folder. This establishes a Cherry Tree prefab with a box collider.

10. In the **Hierarchy** panel, delete the Cherry Tree, unless it is in a place that you want it to be in.

11. Select the CherryTreeCollider prefab in the Prefabs folder.

12. In the **Inspector** panel, click the pull-down menu next to **Tag**. Select the **Add Tag** button.

13. As indicated by the arrow in the following screenshot, click the **+** icon at the bottom of the empty list:

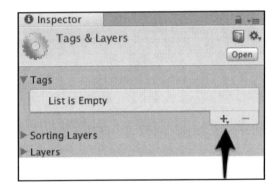

14. In the pop-up window, enter CherryTree as the tag name and click the **Save** button.

15. Select the CherryTreeCollider prefab in the Prefabs folder.

16. In the **Inspector** panel, click the pull-down menu next to **Tag**. Select the CherryTree tag.

Now you are ready to start planting your Cherry Trees. Simply drag the prefab to each area where you want a Cherry Tree. You can create as many or as few as you want. The example provided with this book contains 25 Cherry Trees.

Once your Cherry Trees are where you want them, your hierarchy panel will probably be disorganized. A quick trick to make things more organized is to right-click inside the **Hierarchy** panel and select **Create Empty**. Then, rename the GameObject to Cherry Trees. Lastly, in the **Hierarchy** panel, select all the Cherry Trees and place them in that GameObject. Now that GameObject serves as a folder for viewing purposes. You can collapse and expand the folder as needed.

If you placed your Cherry Trees using a top-down view in the **Scene** view, some of your trees might need to be raised or lowered based on your terrain. You can double-click a Cherry Tree in the **Hierarchy** view to auto-zoom in on the **Scene** view.

Once you complete your work on the Cherry Trees, save your scene and your project.

Planting Cucumber Patches

We previously identified six areas for our Cucumber Patches. We can follow the same approach in placing Cucumber Patches in our game environment as we used for our Cherry Trees. If we took an auto-planting approach to planting our Cucumber Patches, we would likely end up with a lot more Cucumber Patches than we want. So, we will take a manual approach.

We have prefabs in the `Cucumber Patch` folder from our early import. Let's do a few things to prepare these prefabs for our use. Follow these steps:

1. In the **Project** panel, right-click in the `Prefabs` folder and select **Create | Prefab**. Name the prefab `CucumberPatch1`.
2. Repeat step 1 and name this second prefab `CucumberPatch2`.
3. In the **Project** panel, drag the `Patch1prefab` that you imported in the previous section into the **Scene** view. It doesn't matter where.
4. In the **Hierarchy** panel, select the Cucumber Patch you just added to the **Scene** view.
5. In the **Project** panel, ensure that the `Prefabs` folder is selected.
6. Drag the Cucumber Patch from the **Hierarchy** panel to the `CucumberPatch1` prefab in the `Prefabs` folder.
7. Delete the Cucumber Patch from the **Hierarchy** panel.
8. In the **Project** panel, drag the `Patch2prefab` that you imported in the previous section into the **Scene** view. It doesn't matter where.
9. In the **Hierarchy** panel, select the Cucumber Patch you just added to the **Scene** view.
10. In the **Project** panel, ensure that the `Prefabs` folder is selected.

11. Drag the Cucumber Patch from the **Hierarchy** view to the `CucumberPatch2` prefab in the `Prefabs` folder.

12. Delete the Cucumber Patch from the **Hierarchy** panel.

We could have just moved the prefabs we imported to the `Prefabs` folder. Our approach was to duplicate them so that we have the originals available should we need them.

Next, we will prepare the six areas in our game world for the Cucumber Patches. Our goal is to identify the rectangular areas, each with a flat area of ground.

Using the following reference image and the Unity skills you used to create your terrain, we need to flatten the six areas and record their rectangle boundaries:

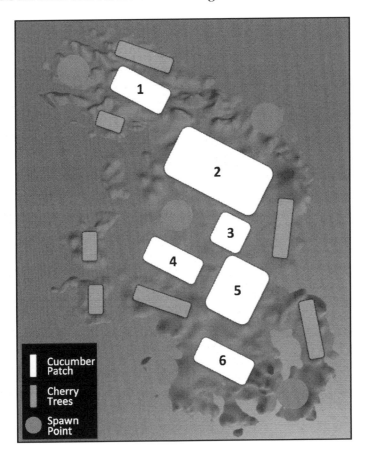

To prepare our Cucumber Patch areas, follow these steps:

1. Use the **Paint Height** tool to flatten a Cucumber Patch area.
2. Select **GameObject | 3D Object | Plane** from the top menu.
3. Position the plane so that it is on the ground, specifically in the flattened area.
4. In the **Inspector** view, set the **Materials | Element 0** parameter to **SpatialMappingOcclusion**. This will make the plane transparent.
5. Once the plane is in place, make note of the transform information.
6. Repeat steps 1 through 5 for the remaining Cucumber Patches.
7. Rename the planes so that you have
   `CucumberPatchArea1`, `CucumberPatchArea2`, `CucumberPatchArea3`, `CucumberPatchArea4`, `CucumberPatchArea5`, and `CucumberPatchArea6`.

When you are completed, you should have six defined areas for your Cucumber Patches. For reference, the six areas used in the book's example are shown in the following table:

Plane	Transform			
`CucumberPatchArea1`		X	Y	Z
	Position	7373	40.03	1689
	Rotation	0	10.082	0
`CucumberPatchArea2`		X	Y	Z
	Position	1211	40.03	1142
	Rotation	0	53.984	0
`CucumberPatchArea3`		X	Y	Z
	Position	1160	40.03	831
	Rotation	0	87.876	0
`CucumberPatchArea4`		X	Y	Z
	Position	892	40.03	849
	Rotation	0	120.877	0

CucumberPatchArea5		X	Y	Z
	Position	1200	40.03	568
	Rotation	0	143.801	0

CucumberPatchArea6		X	Y	Z
	Position	1184	40.03	330
	Rotation	0	103.911	0

Our last step is to group the six Cucumber Patches in the **Hierarchy** panel to help stay organized. As we did with the Cherry Trees, we will right-click inside the **Hierarchy** panel and select **Create Empty**. Then rename the GameObject as Cucumber Patch Areas. Lastly, in the **Hierarchy** panel, select all six Cucumber Patch panes and place them in that GameObject.

In Chapter 8, *Implementing Our Non-Player Characters*, we will use the panes to add Cucumber Patches, Cucumbers, and beetles.

Summary

In this chapter, we spent considerable time making our game environment more robust. We imported and used several assets. We added trees and other objects to our scene. We created 3D objects using Unity's native modeling tools and imported assets from the Unity Asset Store, as well as from the publisher's companion site. Specifically, we added our game's Cherry Trees, and prepared areas for Cucumber Patches.

In Chapter 7, *Implementing Our Player Character*, we will incorporate our game's player character, the Cucumber Man. We will import the character, review the controls, examine the animations, and make the necessary configuration changes to fully use our character in the game. By the end of the chapter, you will be able to start testing the game.

7
Implementing Our Player Character

In *Chapter 6*, *Creating and Importing 3D Objects for Our Game*, we worked on our game environment and added several assets to our game project. We added and planted our cherry trees and prepared six areas for our cucumber patches. We also learned how to import assets from the Unity Asset Store, as well as from third-party sources.

In this chapter, we will incorporate our game's player character, the Cucumber Man. We will import the character, review the controls, examine the animations, and make the necessary configuration changes to fully use our character in the game. By the end of the chapter, you will be able to start testing the game in game-mode.

We will look at the following topics in this chapter:

- Working with Unity's standard asset package
- Importing the game character
- Configuring the player controller
- Fine-tuning our character
- Animating our player character
- Terraforming the terrain for our Cucumber Man

Working with Unity's standard asset package

The game character, the player character, the user-controlled player—these are all terms that are used to refer to our game's main character, the Cucumber Man, which the human player will control. In Unity, we refer to this as the player character. In order to have a player character, we need a controller. In our case, we will use a third-person controller. A third-person controller is a framework used to control a character from the perspective of a third-person camera.

The Unity standard asset package includes a `ThirdPersonController` asset package. The package, as you can see in the following screenshot, contains `Animation`, `Materials`, `Models`, `Scripts`, `Textures`, and `Prefabs`:

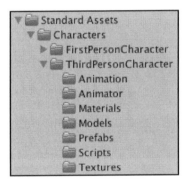

This section demonstrates how to use a character created by Unity. It will not be incorporated into the *Cucumber Beetle* game. By going through the following steps, you will become familiar with the process of using the `ThirdPersonCharacter` provided by Unity:

1. Launch Unity.
2. From the top menu, select **Assets** | **Import Package** | **Characters**.
3. You will be presented with the **Import Unity Package** dialog window. Click the **Import** button.

4. In the **Project** panel, you will see Standard Assets. Navigate to Standard Assets | **Characters** | ThirdPersonCharacter | Prefabs and drag the ThirdPersonController prefab to the **Hierarchy** panel.

5. Double-click on the ThirdPersonController in the **Hierarchy** panel to autofocus on the controller in the **Scene** view. As shown in the following screenshot, the character is encased in a capsule controller:

6. In the hierarchy pane, drag the **Main Camera** so that it is subordinate to the ThirdPersonController. This is required so that the camera follows the player character during gameplay.

7. In the **Scene** view, use the transform tools to position the camera above and behind the character. With the camera selected, your **Camera Preview** window, in the **Scene** view, should look similar to the following screenshot:

Now you can put the game into game-mode and navigate the game world using your keyboard and mouse. As you will see, the default character can move around the world, and the camera will follow.

Using the provided `ThirdPersonController` is great for testing purposes, but you would not want to deploy a game using these standard assets. Although Unity Technologies permits commercial use of their standard assets, using them erodes the uniqueness of your game, so it is recommended that they only be used for testing.

Importing the game character

We will use a custom third-person character controller for our *Cucumber Beetle* game. First, we should make sure there are no conflicting assets in your game project. Let's start by launching Unity and opening your game project based on the work you did in Chapter 6, *Creating and Importing 3D Objects for our Game*. Alternatively, you can load the Starting-Chapter-07 Unity project available from the publisher's companion site. Once your project is loaded in Unity, delete any of the following listed items from the **Hierarchy** panel:

- Camera (you will retain the main camera you first explored in Chapter 5, *Lights, Cameras, and Shadows*)
- `ThirdPersonController`

Once the unnecessary assets are deleted, your **Hierarchy** panel should contain only the assets listed in the following **Hierarchy** panel screenshot:

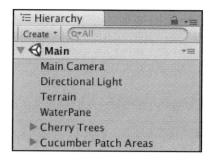

You are now ready to import the asset package for our game's player character, the Cucumber Man. Go through the following steps to import the package:

1. Download the `CucumberMan_Controller.unitypackage` file from the publisher's companion website
2. In Unity, with your game project open, select **Assets** | **Import Package** | **Custom Package** from the top menu
3. Navigate to the location of the asset package you downloaded in step 1 and click the **Open** button
4. When presented with the **Import Asset Package** dialog window, click the **Import** button

As you will notice, the Cucumber Man asset package contains several assets related to the Cucumber Man, including a Controller, Scripts, Prefabs, and other assets. In the next section, we will add the Cucumber Man to our game.

Configuring a player controller

So, far we have taken a lot of time to shape our world and populate it with cherry trees and spawn points, and prepare it for cucumber patches. We have been creating the game world for our player character, the Cucumber Man, to exist in. It is now time to add our Cucumber Man to our game.

Here are the steps to add the Cucumber Man to our game and to configure the controller:

1. In the **Project** panel, select **Prefabs**.
2. Drag the CucumberMan prefab to the **Hierarchy** panel. Use the following screenshot as a reference to ensure that you are dragging the highlighted prefab illustrated in the following screenshot. Note that the subordinate Cucumbor_Man has been intentionally misspelled to help ensure the CucumberMan prefab is used:

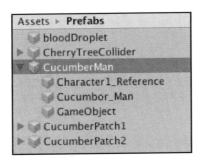

3. In the **Hierarchy** panel, select **Main Camera**.
4. With the **Main Camera** selected, click the **Add Component** button in the **Inspector** panel.
5. Select **Scripts | Camera Follower** to add the **Camera Follower** script to the **Main Camera**.
6. In the **Camera Follower** component of the **Main Camera**, in the **Inspector** panel, change the **Movement Smoothness** to 5.
7. In the **Camera Follower** component of the **Main Camera**, change the **Rotation Smoothness** to 5.
8. In the **Hierarchy** panel, click the gray triangle to the left of CucumberMan. This will expose the subordinate components.
9. Reselect the **Main Camera** in the **Hierarchy** panel.
10. Click the **GameObject** under CucumberMan in the **Hierarchy** panel and drag it to the **Follow Target** field in the **Camera Follower** component of the **Main Camera**.
11. Ensure that the **Can Follow** checkbox is checked.

Your **Camera Follower** component of the main camera should look identical to the following image. If it is not identical, please revisit steps 6 through 11:

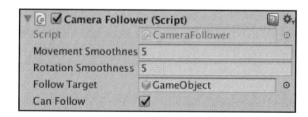

Next, we will edit the **Player Motor (Script)** component of the CucumberMan. Follow these important steps to properly configure the **Player Motor (Script)** component:

1. In the **Hierarchy** panel, select the CucumberMan
2. Expand, if necessary, the **Player Motor (Script)** component of the CucumberMan in the **Inspector** panel
3. Drag the **Main Camera** from the **Hierarchy** panel to the **Cam** field in the **Player Motor (Script)** component of CucumberMan in the **Inspector** panel

Next, let's position the Cucumber Man to a logical start location for our game. Where you place the Cucumber Man is up to you. It is recommended that it be placed on one of the respawn points. Once you know where you want the character to start each game, follow these steps:

1. In the **Hierarchy** panel, select CucumberMan.
2. Using the transform tools, move the character to one of the spawn points.
3. Zoom in and ensure the character's feet are on or slightly above the ground. We still have one more step to make the Cucumber Man our game's playable character.
4. With the CucumberMan still selected, select the **Tag** drop-down menu in the **Inspector** panel and select **Player**. This will make it easier for us to reference collisions. You will learn more about this in Chapter 10, *Scripting Our Points System.*

You can now put the game into game-mode and test the player character. You can use the keyboard keys listed in the following table to control the Cucumber Man:

Keyboard Key	Action
W	Walk Up
A	Walk Left
S	Walk Down
D	Walk Right
E	Throw
Left-Hand *Shift* Key	Run
Spacebar	Jump

In the next section, we will fine-tune the Cucumber Man.

Fine-tuning our character

Now that the Cucumber Man is in our game, we can start experimenting with the character to ensure it looks and behaves the way we want. In this section, we will look at the following refinements to our Cucumber Man:

- Motor controls
- Scale
- Capsule Collider
- Input controls

Fine-tuning the motor controls

You can put the game into game-mode and use the keyboard inputs detailed in the previous section to experiment with the Cucumber Man's movements. One of the things you might have noticed is that the player character does not seem to move very fast. Of course, this is relative to the size of our terrain and the character's size. Let's look at how to increase the speed of our character by reviewing the associated script.

The following code snippet is from the `PlayerMotor.cs` script that you imported with the Cucumber Man. This snippet is the first part of the script, not the entire script. As you can see, there are variables for `JumpPower`, `MoveSpeed`, and `RunSpeed`. Those variables are created in the code and their values can be controlled in the Unity editor:

```
using System.Collections;
using System.Collections.Generic;
using UnityEngine;
using UnityStandardAssets.CrossPlatformInput;

[RequireComponent(typeof(Rigidbody))]
public class PlayerMotor : MonoBehaviour {

  float horizontal, vertical;
  Rigidbody m_Rigidbody;

  public float JumpPower;
  public float MoveSpeed, RunSpeed;

  private float currentJumpPower = 0;
  private float currentMoveSpeed = 0;

  // Use this for initialization
  void Start ()
  {
    m_Rigidbody = GetComponent<Rigidbody>();
    currentMoveSpeed = MoveSpeed;
// m_Cam = Camera.main.transform;
    m_Animator = GetComponent<Animator>();
  }
. . .
```

The following screenshot is from the Cucumber Man's **Inspector** panel. Here, you can see that we have the ability to update the values for **Jump Power**, **Move Speed**, **Run Speed**, **Stationary Turn Speed**, and **Moving Turn Speed**:

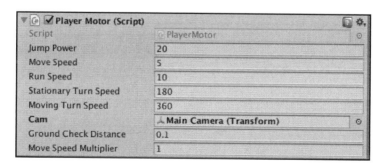

Using the **Player Motor (Script)** component of the Cucumber Man, you can experiment with the values to have the player character's movements respond the way you want them to. You can always refer back to the previous screenshot to reset your values.

You can experiment with the **Player Motor (Script)** parameters while in game-mode. Any changes made in game-mode are not retained when leaving game-mode. This is a great way of experimenting without impacting any saved settings.

Here is a typical set of parameters for the Cucumber Man's motor controls:

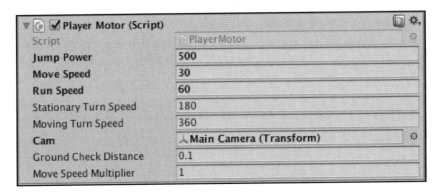

We also have the option of editing the **Move Speed Multiplier** variable to impact all of the motor speed values. You can set this manually in the **Inspector** panel as well as programmatically. To set the multiplier manually, simply edit the value in the **Player Motor (Script)** component of the CucumberMan in the **Inspector** panel. To change this value programmatically, you can edit the PlayerMotor.cs script. The following code snippet is from that script, and represents the later section of that script:

```
. . .
Animator m_Animator;
[SerializeField] float m_MoveSpeedMultiplier = 1f;
public void OnAnimatorMove()
{
    // we implement this function to override the default root motion.
    // this allows us to modify the positional speed before it's applied.
    if (m_IsGrounded && Time.deltaTime > 0)
    {
        Vector3 v = (m_Animator.deltaPosition * m_MoveSpeedMultiplier) /
Time.deltaTime;

        // we preserve the existing y part of the current velocity.
        v.y = m_Rigidbody.velocity.y;
```

```
        m_Rigidbody.velocity = v;
    }
}
.  .  .
```

As you can see in the previous code snippet, m_MoveSpeedMultiplier is set to 1. You can change that value directly in the script as an alternative method to using the Unity editor.

Fine-tuning scale

Our Cucumber Man has a **Transform** that includes **Scale** values for **X**, **Y**, and **Z**. By default, these are all set to **1**. We can easily change the size of our Cucumber Man by decreasing or increasing the scale values. With this approach, you can create copies of the Cucumber Man that are cucumber babies or cucumber giants.

The following screenshot shows three copies of the Cucumber Man. Starting from the left and moving to the right, each Cucumber Man is larger than the last:

Here is a look at the transform settings for each Cucumber Man in the preceding screenshot:

Cucumber Man version	Transform Scale setting		
	X	Y	Z
Cucumber Baby	0.5	.5	.5
Cucumber Man	1	1	1
Cucumber Giant	2	2	2

For our game, we will only have one Cucumber Man, and we want him to be larger than the beetles and smaller than the cherry trees. The default scale of one results in the Cucumber Man's height being ideal. This is evident by his relative size compared to the cherry trees, as indicated in the following screenshot:

In Chapter 8, *Implementing our Non-Player Character*, we will inspect the scale of our Cucumber Beetles and ensure they are appropriately scaled in relation to the size of our Cucumber Man.

Fine-tuning the Capsule Collider

Capsule Colliders have the shape of a pill—that is, a cylinder with rounded ends. We can view the Capsule Collider by selecting our character in the **Hierarchy** panel or the **Scene** view and then reviewing the **Capsule Collider** component in the **Inspector** panel. As shown in the following screenshot, we can edit the **Capsule Collider** by clicking the **Edit Collider** button:

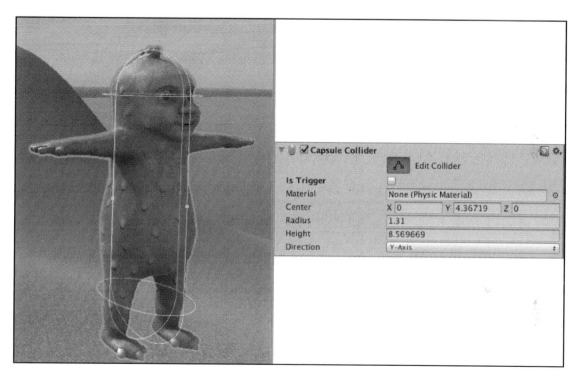

Here is a brief description of each of the Capsule Collider component parameters:

- **Is Trigger**: When we enable this option, the physics engine will ignore the Capsule Collider
- **Material**: We can assign how the Capsule Collider interacts with other colliding game objects
- **Center**: There are **X**, **Y**, and **Z** fields to identify the center of the capsule relative to itself
- **Radius**: The radius of the collider's width

- **Height**: The collider's height
- **Direction**: The orientation of the capsule lengthwise

For greater precision, the Capsule Collider should receive a height adjustment so that the Cucumber Man fits within it, as shown in the following screenshot:

Make any refinements required to ensure that your Cucumber Man's Capsule Collider resembles the preceding screenshot. Once you complete your refinements, be sure to save your work.

All changes to the *Cucumber Man* game detailed in this chapter will be incorporated in the `Starting-Chapter-08.zip` file available at the beginning of `Chapter 8`, *Implementing Our Non-Player Characters*.

Changing and refining input controls

When we develop games using Unity, we have several options for gathering user input during gameplay. Here is a list of those input options:

- Keyboard
- Mouse
- Joystick

- Touchscreen
- Mobile device movement sensors
- Microphone
- Camera

As we stated previously in this chapter, we will be using the keyboard as our sole input device for the *Cucumber Man* game. Let's take a look at where you can make changes to the input controls for your game if you want to experiment or simply want to change the way users interact with the game. We will use Unity's input manager for this.

The input manager for your game project is accessible, as illustrated in the following screenshot, by selecting the **Edit** | **Project Settings** | **Input** drop-down menu selection:

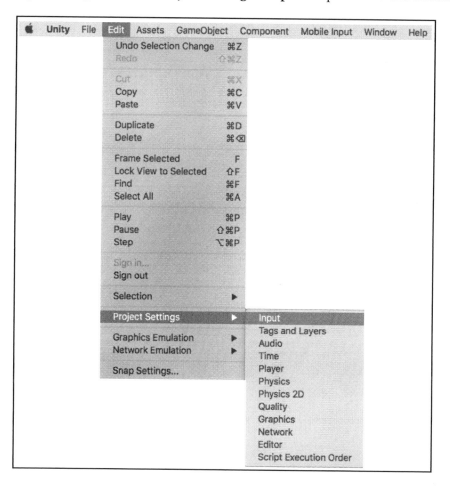

This results in the input manager being displayed in the **Inspector** panel. There, you will find the relevant virtual axes for the game. In the following screenshot, the horizontal virtual axis and vertical virtual axis are displayed side by side. You can see how the keyboard's *W*, *A*, *S*, and *D* keys are set for controlling horizontal and vertical movement. For example, the *W* key is identified in the vertical virtual axis and is assigned to the **Alt Positive** Button, which means it is an alternative button for moving forward. While the primary **Negative** and **Positive** buttons are listed as using the left and right arrow keys for horizontal movement, and the down and up arrow keys are used for vertical navigation, we will implement the *W*, *A*, *S*, and *D* keys as our default method of moving the Cucumber Man character through the game world:

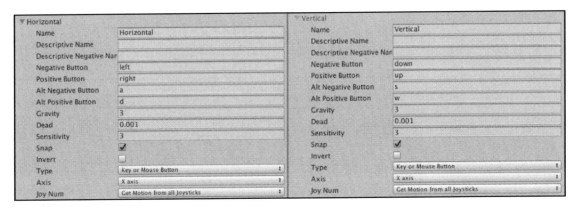

The input manager enables us to determine all of our input controls, and is where you can set your mouse, keyboard, and joystick inputs. An additional setting available in the input manager is for the jump functionality. As shown in the following screenshot, the jump functionality has the keyboard's space bar as the positive input device. You will note that there is no **Negative Button** assigned as it is assumed that the character can only jump up, not down:

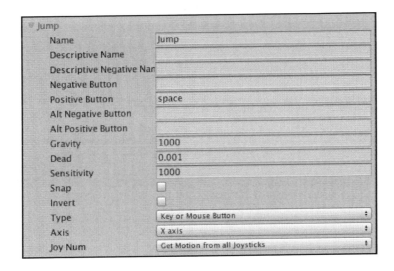

Animating our player character

Your Cucumber Man character controller package includes the necessary assets to support the character's six animations. In this section, we will look at the Cucumber Man's animations, which are listed as follows:

- Idle
- Walk
- Run
- Jump
- Throw
- Die

Reviewing the player controller script

There are a couple of areas in Unity in which we can review the Cucumber Man's animations. Let's first look at the **Player Controller (Script)** component of the CucumberMan **Controller** object. When you select the **CucumberMan** controller in the hierarchy pane, you should see the **Player Controller (Script)** component in the **Inspector** panel. You might need to click the expand button to the left of the component in order to reveal the component's details.

As shown in the following screenshot, each of our character's animations has a state associated with it:

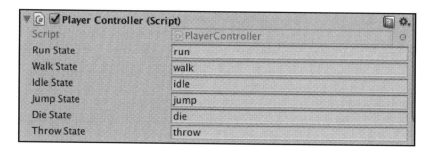

Now, let's review the `PlayerController.cs` script. You can access this file by selecting the **All Scripts** button in the **Project** panel, under **Favorites**. Then, scroll to the **PlayerController (Script)** in the **Project** panel. The first 14 lines of the script are shown in the following code fragment:

```
using System.Collections;
using System.Collections.Generic;
using UnityEngine;

public class PlayerController : MonoBehaviour {

    public string RunState, WalkState, IdleState, JumpState, DieState,
ThrowState;
    bool isWalking, isRunning, isJumping, isIdle, isDie,
forward,left,right,back;
    Animator mAnim;
    // Use this for initialization
    void Start () {
      mAnim = GetComponent<Animator>();
      isIdle = true;
    }
```

The first three lines simply identify the namespaces we want to use in our script. These are `System.Collections`, `System.Collections.Generic`, and `UnityEngine`. Next, we have the class declaration for our `PlayerController` class. The next three lines of code are our variable definitions. As you can see, there is a public string for each of our six animations: `RunState`, `WalkState`, `IdleState`, `JumpState`, `DieState`, and `ThrowState`. There are also several boolean (`bool`) variables including `isWalking`, `isRunning`, `isJumping`, `isIdle`, and `isDie`. We also identify `mAnim` as our animator. We will see how each of these is used later in the script.

The Start() method sets our initial state of isIdle to true and gets a reference to our **Animator** with the mAnim = GetComponent<Animator>(); statement.

The largest method of our PlayerController.cs script is the Update() method. The Update() method is called once per frame. This method is provided in the following code segments, with ellipses (...) to reflect areas where code was removed for brevity. You can refer to the full script in Unity. The first code segment sets the appropriate states to true or false. For example, when the user presses the *W* key and the player is not currently running, the isWalking variable is set to true and the mAnim.SetBool is passed two parameters (WalkState and true). Similar actions are taken for the *A*, *S*, and *D* keys:

```
  . . .
void Update () {
  //Down states
  if( Input.GetKeyDown(KeyCode.W))
  {
    if( !isRunning )
    {
      isWalking = true;
      isIdle = false;
      forward = true;
      mAnim.SetBool(WalkState, true);
      mAnim.SetBool(IdleState, false);
    }
  }
  if( Input.GetKeyDown(KeyCode.A))
  {
      . . .
  }
  if( Input.GetKeyDown(KeyCode.S))
  {
      . . .
  }
  if( Input.GetKeyDown(KeyCode.D))
  {
      . . .
  }
  . . .
```

The next code snippet from the `Update()` method, shown in the following snippet, handles the running animation when the left *Shift* key is pressed. In this instance, the animation is changed from the `WalkState` to the `RunState`:

```
. . .
if( Input.GetKeyDown(KeyCode.LeftShift))
{
  if( isWalking )
  {
    isRunning = true;
    mAnim.SetBool(RunState, true);
    mAnim.SetBool(WalkState, false);
  }
}
. . .
```

The next segment of code, provided in the following snippet, shows how detecting the spacebar input results in the `Jump()` animation running and the `Throw()` animation running when the *E* key is detected:

```
. . .
if( Input.GetKeyDown(KeyCode.Space))
{
  Jump();
}

if( Input.GetKeyDown(KeyCode.E))
{
  Throw();
}
. . .
```

Reviewing the Animator component

There is one final component in the `CucumberMan` **Controller** object to review: the **Animator** component. As you can see in the following screenshot, the **Animator** component has two key properties: **Controller** and **Avatar**:

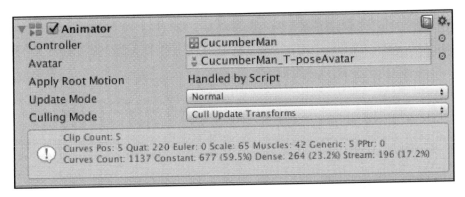

The controller points to the `CucumberMan.controller` file. The file's `.controller` file extension will not be displayed in the component interface, but it is a reference to that file. You can navigate to that file in the project pane. It is located under **Assets | Cucumber Man**. When you double-click that file, it opens in an **Animator** window, as shown in the following screenshot:

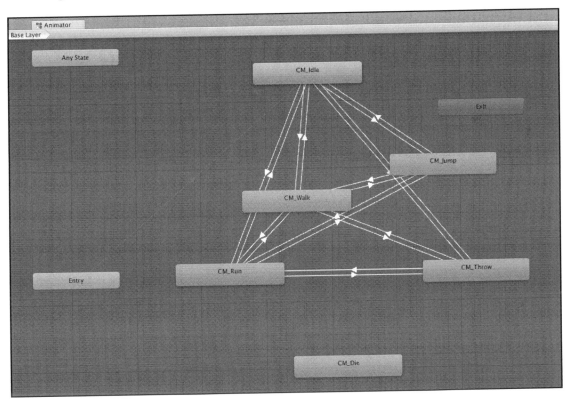

Here, you can see each of the states, one for each animation, along with the possible transitions between them. Each state is labeled with a CM_ prefix to indicate the CucumberMan. These states are listed as follows:

- **CM_Idle**
- **CM_Walk**
- **CM_Run**
- **CM_Jump**
- **CM_Throw**
- **CM_Die**

If the layout of the **Animator** window is jumbled or unclear, you can rearrange the objects in the **Animator** window so they are easy to understand. You accomplish this by clicking on a state, dragging it to where you want it, and releasing the mouse button. The following graphic shows one possible organizational approach to the Cucumber Man's states and transitions. Your approach can differ, if you like:

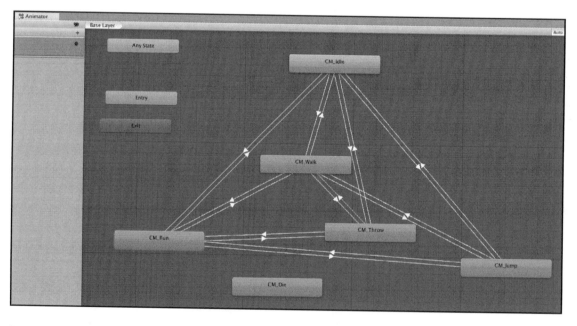

You can leave these transitions as they have been provided to you, or, if you want to, you can make changes using the **Animator** window.

Previewing the animations

You have the option of previewing individual animations without putting the game into game-mode. In the **Project** panel, select **Assets | Cucumber Man** and you will see the individual animations listed. For example, click the `CucumberMan_Throw` animation. This is the `CucumberMan_Throw.fbx` file that is part of the package you imported earlier in this chapter.

With the animation selected, the **Inspector** panel gives you access to the **Model**, **Rig**, and **Animations** tabs. Although you do not need to make any changes here, it is worth your time to explore the various features. When you select the **Animations** tab, you have access to a preview of the animation at the bottom the **Inspector** panel, as illustrated in the following screenshot:

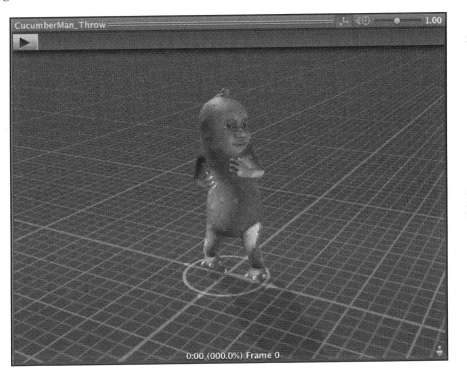

You can click the play button in the top-left corner of the animation preview window to play the animation. The animation will play and loop until you stop the animation.

You can preview each animation by playing the game as well. This is true for all of the animations, except the die animation; we will have to write a script to evoke that animation. We will do this in Chapter 11, *Scripting Victory and Defeat*.

Terraforming the terrain for our Cucumber Man

As you play-test the game, it is advisable to have the Cucumber Man walk, run, and jump where you want the player to be able to do these actions when they play the game. This is a step that is often overlooked or given insufficient attention. Think back to the games you play or have played in the past. Has your character ever been stuck or unable to get to a certain area? Odds are that some of that was a result of inadequate testing.

It is recommend that you work on this. The terrain might be, for example, too steep for the character to climb. Use the skills you learned in Chapter 4, *Creating Our Terrain*, to modify your terrain so that the player character can navigate your game world the way you want it to.

The time you spend on this important step will help ensure the non-player characters, our Cucumber Beetles, can get to the areas you want them to. You will be prompted to check for this in the next Chapter 8, *Implementing Our Non-Player Characters*.

 Now is a great time to save your scene and your project. Remember, save early and save often!

Summary

In this chapter, we incorporated our game's player character, the Cucumber Man. We imported the character, reviewed the controls, examined the animations, and made the necessary configuration changes to fully use our character in the game.

In Chapter 8, *Implementing Our Non-Player Characters*, we will implement our non-player characters, the Cucumber Beetles. We will import and review the assets associated with the beetles and start scripting parts of our game that are specific to the beetles. This will include randomizing the location of cucumber plants and cucumbers.

8
Implementing Our Non-Player Characters

In the previous chapter, we focused on our game's player character, the Cucumber Man. We imported the character, reviewed the controls, examined the animations, and made the necessary configuration changes to fully use our character in the game. We reviewed the player character's animations and the character's animation controller. We also identified scripts relevant to the player character and reviewed several of them. In addition, we made modifications to our game's terrain to better accommodate the player character during gameplay.

In this chapter, we will focus on the non-player characters. Our Cucumber Beetles will serve as our game's non-player characters and will be the Cucumber Man's enemies. We will incorporate Cucumber Beetles in our game through direct placement. We will review the beetles' 11 animations and make changes to the non-player character's animation controller. In addition, we will write scripts to control the non-player characters. We will also add cucumber patches, cucumbers, and cherries to our game world.

In this chapter, we will cover the following topics:

- Understanding the non-player characters
- Importing the non-player characters into our game
- Animating our non-player characters
- Incorporating the non-player characters into our game
- Terraforming the terrain for our Cucumber Beetles
- Adding cucumber patches to our terrain
- Adding cucumbers to our terrain
- Scripting our non-player characters

Understanding the non-player characters

Non-player characters, commonly referred to as NPCs, are simply game characters that are not controlled by a human player. These characters are controlled through scripts, and their behaviors are usually responsive to in-game conditions.

Our game's non-player characters are the Cucumber Beetles. These beetles, as depicted in the following screenshot, have six legs that they can walk on; under special circumstances, they can also walk on their hind legs:

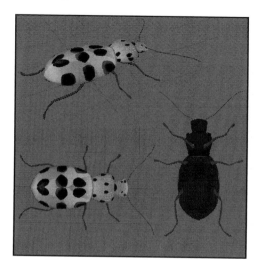

Cucumber Beetles are real insects, and are a threat to cucumbers. They cannot really walk on their hind legs, but they can in our game.

In the next section, you will import a Cucumber Beetle asset package prepared specifically for this game. There will only be one beetle in that asset package. We will, through scripting, make multiple copies of the beetle.

Before you move on to the next section, you should open your Unity game project. Alternatively, you can download the Starting-Chapter-08 Unity project available from the publisher's companion site.

Importing the non-player characters into our game

You are now ready to import the asset package for our game's non-player character, the Cucumber Beetle. Go through the following steps to import the package:

1. Download the `Cucumber_Beetle.unitypackage` file from the publisher's companion website
2. In Unity, with your game project open, select **Assets** | **Import Package** | **Custom Package** from the top menu
3. Navigate to the location of the asset package you downloaded in step 1 and click the **Open** button
4. When presented with the **Import Asset Package** dialog window, click the **Import** button

As you will notice, the `Cucumber_Beetle` asset package contains several assets related to the Cucumber Beetles, including a controller, scripts, a prefab, animations, and other assets:

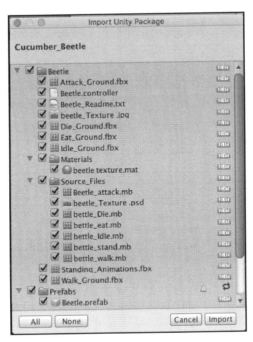

Now that the `Cucumber_Beetle` asset package has been imported into our game project, we should save our project. Use the **File | Save Project** menu option.

Next, let's review what was imported.

In the **Project** panel, under **Assets | Prefabs**, you will see a new `Beetle.Prefab`. Also in the **Project** panel, under **Assets**, you will see a `Beetle` folder. It is important that you understand what each component in the folder is for. Please refer to the following screenshot for an overview of the assets that you will be using in this chapter in regards to the Cucumber Beetle:

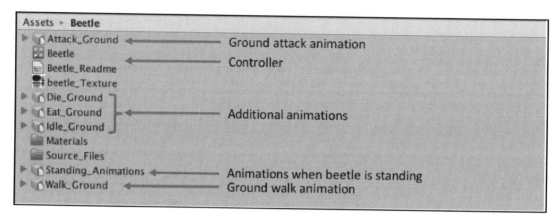

The other assets in the previous screenshot that were not called out include a `readme.txt` file, the texture and materials for the Cucumber Beetle, and the source files. We will review the Cucumber Beetle's animations in the next section.

Animating our non-player characters

Several Cucumber Beetle animations have been prepared for use in our game. Here is a list of the animation names as they appear in our project, along with brief descriptions of how we will incorporate the animation into our game. The animations are listed in alphabetical order by name:

Animation Name	Usage Details
Attack_Ground	The beetle attacks the Cucumber Man's feet from the ground
Attack_Standing	The beetle attacks the Cucumber Man from a standing position
Die_Ground	The beetle dies from the starting position of on the ground

Die_Standing	The beetle dies from the starting position of standing on its hind legs
Eat_Ground	The beetle eats cucumbers while on the ground
Idle_Ground	The beetle is not eating, walking, fighting, or standing
Idle_Standing	The beetle is standing, but not walking, running, or attacking
Run_Standing	The beetle runs on its hind legs
Stand	The beetle goes from an on-the-ground position to standing (it stands up)
Walk_Ground	The beetle walks using its six legs
Walk_Standing	The beetle walks on its hind legs

You can preview these animations by clicking on an animation file, such as
Eat_Ground.fbx, in the **Project** panel. Then, in the **Inspector** panel, click the play button
to watch the animation.

There are 11 animations for our Cucumber Beetle, and we will use scripting, later in this
chapter, to determine when an animation is played.

In the next section, we will add the Cucumber Beetle to our game.

Incorporating the non-player characters into our game

First, let's simply drag the Beetle.Prefab from the Assets/Prefab folder in the **Project**
panel to our game in **Scene** view. Place the beetle somewhere in front of the Cucumber Man
so that the beetle can be seen as soon as you put the game into game mode.

A suggested placement is illustrated in the following screenshot:

When you put the game into game mode, you will notice that the beetle cycles through its animations. If you double-click the `Beetle.controller` in the `Assets | Beetle` folder in the **Project** panel, you will see, as shown in the following screenshot, that we currently have several animations set to play successively and repeatedly:

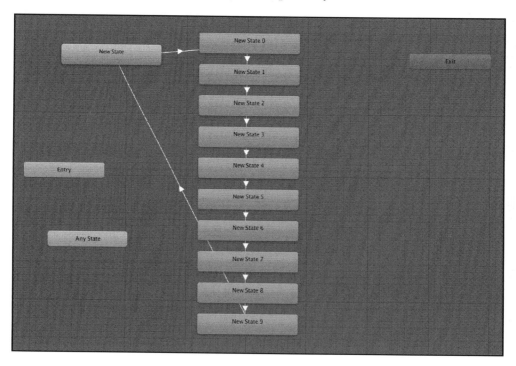

This initial setup is intended to give you a first, quick way of previewing the various animations. In the next section, we will modify the animation controller.

Working with the Animation Controller

We will use an Animation Controller to organize our NPCs' animations. The Animation Controller will also be used to manage the transitions between animations.

Before we start making changes to our Animation Controller, we need to identify what states our beetle has and then determine what transitions each state can have in relation to other states.

 Animation states can be referred to as the character's state of animation. For example, walking is a state, as are running and jumping.

Here are the states that the beetle can have, each tied to an animation:

- Idle on Ground
- Walking on Ground
- Eating on Ground
- Attacking on Ground
- Die on Ground
- Stand
- Standing Idle
- Standing Walk
- Standing Run
- Standing Attack
- Die Standing

With the preceding list of states, we can assign the following transitions:

- From Idle on Ground to:
  - Walking on Ground
  - Running on Ground
  - Eating on Ground
  - Attacking on Ground
  - Stand
- From Stand to:
  - Standing Idle
  - Standing Walk
  - Standing Run
  - Standing Attack

Reviewing the transitions from Idle on Ground to Stand demonstrates the type of state-to-state transition decisions you need to make for your game.

Let's turn our attention back to the **Animation Controller** window. You will notice that there are two tabs in the left panel of that window: **Layers** and **Parameters**. The **Layers** tab shows a **Base Layer**. While we can create additional layers, we do not need to do this for our game. The **Parameters** tab is empty, and that is fine. We will make our changes using the **Layout** area of the **Animation Controller** window. That is the area with the grid background.

Let's start by making the following changes. For all 11 **New State** buttons, do the following:

1. Left-click the state button
2. Look in the **Inspector** panel to determine which animation is associated with the state button
3. Rename the state name in the **Inspector** panel to reflect the animation.
4. Click the return button
5. Double-check the state button to ensure your change was made

When you have completed the preceding five steps for all 11 states, your **Animation Controller** window should match the following screenshot:

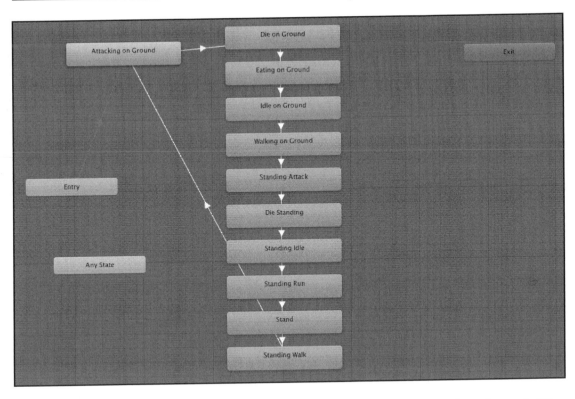

If you were to put the game into game mode, you would see that nothing has changed. We only changed the state names so they made more sense to us. So, we have some more work to do with the **Animation Controller**.

Currently, the Attacking on Ground state is the default. That is not what we want. It makes more sense to have the **Idle on Ground** state to be our default. To make that change, right-click the **Idle on Ground** state and select **Set as Layer Default State**:

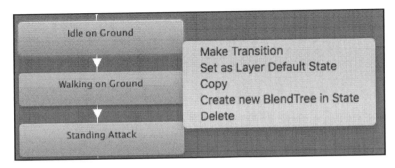

Next, we need to make a series of changes to the state transitions. There are a lot of states and there will be a lot of transitions. In order to make things easier, we will start by deleting all the default transitions. To accomplish this, left-click each white line with an arrow and press your keyboard's *Delete* key. Do not delete the orange line that goes from **Entry** to **Idle on Ground**.

After all transitions have been deleted, you can drag your states around so you have more working room. You might temporarily reorganize them in a manner similar to what is shown in the following screenshot:

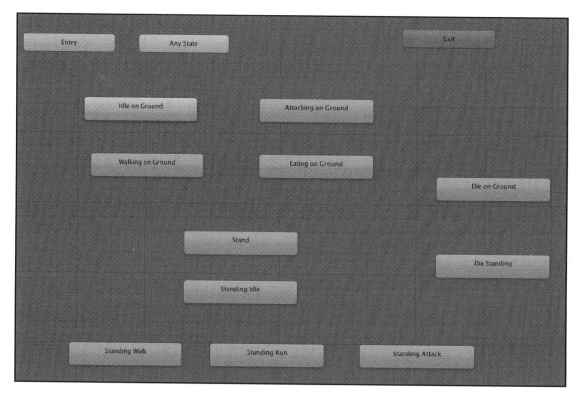

Our next task is to create all of our state transitions. Follow these steps for each state transition you want to add:

1. Right-click the originating state.
2. Select **Create Transition**.
3. Click on the destination state.

Once you have made all your transitions, you can reorganize your states to declutter the Animation Controller's layout area. A suggested final organization is provided in the following screenshot:

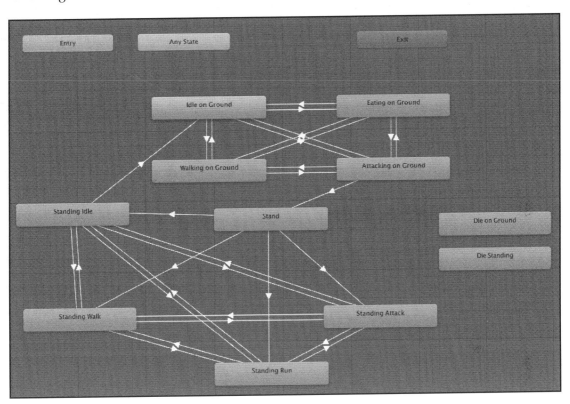

As you can see in our final arrangement, we have 11 states and over two dozen transitions. You will also note that the **Die on Ground** and **Die Standing** states do not have any transitions. In order for us to use these animations in our game, they must be placed into an **Animation Controller**.

Let's run a quick experiment:

1. Select the **Beetle** character in the **Hierarchy** panel.
2. In the **Inspector** panel, click the **Add Component** button.
3. Select **Physics | Box Collider**.
4. Click the **Edit Collider** button.

5. Modify the size and position of the box collider so that it encases the entire beetle body.

6. Click the **Edit Collider** button again to get out of edit mode.

Your box collider should look similar to what is depicted in the following screenshot:

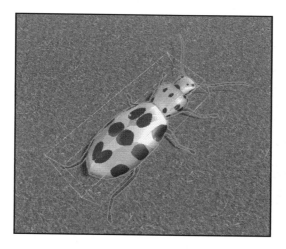

Next, let's create a script that invokes the Die on Ground animation when the Cucumber Man character collides with the beetle. This will simulate the Cucumber Man stepping on the beetle. Follow these steps:

1. Select the **Beetle** character in the **Hierarchy** panel.
2. In the **Inspector** panel, click the **Add Component** button.
3. Select **New Script**.
4. Name the script BeetleNPC.
5. Click the **Create and Add** button.
6. In the project view, select **Favorites | All Scripts | BeetleNPC**.
7. Double-click the BeetleNPC script file.
8. Edit the script so that it matches the following code block:

```
using System.Collections;
using System.Collections.Generic;
using UnityEngine;

public class BeetleNPC : MonoBehaviour {

    Animator animator;
```

```
// Use this for initialization
void Start () {
    animator = GetComponent&lt;Animator>();
}

// Collision Detection Test
void OnCollisionEnter(Collision col)
{
    if (col.gameObject.CompareTag("Player"))
    {
        animator.Play("Die on Ground");
    }
}
}
```

This code detects a collision between the Cucumber Man and the beetle. If a collision is detected, the `Die on Ground` animation is played. As you can see in the following screenshot, the Cucumber Man defeated the Cucumber Beetle:

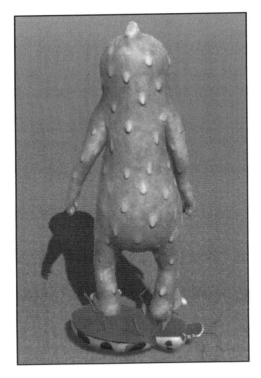

This short test demonstrated two important things that will help us further develop this game:

- Earlier in this section, you renamed all the states in the **Animation Controller** window. The names you gave the states are the ones you will reference in code.
- Since the animation we used did not have any transitions to other states, the Cucumber Beetle will remain in the final position of the animation unless we script it otherwise. So, if we had 100 beetles and defeated them all, all 100 would remain on their backs in the game world.

This was a simple and successful scripting test for our Cucumber Beetle. We will need to write several more scripts to manage the beetles in our game. First, there are some game world modifications we will make.

Terraforming the terrain for our Cucumber Beetles

Our game world is currently very large and appropriate for the game we envisioned. In order to efficiently demonstrate how to script the Cucumber Beetles, we will designate a sandbox area of our game and confine the Cucumber Beetles to that area. We will also need to move some cherry trees there.

We will make the following sequential modifications to our game's terrain:

- Designate a sandbox area
- Plant additional cherry trees
- Create spawning sites

Designating a sandbox area

We do not necessarily want to make major modifications to our game's terrain. We previously spent considerable time planning, creating, and fine-tuning the terrain. Instead, we will select one of the large, flat areas to act as a sandbox. If you do not have any large, flat areas, you can select one of your flat areas and make it a bit bigger.

The following image suggests a size relative to our current game world. The white box towards the bottom center of the image represents an ideal size:

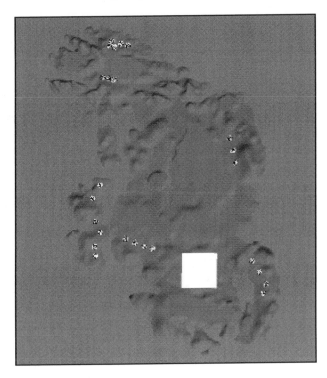

Now that we know where our sandbox will be, let's prepare the **Hierarchy** panel for any new items we create for the sandbox. Simply right-click in an empty area of the **Hierarchy** panel and select **Create Empty**. With that new GameObject selected, rename it in the **Inspector** panel as Sandbox.

Planting additional cherry trees

Since our sandbox is a smaller representation of our larger game environment, we will need one or more cherry trees. As you will recall, the Cucumber Man will collect cherries from the cherry trees and use them to launch ranged attacks on the Cucumber Beetles.

In Chapter 6, *Creating and Importing 3D Objects for Our Game*, we imported our Cherry Tree object and modified it for our game. Now, we can simply add additional cherry trees to our sandbox area. You can drag the **CherryTreeCollider** from **Projects | Assets | Prefabs** directly into your sandbox area in the **Scene** view.

Next, you will want to zoom into the sandbox area, using the Scene view, to ensure that your trees are not above the ground or in need of additional adjustments.

Once your additional cherry trees are in place, each new cherry tree will be accessible in the **Hierarchy** panel. Click each newly created cherry tree and drag it to the Sandbox object you previously created. We are using the Sandbox object for organizational purposes only.

Creating spawning sites

Within the sandbox area, select three areas to serve as spawn points. Where you create them is up to you. Placing them at equal distances from one another would be a good approach. To make these spawn points obvious, let's create a spawn pad and then copy it and place it at various points in the sandbox.

Here are the steps to create the spawn pad:

1. In the **Hierarchy** panel, right-click **Sandbox** and select **3D Object | Cylinder**.
2. In the **Inspector** panel, rename the **Cylinder** to SpawnPad1.
3. Click **Transform | Scale** and change the scale of SpawnPad1 as follows:
   - x = 3
   - y = 0.05
   - z = 3
4. Test the scale of the pad by placing it under the Cucumber Man. It should look similar to what is shown in the following screenshot. Make adjustments so that your pad matches what you see here:

5. With `SpawnPad1` selected, deselect the **Mesh Renderer | Receive Shadows** checkbox in the **Inspector** view. This will prevent shadows from being cast onto our spawn pad. This step is not terribly important, but helps make our spawn pad seem nonorganic, and since we will be spawning the Cucumber Man on this pad, it adds a nice visual element.

6. Using the transform tools, adjust the position of the pad so that it is under the bottom of the Cucumber Man's feet, just at or above the grass level.

7. With `SpawnPad1` selected, click the small circle to the right of the **Materials | Element 0 | Missing (Material)** input box in the **Inspector** panel:

8. Select a material of your choice from the **Select Material** dialog window.

9. Finally, deselect the **Capsule Collider** component in the **Inspector** panel. We will not need this.

You now have your first spawn pad. Make two further copies, ensuring that they are named `SpawnPad1`, `SpawnPad2`, and `SpawnPad3`. In the **Hierarchy** panel, ensure that they are all in your `Sandbox` object.

Our last task is to put the three spawn pad instances where we want them in the `Sandbox` area in **Scene** view.

This is a good time to save your scene and your project.

Adding cucumber patches to our terrain

In `Chapter 6`, *Creating and Importing 3D Objects for Our Game*, we used planes to designate six cucumber patch areas. In this section, we will make a seventh cucumber patch and use it in our sandbox area. We will also plant cucumber patches inside the new cucumber patch area.

Creating a cucumber patch area in the sandbox

This section guides you through the steps necessary to create a cucumber patch area in the sandbox. In the **Hierarchy** panel, you should have a `Cucumber Patch Areas` game object that contains every size of cucumber patch, each one a 3D object of the `plane` type. If you do not have these objects, which are shown in the following screenshot, either revisit `Chapter 6`, *Creating and Importing 3D Objects for Our Game*, or download the `Starting-Chapter-08` Unity project available from the publisher's companion site:

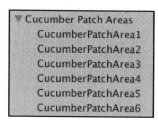

Here are the steps to create a sandbox area in our game:

1. In the **Hierarchy** panel, expand the `Cucumber Patch Areas` game object to expose the six planes. Remember, we created the `Cucumber Patch Areas` game object to serve as a visual organizing folder for our convenience.

2. Double-click each plane (`CucumberPatchArea1`, `CucumberPatchArea2`, `CucumberPatchArea3`, `CucumberPatchArea4`, `CucumberPatchArea5`, and `CucumberPatchArea6`). When you double-click an object in the **Hierarchy** panel, the **Scene** view will be focused on it.

3. Identify which cucumber patch area is already in your sandbox.

4. In the **Hierarchy** panel, right-click the identified cucumber patch and select **Duplicate**.

5. Rename the duplicated cucumber patch as `CucumberPatchAreaSandbox`.

6. In the **Hierarchy** panel, drag the `CucumberPatchAreaSandbox` to subordinate it under the `Sandbox` game object.

7. With the `CucumberPatchAreaSandbox` plane selected, modify the shape to fit the sandbox area. Use the transform tools for this.

8. Modify the terrain section of the sandbox, if necessary, so that the terrain inside the confines of the `CucumberPatchAreaSandbox` is flat and can receive cucumber patches.

You may have to use the **Raise / Lower Terrain** and **Smooth Height** terrain tools to ensure the area with the `CucumberPatchAreaSandbox` is flat. The following screenshot shows the orange-outlined `CucumberPatchAreaSandbox` area, two cherry trees, and the three spawn pads indicated in red. Smaller and more difficult to see are the Cucumber Man and one Cucumber Beetle. Your sandbox does not need to look exactly like this, but should have the same components as shown in the following screenshot:

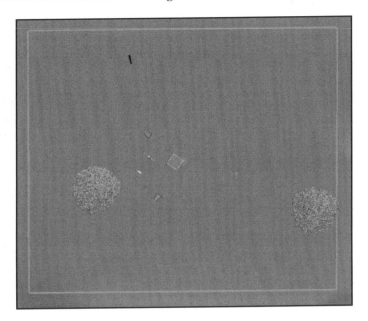

Planting cucumber patches

We will use our cucumber patches, the `CucumberPatch1` and `CucumberPatch2` prefabs, to create cucumber patch areas in the sandbox. These areas will serve as cover for our cucumbers. In this section, we will create an empty game object to encapsulate a series of cucumber patches. Let's get started:

1. Right-click the **Sandbox** in the **Hierarchy** panel and select **Create Empty**.
2. Rename the new GameObject as `cucumberPatches`.
3. Drag several `CucumberPatch1` prefabs onto the scene, in your sandbox.

4. Drag several `CucumberPatch2` prefabs onto the scene, in your sandbox.

5. In the **Hierarchy** panel, move all the newly created cucumber patches to the `cucumberPatches` game object under Sandbox. This is merely to keep the **Hierarchy** panel organized.

6. Expand the `cucumberPatches` game object in the **Hierarchy** panel.

7. Select all of the cucumber patches you added and use *Ctrl + C* and *Ctrl + V* to copy and paste them, respectively. The copied results will be highlighted in the **Hierarchy** panel and accessible in the **Scene** view.

8. In the **Scene** view, use the transform tools to relocate the copied group of cucumber patches.

9. Repeat steps 7 and 8 until you are satisfied with your sandbox.

An example of what your sandbox might look like with the newly created cucumber patches is provided in the following screenshot. Your sandbox will be different, and that is okay:

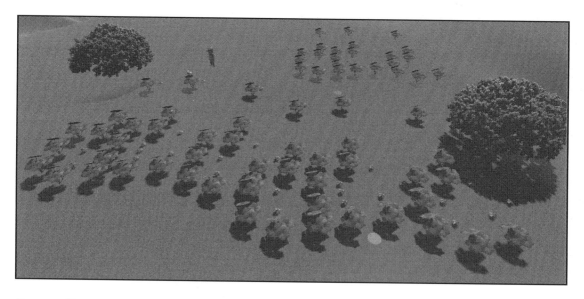

Our sandbox now has sufficient cucumber patches. In the next section, we will focus on cucumbers.

Adding cucumbers to our terrain

Cucumbers will be used in our game to give the beetles something to search for and to eat. We will place several cucumbers in the sandbox area and, in `Chapter 10`, *Scripting Our Points System*, keep track of how many there are during gameplay. In this section, we will prepare the cucumbers for our use and populate them in our game.

You previously downloaded the necessary assets for the cucumber. As you can see in the following screenshot, `Cucumber` is accessible in the `Assets/Cucumber` folder. You will note that when we select `Cucumber`, the bottom of the **Project** panel identifies the `Cucumber` file as a `.fbx` file:

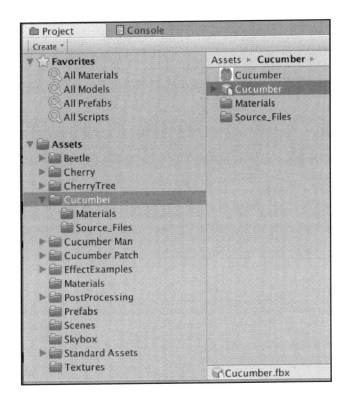

The .fbx file was exported from the 3D modeling software so we can use it in our game. When that asset is selected, the inspector view shows **Import Settings**. We want access to the transform, mesh renderer, and other components, so we will turn it into a prefab and make some changes. Here are some initial steps:

1. Drag the Cucumber.fbx file from **Assets | Cucumber** to the **Hierarchy** panel
2. With the Cucumber selected in the **Hierarchy** panel, drag it to the Assets/Prefabs folder in the **Project** panel
3. Delete the Cucumber from the **Hierarchy** panel
4. In the **Project** panel, select **Assets | Prefabs | Cucumber**

When we select the Cucumber file we just moved from the **Hierarchy** panel to the Prefabs folder, the bottom of the **Project** panel, shown in the following screenshot, identifies Cucumber as a prefab:

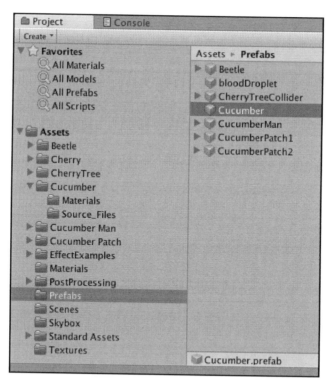

Now, when we look in the **Inspector** panel, we have access to the components we need to further prepare the cucumber for use in our game. Let's make a few changes to the prefab:

1. In the **Inspector** panel, select **Tag | Add Tag**.
2. In the **Tags & Layers** interface, click the plus icon to the right of the view. As shown in the following screenshot, beneath the plus icon is the **CherryTree** tag and to the right:

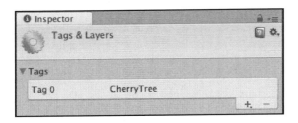

3. Enter the name **Cucumber**.
4. Click the **Save** button.
5. Select the **Assets | Prefabs | Cucumber** prefab in the **Project** panel.
6. In the **Inspector** panel, select **Tag | Cucumber**.

Now that our cucumber prefab has a tag, all copies of it will have that same tag. This tag will facilitate the following for us regarding gameplay:

*   Easily count how many cucumbers are left in the game
*   Identify when a beetle has found a cucumber

We have one more modification to make for our cucumber prefab—add a collider:

1. Select the **Assets | Prefabs | Cucumber** prefab in the **Project** panel
2. In the **Inspector** panel, click the **Add Component** button
3. Select **Physics | Box Collider**

Next, we can add cucumbers to our sandbox area. First, let's take the same approach as we did for the cucumber patches in regards to organization:

1. Right-click the **Sandbox** in the **Hierarchy** panel and select **Create Empty**.
2. Rename the new GameObject to cucumbers.

3. Drag several `Cucumber` prefabs onto the scene, in your sandbox. You can also drag a single prefab into the **Scene** view and make copies of it using the shortcut *Ctrl + D*, which will duplicate all currently selected objects.

4. Using the transform tools, rotate, resize, and relocate the cucumbers.

5. Ensure you have at least 10 cucumbers in your sandbox area.

6. In the **Hierarchy** panel, move all the newly created cucumbers to the `cucumbers` game object under **Sandbox**. This is merely to keep the **Hierarchy** panel organized.

Once you have your cucumbers dispersed throughout the sandbox area of your game world, you are ready to start scripting the Cucumber Beetles. We will take care of this in the next section.

 This is a good time to save your scene and your project.

Scripting our non-player characters

In this section, we will write the necessary scripts to manage the Cucumber Beetles in our game. Specifically, we will write scripts to accomplish the following:

- Beetle patrol
- Beetle finds and eats cucumber
- Beetle attacks player on the ground
- Beetle stands to attack

Getting organized

Since we are writing several scripts, we should stay organized. We can click **Favorites | All Scripts** in the **Project** panel to get a list of all the scripts in our project, but there are a lot of them, most of which we will not edit for our game. So, let's create a folder in the **Project** panel to organize our custom scripts. Here are the steps:

1. In the **Project** panel, right-click the `Assets` folder

2. Select **Create | Folder**

3. Name the new folder `Custom Scripts`

Now that we have a folder for our custom scripts, let's move a few:

1. In the **Project** panel, click **Favorites** | **All Scripts**.
2. Scroll until you find the `BeetleNPC` script we created earlier in this chapter.
3. Drag the `BeetleNPC` script to our `Custom Scripts` folder. This moves the `BeetleNPC` script to the designated folder. You will still see it in **Favorites** | **All Scripts** because this feature shows all scripts regardless of their location.
4. Move the `CameraFollower` script to the `Custom Scripts` folder.
5. Move the `PlayerController` script to the `Custom Scripts` folder.
6. Move the `PlayerMotor` script to the `Custom Scripts` folder.

When you are done moving scripts, your `Cucumber Scripts` folder should be the same as the following screenshot:

Our beetles will have the following behaviors in our game:

- Search for cucumbers (patrol)
- Eat cucumbers when found
- Defend itself from the Cucumber Man on the ground
- Stand to defend itself from the Cucumber Man

The next sections will show you how to script these behaviors.

Beetle patrol

Beetles in our game will search for cucumbers within the sandbox area. In this section, we will write a script to manage their patrol. Let's take some preparatory steps.

We will get started by creating a character controller for our `Beetle` prefab. Here are the steps:

1. In the **Project** panel, select **Assets** | **Prefabs** and click on the `Beetle` prefab
2. In the **Inspector** panel, click the **Add Component** button
3. Select **Physics** | **Character Controller**

 Be sure that you add the character controller to the `Beetle` prefab, not a beetle that you have in your scene.

We do not need to make any changes to the default character controller, but we do need to have one.

Next, let's make things easy on us and create some temporary containing walls for the beetles. You can simply add 3D cube game objects and, using the transform tools, orientate them so that they border the sandbox, or a part of the sandbox. You can put your walls inside an empty game object called `Walls` and, in the **Hierarchy** panel, organize them inside the `Sandbox` game object. A representative example is shown in the following screenshot:

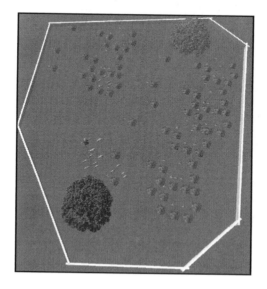

Okay, now we are ready to start scripting our beetle's patrol. To get started, right-click the **Assets | Custom Scripts** folder in the **Project** panel. Select **Create | C# Script**, then name the script `BeetlePatrol`. This creates a C# script for us in our `Custom Scripts` folder. We will walk through this script from top to bottom in small chunks.

This first section of code simply imports `System.Collections`, `System.Collections.Generic`, and the `UnityEngine`. The section also has our `BeetlePatrol` class header:

```
using System.Collections;
using System.Collections.Generic;
using UnityEngine;

public class BeetlePatrol : MonoBehaviour {
```

Our variables are provided in the next section. The first variable, `isDie`, is a global variable the we will use to determine whether the Cucumber Beetle should stop patrolling. The remaining variables are local. Their use will be self-evident after reviewing subsequent code sections:

```
// Variables
public static bool isDie = false;

public float speed = 5;
public float directionChangeInterval = 1;
public float maxHeadingChange = 30;

Animator beetleAnim;

CharacterController controller;
float heading;
Vector3 targetRotation;
```

The next section of code is our `Start()` method, which only runs at the beginning of the game. This code sets the initial rotation for the beetle's patrol:

```
void Start () {

    controller = GetComponent&lt;CharacterController>();
    beetleAnim = GetComponent&lt;Animator> ();
    // Set random initial rotation
    heading = Random.Range(0, 360);
    transform.eulerAngles = new Vector3(0, heading, 0);

    StartCoroutine(NewHeading());
}
```

Our `Update()` method, shown in the following code, is our next section. This code will be executed once per game frame. Here, you can see that if condition `isDie` is `false` (or not `true`), then the code will be executed:

```
void Update () {

    if (!isDie) {
        transform.eulerAngles = Vector3.Slerp (transform.eulerAngles,
    targetRotation,
            Time.deltaTime * directionChangeInterval);
        var forward = transform.TransformDirection (Vector3.forward);
        controller.SimpleMove (forward * speed);
    }

}
```

This last section of code provides two methods. The `NewHeading()` and `NewHeadingRoutine()` methods calculate a new direction for the beetle to move towards:

```
IEnumerator NewHeading () {

    while (true) {
        NewHeadingRoutine();
        yield return new WaitForSeconds(directionChangeInterval);
    }
}

void NewHeadingRoutine () {

    var floor = transform.eulerAngles.y - maxHeadingChange;
    var ceil  = transform.eulerAngles.y + maxHeadingChange;
    heading = Random.Range(floor, ceil);
    targetRotation = new Vector3(0, heading, 0);
}

} // this is the end of the Beetle Patrol class
```

Save your script. Next, we need to associate it with the `Beetle` prefab. With the prefab selected, click the **Add Component** button in the **Inspector** panel. Then, select **Scripts | Beetle Patrol**.

You can drag multiple beetles into your scene and test the game. You should see them wandering around your sandbox, remaining confined by the walls you built.

Beetle finds and eats cucumber

Earlier in this chapter, we created a `BeetleNPC` script file and attached it to our `Beetle` prefab. That script detected collisions with the Cucumber Man. In this section, we will modify that script so that it can also detect when it collides with a cucumber.

Let's first ensure that the cucumbers are properly set up. Check that the is selected (checked) in the cucumber's **Box Collider** component in the **Inspector** panel. Next, make several copies of your cucumber throughout the sandbox area of your scene. You can place them in close proximity to your beetles for easier testing. See the following screenshot for an optimal test configuration:

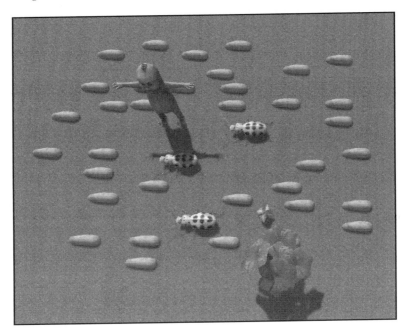

The `BeetleNPC` script needs a new variable and two methods, one of which will be used as a coroutine. Let's get started with the new variable. As you can see in the following code snippet, we now have a second variable, `cucumberToDestroy`. We will use that to reference the cucumber that the beetle ate:

```
Animator animator;
public GameObject cucumberToDestroy;
```

Next, we will add an OnTriggerEvent() method that is similar to the OnCollissionEnter that we previously created in this chapter. As you can see, we are testing to see whether the beetle collided with a cucumber. When that is detected, we have four lines of code that are executed. The first line points the cucumberToDestroy variable to the specific cucumber the beetle collided with. The next line sets the isEating value to true. We will update the BeetlePatrol script to accommodate that change. The third statement plays the eating animation. The final statement calls the DestroyCucumber function, which we will look at next:

```
void OnTriggerEnter(Collider theObject) {
    if (theObject.gameObject.CompareTag ("Cucumber")) {
        cucumberToDestroy = theObject.gameObject;
        BeetlePatrol.isEating = true;
        animator.Play ("Eating on Ground");
        StartCoroutine ("DestroyCucumber");
    }
}
```

The last change to the BeetleNPC script is the DestroyCucumber() function. We are using this function to delay the destruction of the cucumber. This simulates the amount of time it takes for the beetle to eat the cucumber. You can change the parameter of WaitForSecondsRealTime to your liking. That parameter represents real-world seconds. Once the delay is over, the object is destroyed and the isEating variable is set to false:

```
IEnumerator DestroyCucumber() {

    yield return new WaitForSecondsRealtime (4);
    Destroy (cucumberToDestroy.gameObject);
    BeetlePatrol.isEating = false;
}
```

We have two changes to make to our BeetlePatrol script. First, as you can see in the following code, we will add the new isEating variable:

```
public static bool isDie, isEating = false;
```

Our final change to the BeetlePatrol script is to update the conditional statement, as shown in the following code. Now, we will stop the patrol if the beetle is dying or eating:

```
void Update () {

    if (!isDie && !isEating) {
        transform.eulerAngles = Vector3.Slerp (transform.eulerAngles,
targetRotation,
```

```
                    Time.deltaTime * directionChangeInterval);
            var forward = transform.TransformDirection (Vector3.forward);
            controller.SimpleMove (forward * speed);
        }
    }
```

Beetle attacks player on the ground

Currently, when our Cucumber Man collides with a Cucumber Beetle, the **Die** animation is played, but no other behaviors are implemented. In this section, we will modify the necessary scripts for the following to occur each time the Cucumber Man collides with a Cucumber Beetle:

- Beetle faces Cucumber Man
- Beetle attacks Cucumber Man for specified time
- Beetle's die animation plays
- Beetle is removed from game

We will use the following three lines of code inside our `OnCollisionEnter()` method to force the beetle to face the Cucumber Man when there is a collision. As you can see from the following code, we create a variable to make it easy to reference the Cucumber Man and then a second variable for the Cucumber Man's current transform. The third line of code tells the current Cucumber Beetle to face the Cucumber Man:

```
var cm = GameObject.Find ("CucumberMan");
var tf = cm.transform;
this.gameObject.transform.LookAt (tf);
```

Now, we just need to edit the `OnCollisionEnter` method to include two statements. The first statement plays the Attacking on Ground animation. The second statement makes a call to the function that will destroy the current Cucumber Beetle. Here are those two lines of code:

```
animator.Play ("Attacking on Ground");
StartCoroutine ("DestroySelf");
```

The last change to the `BeetleNPC` script is the `DestroySelf()` function. We are using this function to simulate the battle and end of life for the current Cucumber Beetle. There are three statements inside the function. The first statement simulates the attack time. The second statement plays the `Die on Ground` animation. The final line destroys the game object, which is the current Cucumber Beetle:

```
IEnumerator DestroySelf() {

    yield return new WaitForSecondsRealtime (4);
    animator.Play ("Die on Ground");
    Destroy (this.gameObject, 4);
}
```

We have two changes to make to our `BeetlePatrol` script. First, as you can see in the following code, we will add the new `isAttacking` variable:

```
public static bool isDie, isEating, isAttacking =</span> false;
```

Our final change to the `BeetlePatrol` script is to update the conditional statement, as shown in the following code. Now, we will stop the patrol if the beetle is dying, eating, or attacking:

```
void Update () {

    if (!isDie && !isEating && !isAttacking)) {
        transform.eulerAngles = Vector3.Slerp (transform.eulerAngles,
            targetRotation, Time.deltaTime * directionChangeInterval);
        var forward = transform.TransformDirection (Vector3.forward);
        controller.SimpleMove (forward * speed);
    }
}
```

We will make additional modifications to the scripts and behaviors in Chapter 10, *Scripting Our Points System*.

Beetle stands to attack

You will recall that the Cucumber Man has the ability to throw cherries at the Cucumber Beetles. This is a ranged attack, and if the Cucumber Beetle were to start walking or running on the ground toward the Cucumber Man to attack, it is likely the beetle would die before reaching the Cucumber Man.

So, if a beetle is hit by a cherry, we want the following to occur:

- Beetle faces Cucumber Man
- Beetle stands
- Beetle runs, while standing, towards the Cucumber Man
- Beetle attacks Cucumber Man while standing

You can review the animations if you need a refresher on what they look like.

We will make some significant changes to our `BeetleNPC` script. The updated script is presented in the following code in its entirety, divided by sequential sections with explanations.

This section shows the imports and class-level variables. You will notice that the last three variables (`cherryHit`, `smoothTime`, and `smoothVelocity`) are new. We will use `cherryHit` to keep track of the sequence leading up to the beetle's death. The remaining two variables will be used to control how fast and smooth the beetle travels to the Cucumber Man:

```
using System.Collections;
using System.Collections.Generic;
using UnityEngine;

public class BeetleNPC : MonoBehaviour {

    Animator animator;
    public GameObject cucumberToDestroy;
    public bool cherryHit = false;
    public float smoothTime = 3.0f;
    public Vector3 smoothVelocity = Vector3.zero;
```

No change was made to the `Start()` method:

```
void Start () {
    animator = GetComponent&lt;Animator>();
}
```

We are now using the Update() method for the first time. This is necessary so that every frame in which the beetle can travel toward the Cucumber Man is shown. You can also see that we are using the cherryHit variable in our conditional statement:

```
void Update () {
    if (cherryHit) {
        var cm = GameObject.Find ("CucumberMan");
        var tf = cm.transform;
        this.gameObject.transform.LookAt (tf);

        animator.Play ("Standing Run");

        transform.position = Vector3.SmoothDamp (transform.position,
tf.position,
            ref smoothVelocity, smoothTime);
    }
}
```

The next section of our script is the OnCollisionEnter() method. We moved the statements we previously had in this method so that they are encapsulated in an if statement. If the cheeryHit is false, then the original code will be executed, otherwise the two lines of code after the else statement will be executed. We see there that we caused two animations to play:

```
void OnCollisionEnter(Collision col) {
    if (col.gameObject.CompareTag ("Player")) {

        if (!cherryHit) {
            BeetlePatrol.isAttacking = true;

            var cm = GameObject.Find ("CucumberMan");
            var tf = cm.transform;
            this.gameObject.transform.LookAt (tf);

            animator.Play ("Attacking on Ground");
            StartCoroutine ("DestroySelfOnGround");
        } else {
            animator.Play ("Standing Attack");
            StartCoroutine ("DestroySelfStanding");
        }
    }
}
```

The next section of code is the `OnTriggerEnter()` method that we previously created for handling collisions with cucumbers. As you can see from the following code, we added an `else if` statement to check whether we collided with a `gameObject` with a tag of `Cherry`. When that condition is `true`, we set the `isAttacking` Boolean variable to `true` so that the forward motion driven by the `BeetlePatrol` script will stop. We also set the `cherryHit` value to `true` and play the animation that shows the beetle standing:

```
void OnTriggerEnter(Collider theObject) {
    if (theObject.gameObject.CompareTag ("Cucumber")) {

        cucumberToDestroy = theObject.gameObject;
        BeetlePatrol.isEating = true;
        animator.Play ("Eating on Ground");
        StartCoroutine ("DestroyCucumber");
    } else if (theObject.gameObject.CompareTag ("Cherry")) {
        BeetlePatrol.isAttacking = true;
        cherryHit = true;
        animator.Play ("Stand");
    }
}
```

The last section of our `BeetleNPC` script contains three `Destroy`-related functions. You are already familiar with `DestroyCucumber()`. We renamed the `DestroySelf()` function as `DestroySelfOnGround()` and added the new `DestroySelfStanding()`:

```
IEnumerator DestroyCucumber() {
    yield return new WaitForSecondsRealtime (4);
    Destroy (cucumberToDestroy.gameObject);
    BeetlePatrol.isEating = false;
}

IEnumerator DestroySelfOnGround() {

    yield return new WaitForSecondsRealtime (4);
    animator.Play ("Die on Ground");
    Destroy (this.gameObject, 4);
}

IEnumerator DestroySelfStanding() {

    yield return new WaitForSecondsRealtime (4);
    animator.Play ("Die Standing");
```

```
        Destroy (this.gameObject, 4);
        cherryHit = false;
    }

    } // End of BeetleNPC.cs
```

In order to test this functionality, we will need to have some cherries in our scene. Start by downloading the `Cherries.unitypackage` asset package from the publisher's site. This package includes a `Cherry.prefab` file that is already set up to work in our game. It has a `Cherry` tag and a `Box Collider` with `Is Trigger` checked.

In `Chapter 10`, *Scripting Our Points System*, we will add the ability for the Cucumber Man to throw cherries. For now, let's place a bunch of them in our sandbox for testing. One approach, as illustrated in the following screenshot, is to surround a beetle with cherries. This will make our testing easier and faster:

 This is a good time to save your scene and your project.

Summary

In this chapter, we focused on the Cucumber Beetles, our game's non-player characters. We reviewed the beetles' 11 animations and made changes to the non-player characters' animation controller. In addition, we wrote scripts to control the non-player characters. Our scripts resulted in several beetle behaviors: patrolling, cucumber consumption, fighting on the ground, and, when hit by a cherry, standing, running, and attacking on hind legs. We also added cucumber patches, cucumbers, and cherries to our game world.

In Chapter 9, *Adding a Heads-Up Display*, we will design, develop, and incorporate a **Heads-Up Display (HUD)** in our game. We will create text and graphics that provide visual indicators of points, health, and additional information to help the player maintain situational awareness during gameplay.

9
Adding a Heads-Up Display

In the last chapter, we configured our non-player character, the Cucumber Beetle, and reviewed its 11 animations. We significantly reconfigured the non-player character's animation controller. We also planned and wrote scripts to control the non-player character's in-game behaviors, which included patrolling, cucumber consumption, fighting on the ground, and fighting on hind legs. In addition, we added cucumber patches, cucumbers, and cherries to our game world.

In this chapter, we will design, develop, and incorporate a **Heads-Up Display (HUD)** in our game. We will use a canvas to create text and graphics that provide visual indicators of points, health, and additional information to help the player maintain situational awareness during gameplay. We will also implement a mini-map using a Unity camera.

In this chapter, we will cover the following:

- Designing our HUD
- Working with a canvas
- Creating a mini-map
- Scripting for dynamic content

Designing our Heads-Up Display

As you will remember from Chapter 3, *Designing the Game*, we determined that we would have six on-screen components: health, lives, score, cherries, cucumbers, and Cucumber Beetles. That design will now be modified to include a mini-map in the lower-right-hand corner of the screen:

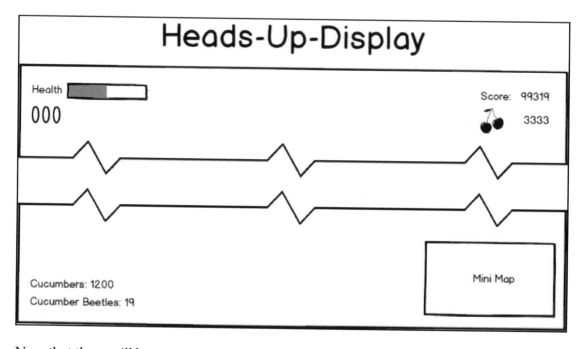

Now that there will be seven components to our HUD, let's review each of them, organized by region:

- **Top-left**:
    - **Player Health**: This will consist of a text label indicating *Health* and a health meter tied to the Cucumber Man's health.
    - **Lives**: We will have a visual indication of the Cucumber Man's remaining lives. The player will start with three lives.
- **Top-right**:
    - **Score**: We will add a text label indicating the score and then have the player's actual score updated here.
    - **Cherries**: The number of cherries the Cucumber Man has will be updated and displayed here.

- **Bottom-right**:
    - **Mini-Map**: This will be a mini-map that shows an overview of the game map with indicators of where the Cucumber Beetles are.
- **Bottom-left**:
    - **Cucumbers**: We will include a text label, along with the number of cucumbers left in the game.
    - **Cucumber Beetles**: This final area of the HUD will feature a text label and the number of Cucumber Beetles left in the game.

Now that we have a clear design for our HUD, we are ready to create it. Before you move on to the next section, you should open your Unity game project. Alternatively, you can download the `Starting-Chapter-09` Unity project available from the publisher's companion site.

Working with a canvas

In Unity, we can use a canvas as a container for UI components. Canvases are GameObjects, and the UI components are the visual components we want on the screen during gameplay. In this section, we will create a canvas and then add and configure the necessary UI components to match our HUD's design from the previous section.

Adding the canvas

Here are the steps for adding a canvas for our UI:

1. Right-click in an empty area of the **Hierarchy** panel and select **UI | Canvas**. You can review the details of the canvas in the **Inspector** panel.

    You will note, in the **Hierarchy** panel, that Unity created an `EventSystem` when you created your canvas. This system is used to manage user input.

2. Change the new canvas GameObject's name from `Canvas` to `HUD_Canvas`. Using self-descriptive names for our GameObjects is considered good development practice. No other changes to any of the canvas properties are necessary.

Adding the health bar UI components

Next, we will create the UI components to display the Cucumber Man's health:

1. Right-click the **HUD_Canvas** GameObject in the **Hierarchy** panel and select **UI | Text**. This will create a text object subordinate to the canvas.
2. Rename the text component as Health_Label.
3. Right-click the **HUD_Canvas** GameObject in the **Hierarchy** panel and select **UI | Slider**. This will create a slider object subordinate to the canvas.
4. Rename the slider component as Health_Slider.

So far, we have created a canvas with text and slider components. Next, we will orient the UI components on the canvas to match the placement in our HUD design from the previous section:

1. In the **Hierarchy** panel, double-click the **HUD_Canvas**. This will focus the canvas in the **Scene** view, and this will give you an overview of how your canvas looks.
2. In the **Hierarchy** panel, double-click the **Health_Label**. Now, you can see both the text and slider components we created.
3. Zoom out until you can see the entire canvas in the **Scene** view.
4. Toggle the **2D** view on in the **Scene** view. This will make orientating our UI components on our canvas much easier:

5. Ensure that the **Health_Label** is selected in the **Hierarchy** panel.
6. In the **Inspector** panel, change the **Text** value of the **Text (Script)** component to Health. See the following screenshot for details:

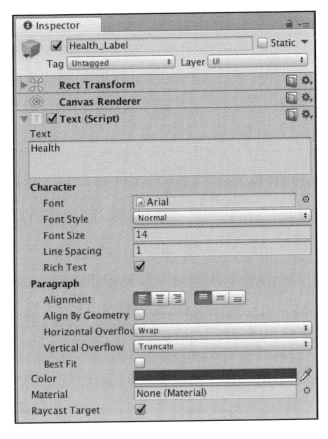

7. Drag the **Health_Label** to the top-left corner of the canvas.

8. In the **Text (Script)** component, make the following changes, or select other settings to your liking. You can experiment with the game in game-mode to see how this will look during the game:

Property	Value
Font	Arial
Font Style	Bold
Font Size	16
Color	Dark Blue

9. Either in the **Inspector** panel or in the **Scene** view, resize the rectangle encasing of your **Health_Label** UI text component so that there is not excessive blank space above, below, or to the right of the text.

10. Relocate the **Health_Slider** so that it is immediately to the right of the **Health_Label** text.

11. In the **Inspector** panel, make the following changes to the **Slider (Script)** component:
    - Deselect the **Interactable** checkbox
    - Change the **Max Value** to 100
    - Select the **Whole Numbers** checkbox

12. In the **Hierarchy** panel, expand the **Health_Slider** object to reveal the subordinate parts as follows:

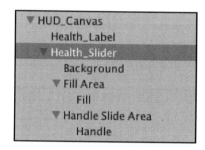

13. In the **Hierarchy** panel, select **HUD_Canvas | Health_Slider | Background**.

14. In the **Inspector** panel, select **Image (Script) | Color** and change the color to red. This will serve as our health meter's background.

15. In the **Hierarchy** panel, select **HUD_Canvas | Health_Slider | Fill Area | Fill**.

16. In the **Inspector** panel, select **Image (Script) | Color** and change the color to green. This will serve as our health meter's fill area.

The final two steps for our health meter will be to increase the height and to remove the slider handle:

1. In the **Hierarchy** panel, select **HUD_Canvas | Health_Slider.**

2. In the **Inspector** panel, select **Rect Transform | Height** and change the height to 30.

3. In the **Hierarchy** panel, select **HUD_Canvas | Health_Slider | Handle Slide Area | Handle**.

4. Deselect the **Image (Script)** component. This will remove the slider's handle from the UI.

5. In the **Scene** view, adjust the **Health_Label** and **Health_Slider** so that they are aligned with each other in the top-left-hand corner of the canvas.

Your finished work should look similar to the following screenshot from the **Game** view:

Make any necessary adjustments before moving on to the next section.

Creating the Lives Remaining UI components

In this section, we will add three images of the Cucumber Man's head beneath the health label and meter, each image representing a life remaining:

1. Download the `cmLives.png` file from the publisher's website

2. Drag that image into the `Assets | Cucumber Man` folder in the **Project** panel

3. Select the imported image and, in the **Inspector** panel, change the **Texture Type** to **Sprite (2D and UI)**

4. In the **Hierarchy** panel, right-click the `HUD_Canvas` and select **UI | Image**

5. In the **Inspector** panel, click the small circle to the right of the setting under **Image (Script) | Source Image**

6. Select the `cmLives.png` image you added in step 2

7. In the **Inspector** panel, rename this image as `Life1`

8. Click **Rect Transform | Scale** and change the scale of **Life1** to `0.4` for **X**, **Y**, and **Z**

9. In the **Scene** view, reposition the **Life1** image so that it is directly preceding the health label

10. In the **Hierarchy** panel, right-click and duplicate **Life1** twice, and rename the copies `Life2` and `Life3`

11. In the **Scene** view, reposition the three images so that they are in sequential order and aligned in a visually pleasing manner

Your finished work should look similar to the following screenshot from the **Game** view:

Make any necessary adjustments before moving on to the next section.

Adding the scoring UI components

The upper-right corner of our game's interface and canvas, will contain the scoring information. This section demonstrates how to create the necessary UI components:

1. Right-click the **HUD_Canvas** GameObject in the **Hierarchy** panel and select **UI | Text**. We will use this text object for our score label.

2. Rename the text component as `Score_Label`.

3. In the **Inspector** panel, change the **Text** value of the **Text (Script)** component to `Score`.

4. In the **Text (Script)** component, make the following changes or select other settings as you wish. You can experiment with the game in game mode to see how this will look during the game:
   - **Font Style: Bold**
   - **Font Size: 16**
   - **Color: Dark Blue**

5. Either in the **Inspector** panel or in **Scene** view, resize the rectangle encasing your `Score_Label` UI text component so that there is no excessive blank space above, below, or to the right of the text.

6. Right-click the **HUD_Canvas** GameObject in the **Hierarchy** panel and select **UI | Text**. We will use this text object to display the current score.

7. Rename the text component as `Score_Value`.

8. In the **Inspector** panel, change the **Text** value of the **Text (Script)** component to `000000000`. This will help us determine the layout.

9. Either in the **Inspector** panel or in **Scene** view, resize the rectangle encasing your `Score_Value` UI text component so that there is no excessive blank space above, below, or to the right of the text.

10. Repeat step 4 for the `Score_Value` text component.

Now that you have the two score-related UI text components have been added to your canvas, you are ready to reposition them on the screen.

1. In the **Scene** view, adjust the **Score_Label** and **Score_Value** text objects so that their rect transform is sized to encase the text values

2. Lastly, reposition the two text objects in **Scene** view so that they are aligned with each other in the top-right corner of the canvas

Your finished work should look similar to the following screenshot from the **Game** view.

Make any necessary adjustments before moving on to the next section.

Adding the cherry UI components

In this section, we will add an image of cherries and a text object for displaying the number of cherries the Cucumber Man has.

We will start by adding the cherry image:

1. Download the `Cherries.png` file from the publisher's website

2. Drag that image into the `Assets | Cherry` folder in the **Project** panel

3. Select the imported image and, in the **Inspector** panel, change the **Texture Type** to **Sprite (2D and UI)**

4. In the **Hierarchy** panel, right-click the **HUD_Canvas** and select **UI | Image**
5. In the **Inspector** panel, click the small circle to the right of the setting under **Image (Script) | Source Image**
6. Select the `Cherries.png` image you added in step 2
7. In the **Inspector** panel, rename this as `Cherries`
8. Click **Rect Transform | Scale** and change the scale of **Cherries** to 0.4 for **x**, **y**, and **z**
9. In the **Scene** view, reposition the **Cherries** image directly below the start of the **Score_Value** text object

Next, we will add the text object to hold the cherry count:

1. Right-click the **HUD_Canvas** GameObject in the **Hierarchy** panel and select **UI | Text**.
2. Rename the text component as `Cherries_Count`.
3. In the **Inspector** panel, change the **Text** value of the **Text (Script)** component to `0000`. This will help us determine the layout.
4. In the **Text (Script)** component, change the **Font Style** to **Bold**, the **Font Size** to **16**, and the **Color** to **Red**, or select other settings to your liking.
5. Either in the **Inspector** panel or in the **Scene** view, resize the rectangle encasing your `Cherries_Count` UI text component so that there is no excessive blank space above, below, or to the right of the text.
6. In the **Scene** view, reposition the `Cherry_Count` text object to the right of the `Cherries` image object.

Your finished work should look similar to the following screenshot from the game view:

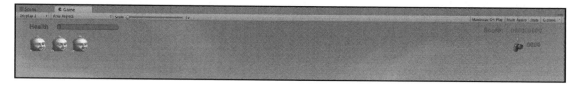

Make any necessary adjustments before moving on to the next section.

Adding the cucumber and Cucumber Beetle UI components

In this section, we will add four UI text components to the lower-left-hand corner of our canvas. These text components will be used for the following:

- Cucumber label
- Cucumber count value
- Cucumber Beetles label
- Cucumber Beetles count value

At this point, you should be comfortable with adding UI text components to your canvas, so this section will be brief. Feel free to consult previous sections to review the steps involved:

1. Create a text object for the cucumber label:
    1. Right-click the **HUD_Canvas** GameObject in the **Hierarchy** panel and select **UI** | **Text**
    2. Rename the text component as `Cucumbers_Label`
    3. Change the **Text** value of the **Text (Script)** component to **Cucumbers**
    4. In the **Text (Script)** component, change the **Font Style** to **Bold**, the **Font Size** to **16**, and the **Color** to **Blue**
    5. Either in the **Inspector** panel or in the **Scene** view, resize the rectangle encasing your **Cucumbers_Label** UI text component so that there is no excessive blank space above, below, or to the right of the text
    6. In the **Scene** view, reposition the **Cucumbers_Label** text object to reflect the HUD design from earlier in this chapter

2. Create a text object for the Cucumber Beetles label:
    1. Right-click the **HUD_Canvas** | **Cucumbers_Label** GameObject in the **Hierarchy** panel and select **Duplicate**
    2. Rename the duplicated text component to `Beetles_Label`
    3. Change the **Text** value of the **Text (Script)** component to `Cucumber Beetles`

4. Either in the **Inspector** panel or in the **Scene** view, resize the rectangle encasing your **Beetles_Label** UI text component to ensure it is wide enough to display the entire text

5. In the **Scene** view, reposition the **Beetles_Label** text object to reflect the HUD design from earlier in this chapter

3. Create a text object for the cucumber count:
    1. Right-click the **HUD_Canvas | Cucumbers_Label** GameObject in the **Hierarchy** panel and select **Duplicate**
    2. Rename the duplicated text component as `Cucumber_Count`
    3. Change the **Text** value of the **Text (Script)** component to `0000`
    4. Either in the **Inspector** panel or in the **Scene** view, resize the rectangle encasing your **Cucumber_Count** UI text component so that there is no excessive blank space above, below, or to the right of the text
    5. In the **Text (Script)** component, change the **Color** to **Red**
    6. In the **Scene** view, reposition the **Cucumber_Count** text object to reflect the HUD design from earlier in this chapter

4. Create a text object for the Cucumber Beetle count:
    1. Right-click the **HUD_Canvas | Cucumber_Count** GameObject in the **Hierarchy** panel and select **Duplicate**
    2. Rename the duplicated text component as `Beetle_Count`
    3. In the **Scene** view, reposition the **Beetle_Count** text object to reflect the HUD design from earlier in this chapter

Your finished work should look similar to the following screenshot from the **Game** view:

Make any necessary adjustments before moving on to the next section.

Creating a mini-map

In Chapter 5, *Lights, Cameras, and Shadows,* you learned about how to use cameras for mini-maps. In this section, we will implement a mini-map for our game. This mini-map will provide a top-down view of our game, centered on the sandbox area you created in Chapter 8, *Implementing Our Non-Player Character.* The player can use this mini-map as a radar to help find Cucumber Beetles in the sandbox.

First, we need to turn the **Scene** view 2D toggle off. This will put the **Scene** view back into 3D mode.

Here are the steps for creating a mini-map in our game:

1. Right-click on an empty area of the **Hierarchy** panel and select **Camera**
2. Rename the camera as Camera_Minimap
3. Double-click the **Camera_Minimap** camera in the **Hierarchy** panel to focus on that object in the **Scene** view
4. Change the **Transform** | **Rotation** | **X** value to 90, so it is looking at the ground
5. In the **Scene** view, use the transform tools to position the camera so that it covers your sandbox
6. You can use the **Camera Preview** to help determine what will be visible during gameplay

The following screenshot shows a **Camera Preview** that covers the entire sandbox area, bordered with white rectangular walls:

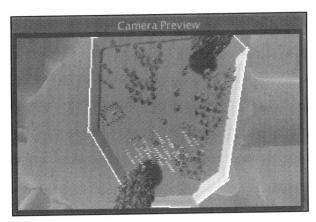

Now that the **Camera_MiniMap** camera has been added to our scene, we need to ensure it is not treated like our main camera. Here are the steps:

1. In the **Project** panel, under **Assets**, right-click the `Textures` folder and select **Create | Render Texture**
2. Rename the new render texture `Render_Texture_Minimap`
3. Select the **Camera_Minimap** camera in the **Hierarchy** panel
4. In the **Inspector** panel, click the small circle to the right of the **Camera | Target Texture** property
5. Select the `Render_Texture_Minimap` texture you created

The minimap camera is now properly configured. Our next set of steps require us to modify our **HUD_Canvas**. We will accomplish this with the following steps:

1. In the **Hierarchy** panel, drag the **Camera_Minimap** object so that it is subordinate to the **HUD_Canvas**
2. Right-click the **HUD_Canvas** and select **UI | Raw Image**
3. Rename the new raw image UI component as `RawImage_Minimap`
4. In the **Inspector** panel, click the small circle to the right of the **Raw Image (Script) | Texture** property
5. Select the `Render_Texture_Minimap` texture you created
6. Toggle the **Scene** view 2D toggle on
7. Double-click the **HUD_Canvas** in the **Hierarchy** panel, then zoom in so you can see a close-up of the canvas
8. Relocate the **RawImage_Minimap** so that it is in the lower-right-hand corner of the canvas
9. Change the **Rect Transform | Scale** to 2 for **X**, **Y**, and **Z**

You are now ready to test your game in game mode. You should see the mini-map in the bottom-right-hand corner of the screen, illustrated in the following screenshot:

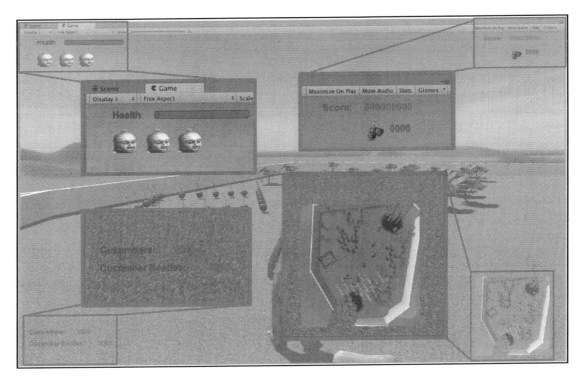

You can use this mini-map as a great starting point as you work to refine how it looks in the game. Some options for refinement include giving the mini-map more contrast with the game world and showing red dots for Cucumber Beetles instead of only showing the entire terrain.

Scripting for dynamic content

Now that your HUD has been completed, it is time to consider how the information on the HUD is updated. The following elements of our HUD require scripting so that they are dynamically updated during the game:

- Cucumber Man's health
- Number of Cucumber Man lives remaining
- Points

- Number of cherries in Cucumber Man's inventory
- Number of cucumbers
- Number of Cucumber Beetles

In this section, we will lay the groundwork for updating the HUD information.

Scripting the cucumber count

Let's start with our cucumber count:

1. In the **Hierarchy** panel, select **HUD_Canvas | Cucumber_Count**
2. In the **Inspector** panel, click the **Add Component** button
3. Select **New Script** and name the script `CucumberManager`
4. Edit the script

With the script open, make the necessary modifications to match the script provided, as follows:

```
using System.Collections;
using System.Collections.Generic;
using UnityEngine;
using UnityEngine.UI;

public class CucumberManager : MonoBehaviour {

    public int currentCucumberCount;
    Text Cucumber_Count;
    public GameObject[] cucumbers;


    void Awake () {

        Cucumber_Count = GetComponent&lt;Text> ();
        currentCucumberCount = 0;
    }


    void Update () {

        cucumbers = GameObject.FindGameObjectsWithTag ("Cucumber");
        Cucumber_Count.text = cucumbers.Length.ToString();
    }
}
```

As you can see, we are using the `UnityEngine.UI` namespace. Inside the `CucumberManager` class, we declare three variables, establish an initial count of zero in the `Awake()` method, and then count the amount of cucumbers every frame in `Update()`, providing an on-screen update of the number of cucumbers left in the game. The ease with which we were able to program this was partially due to our assigning of the `Cucumber` tag to all of our cucumbers.

Scripting the beetle count

As you might imagine, the script for counting beetles will be very similar to the method we used for counting cucumbers. This time, we will add a `BeetleManager` script to our `Beetle_Count` UI component. Here is the required script:

```
using System.Collections;
using System.Collections.Generic;
using UnityEngine;
using UnityEngine.UI;

public class BeetleManager : MonoBehaviour {

    public int currentBeetleCount;
    Text Beetle_Count;
    public GameObject[] beetles;


    void Awake () {

        Beetle_Count = GetComponent&lt;Text> ();
        currentBeetleCount = 0;
    }


    void Update () {

        beetles = GameObject.FindGameObjectsWithTag ("Beetle");
        Beetle_Count.text = beetles.Length.ToString ();
    }
}
```

This code is very similar to our `CucumberManager` script. The only difference is the GameObject tag and our variable names.

If this script does not work for you, ensure that your beetles are assigned the `Beetle` tag.

The remaining scripting of our HUD will be accomplished in subsequent chapters. In `Chapter 10`, *Scripting Our Points System*, we will write scripts for the points and number of cherries in Cucumber Man's inventory. In `Chapter 11`, *Scripting Victory and Defeat*, we will write the necessary scripts to update the health slider and the number of Cucumber Man lives that remain.

Be sure to save your Unity scene and project!

Summary

In this chapter, we designed, developed, and incorporated a HUD in our game. We used a canvas GameObject to create text and graphics that provide visual indicators of points, health, and additional information to help the player maintain situational awareness during gameplay. In addition to this, we wrote scripts to update key components of the HUD. We also implemented a mini-map using a Unity camera.

In `Chapter 10`, *Scripting Our Points System*, we will design, script, and implement our game's point system. This will include providing frame-by-frame updates to key on-screen components of the game's HUD.

10

Scripting Our Points System

In the last chapter, we designed, developed, and incorporated a **Heads-Up Display (HUD)** in our game. We used a canvas game object to create text and graphics that provide visual indicators of points, health, and additional information to help the player maintain situational awareness during game play. In addition, we wrote scripts to update key components of the HUD. We also implemented a mini-map using a second camera in our game scene.

In this chapter, we will design, script, and implement our game's point system. This will include providing frame-by-frame updates to key on-screen components of the game's HUD.

Specifically, we will write scripts for the following in this chapter:

- Collecting cherries from trees
- Adding the cherry-throwing capability
- Adding points based on cherry collection and combat hits

Collecting cherries from trees

In this section, we will make the necessary adjustments to our game objects and script functionality that enable the collection of cherries from cherry trees. More specifically, we will create the following gameplay:

- Detect collisions of Cucumber Man and cherry trees
- Simulate collection of cherries
- Update inventory and HUD with cherry count

Before we get started, you should open your Unity game project. Alternatively, you can download the **Starting-Chapter-10** Unity project available from the publisher's companion site.

Detecting collisions of Cucumber Man and cherry trees

In this section, we will enable and test collisions between the Cucumber Man and cherry trees. Our first step is to ensure the cherry trees in our sandbox area all have the `CherryTree` tag. We previously created the tag name, so we only need to apply it to the trees in our sandbox. Here are the steps:

1. In the **Hierarchy** panel, select a **Cherry Tree** that is inside your sandbox area
2. In the **Inspector** panel, click the drop-down box to the left of the **Tag** label
3. Select the **CherryTree** tag
4. Repeat steps 1 through 3 for each **Cherry Tree** GameObject in your sandbox area
5. Optionally, repeat steps 1 through 3 for all the **Cherry Tree** GameObjects in the **Hierarchy** view, not just the ones in your sandbox area

Next, we will create a `CucumberManManager` script to handle the collisions with the cherry trees. Here are the steps to create that script:

1. In the **Hierarchy** panel, select the **CumcuberMan** player character
2. In the **Inspector** panel, scroll to the bottom and click the **Add Component** button
3. Select **New Script**
4. Name the script `CucumberManManager`
5. Click the **Create and Add** button
6. In the **Project** panel, click **Favorites | All Scripts**
7. Drag the `CucumberManManager` script to the `Assets | Custom Scripts` folder
8. Double-click the `CucumberManManager` script to open it in an editor
9. Edit the script so that it matches the code provided here:

```
using System.Collections;
using System.Collections.Generic;
using UnityEngine;

public class CucumberManManager : MonoBehaviour {
```

```
void OnTriggerEnter(Collider theObject) {
    if (theObject.gameObject.CompareTag ("CherryTree")) {

        // Do something

    }
}
}
```

The preceding script is a C# script with an `OnTriggerEnter()` method. As you can see, we check the tag of what the Cucumber Man collided with to see if that game object has a tag of `CherryTree`.

Next, we need to do something when that collision is detected. We will handle that in the next section.

Simulating the collection of cherries

In this section, we will continue working on the `CucumberManManager` script to simulate the collection of cherries.

If you do not already have the script open, open it now in an editor. We will review the updated code in five sequential sections.

Our first section, shown here, imports the three necessary namespaces.

```
using System.Collections;
using System.Collections.Generic;
using UnityEngine;

public class CucumberManManager : MonoBehaviour {

    public static int currentCherryCount;
    public int tempCurrentCherryCount;
    public bool collectingCherries;
```

The fourth line of code is the class declaration statement. The last three lines of code in this section are the class variables. Here is a brief description of each:

- `currentCherryCount`: Keep the current number of cherries in the Cucumber Man's inventory
- `tempCurrentCherryCount`: Used to limit cherry collection to one per second
- `collectingCherries`: Used to determine whether the inventory counter should be active

Our second section, shown as follows, features the `Awake()` method. This method is used to initialize our variables at the start of the game:

```
void Awake () {

    currentCherryCount = 0;
    tempCurrentCherryCount = 0;
    collectingCherries = false;

}
```

Our third section, shown here, features the `Update()` method. This method is executed once per frame. We have an if/else statement nested in an outer if statement. This outer statement checks to see whether the `collectingCherries` Boolean value is true. If it is, the inner if/else statement block is evaluated.

The inner if/else block checks to see whether the `tempCurrentCherryCount` variable's value is greater than or equal to `60`. If it is, then the `currentCherryCount` value is incremented by one; otherwise, the `tempCurrentCherryCount` value is incremented by one. The `Update()` method is called once per frame and frame rates can vary. So, we are essentially adding one cherry to the Cucumber Man's inventory every 60 frames:

```
void Update () {

    if (collectingCherries) {
        if (tempCurrentCherryCount >= 60) {
            currentCherryCount = currentCherryCount + 1;
            tempCurrentCherryCount = 0;

        } else {
            tempCurrentCherryCount = tempCurrentCherryCount + 1;
        }
    }

}
```

Our fourth section, shown in the following code block, contains the `OnTriggerEnter()` method we started in the last section. We edited this method to include an if statement that checks to see whether the Cucumber Man has entered a collision with a cherry tree. If so, the `collectingCherries` Boolean variable is set to `true` and one cherry is added to the inventory:

```
void OnTriggerEnter(Collider theObject) {
    if (theObject.gameObject.CompareTag ("CherryTree")) {
```

```
        collectingCherries = true;
        currentCherryCount = currentCherryCount + 1;
    }
}
```

Our fifth section, shown as follows, has the `OnTriggerExit()` method. This event is fired when the Cucumber Man stops colliding with the cherry trees. When this occurs, we set the `collectingCherries` Boolean value to `false`:

```
void OnTriggerExit(Collider theObject) {
    if (theObject.gameObject.CompareTag ("CherryTree")) {
        collectingCherries = false;
    }
}

} // end of CucumberManManager.cs
```

Updating the inventory and HUD with cherry count

We now have a system in place for adding cherries to the Cucumber Man's inventory based on his collision with cherry trees. Next, we need to update the appropriate UI text component with the current inventory amount. We will take care of this important task in this section.

Here are the steps to create that script:

1. In the **Hierarchy** panel, select the `HUD_Canvas` | `Cherries_Count` UI text component
2. In the **Inspector** panel, scroll to the bottom and click the **Add Component** button
3. Select **New Script**
4. Name the script `CherryManager`
5. Click the **Create and Add** button
6. In the **Project** panel, click **Favorites** | **All Scripts**
7. Drag the `CherryManager` script to the `Assets` | `Custom Scripts` folder
8. Double-click the `CherryManager` script to open it in an editor
9. Edit the script so that it matches the code provided here

An explanation of this code is provided immediately following the code block:

```
using System.Collections;
using System.Collections.Generic;
using UnityEngine;
using UnityEngine.UI;

public class CherryManager : MonoBehaviour {

    Text Cherries_Count;

    void Awake () {

        Cherries_Count = GetComponent<Text> ();

    }


    void Update () {

        Cherries_Count.text =
CucumberManManager.currentCherryCount.ToString ();

    }
}
```

The first four lines of code import the appropriate namespaces.

The next line of code is the class declaration: `public class CherryManager : MonoBehaviour {`.

Next is the single class variable, a `text` object named `Cherries_Count`.

The first method in the class is the `Awake()` method. We use this method to create a reference to the `Cherries_Count` UI text component.

The last section of our `CherryManager` class is the `Update()` method. That method has a single statement used to convert the `currentCherryCount` from an `int` to a string and update the HUD.

You can play-test the game to validate the functionality. Simply navigate the Cucumber Man to a cherry tree and watch the inventory of cherries increase. It is important for us to have a method of collecting cherries because the player can press the *E* key on the keyboard to throw a cherry. We will program that functionality in the next section.

Now is a great time to save your scene and project.

Adding the cherry-throwing capability

In Chapter 7, *Implementing our Player Character*, we demonstrated the Cucumber Man's throw animation using the *E* keyboard key. In this section, we will make the necessary changes to instantiate a cherry in the Cucumber Man's right hand when the *E* keyboard key is pressed and then allow it to be launched. We will check to ensure the Cucumber Man has at least one cherry in his inventory so we know whether a cherry should be instantiated or not. Okay, let's get started.

Creating a spot for the cherry

The following steps demonstrate how to create a spot for the cherry on the Cucumber Man's right hand.

1. In the **Hierarchy** panel, expand the CucumberMan object until you see Character1_RightHand.

2. Right-click Character1_RightHand and select **Create Empty**.

3. Rename the new GameObject to cherrySpot. This will be the spot where we render the cherry.

Your CucumberMan object's hierarchy should look as follows:

```
▼ ◆ Main*
    Main Camera
    ► Beetle
    ▼ CucumberMan
        ▼ Character1_Reference
            ▼ Character1_Hips
                ► Character1_LeftUpLeg
                ► Character1_RightUpLeg
                ▼ Character1_Spine
                    ▼ Character1_Spine1
                        ▼ Character1_Spine2
                            ► Character1_LeftArm
                            ► Character1_Neck
                            ▼ Character1_RightArm
                                ▼ Character1_RightForeArm
                                    ▼ Character1_RightHand
                                        ► Character1_RightHandIndex1
                                        ► Character1_RightHandMiddle1
                                        ► Character1_RightHandRing1
                                        ► Character1_RightHandThumb1
                                        cherrySpot
```

4. Using the transform tools, move the `cherrySpot` GameObject so that it is inside the Cucumber Man's right hand. Your placement should be similar to what is displayed here:

We will need to add a `Rigidbody` to the `Cherry` prefab so we can instantiate and throw it during runtime.

1. In the **Project** panel, select **Assets | Cherry |** `Cherry.Prefab`
2. In the **Inspector** panel, click the **Add Component** button
3. Select **Physics | Rigidbody**
4. Uncheck the **Use Gravity** option
5. Expand the **Constraints** section of the **Rigidbody** component
6. Check all **Freeze Position** and **Freeze Rotation** boxes

Next, we will add the `Cherry` prefab to our scene.

1. Drag the **Cherry** prefab from the **Project** panel to the **Hierarchy** panel, making it subordinate to the **cherrySpot** game object.

2. In **Scene** view, zoom in and adjust the location of the **cherrySpot** so the cherry looks as if the Cucumber Man is holding it. A suggested placement is shown here:

Writing a CherryControl script

Next, we will add a script to the cherry prefab to support the creation and release of the cherry with respect to the Cucumber Man's hand.

1. In the **Project** panel, select **Assets | Cherry |** `Cherry.Prefab`
2. In the **Inspector** panel, click the **Add Component** button
3. Select **New Script** and name the script **CherryControl**
4. Click the **Create and Add** button
5. In the **Project** panel, drag the new script into the `Assets | Custom Scripts` folder
6. Edit the script so that it matches what is provided in the following code block

The first part of the script consists of the namespace import statements and the class declaration:

```
using System.Collections;
using System.Collections.Generic;
using UnityEngine;

public class CherryControl : MonoBehaviour {
```

The next section contains the class variables. We have one `Rigidbody`, two floats, and a `GameObject`:

```
public Rigidbody cherry;
public float throwDistance = 2000000000f;
public float time2Die = 4.0f;

GameObject cucumberHand;
```

The `Update()` method, shown here, checks to see whether the *E* keyboard key is pressed and whether the Cucumber Man has at least one cherry:

```
void Update () {

    int count = CucumberManManager.currentCherryCount;

    if (Input.GetKeyDown (KeyCode.E)) {

        if (count >= 1) {

            ThrowACherry ();
        }
    }
}
```

The last section of the code is the `ThrowACherry()` method. As you can see, we clone the cherry at the Cucumber Man's hand, turn gravity on, release the constraints, and push it forward using the `AddForce()` method. Next, we use the `Destroy()` method to destroy the cloned cherry in four seconds. The last statement decrements the Cucumber Man's cherry inventory:

```
public void ThrowACherry () {

    Rigidbody cherryClone = (Rigidbody)Instantiate
            (cherry, transform.position, transform.rotation);
    cherryClone.useGravity = true;
    cherryClone.constraints = RigidbodyConstraints.None;
    cherryClone.AddForce(transform.forward * throwDistance);
```

```
        Destroy (cherryClone.gameObject, time2Die);

        CucumberManManager.currentCherryCount =
CucumberManManager.currentCherryCount - 1;
    }
}
```

Adding points based on cherry collection and combat hits

In this section, we will edit the appropriate scripts so that the Cucumber Man can earn points, related to cherries, based on the following criteria:

In-game event	Points
Cucumber Man picks cherry	+ 5
Cucumber Man hits beetle with cherry	+ 10

Creating a points manager script

In this section, we will create and edit a script to manage our points and to display them on our game's HUD. Here are the steps:

1. In the **Hierarchy** panel, select the **HUD_Canvas** | **Score_Value**
2. In the **Inspector** panel, click the **Add Component** button
3. Select **New Script** and name the script PointsManager
4. In the **Project** panel, click **Favorites** | **All Scripts**
5. Drag the **PointsManager** script to the **Assets** | Custom Scripts folder
6. Double-click the **PointsManager** script to open it in an editor
7. Edit the script so that it matches the following code

The first section of the code contains the namespace import statements and the PointsManager class declaration:

```
using System.Collections;
using System.Collections.Generic;
using UnityEngine;
```

```
using UnityEngine.UI;

public class PointsManager : MonoBehaviour {
```

The next section of the script declares two class variables; one for the current score and the other is a reference to the `Text` UI component that displays the score during game play:

```
public static int currentScore;
Text score;
```

The first method in our class is the `Awake()` method. We use this method to initialize our variables:

```
void Awake () {
    score = GetComponent<Text> ();
    currentScore = 0;
}
```

The last section of our class is the `Update()` method. Here, we have a single statement that converts the current score to a string and then updates the HUD:

```
void Update () {

    score.text = currentScore.ToString ();
}
}
```

Adding points for each cherry picked

In this section, we will edit the appropriate script to add five points for each cherry picked. Here are the steps:

1. In the **Project** panel, select the **Custom Scripts | CucumberManManager**
2. Edit the script
3. Add the following class variable: public `PointsManager _ptsManager;`
4. Add the following lines of code inside the nested if statement in the `Update()` method:

```
_ptsManager = GameObject.Find ("Score_Value").GetComponent<PointsManager> ();
PointsManager.currentScore = PointsManager.currentScore + 5;
```

The two lines of preceding code create a reference to the `PointsManager` script and, on the second line, increments the `currentScore` by 5.

The updated `CucumberManManager` script should be as follows:

```
using System.Collections;
using System.Collections.Generic;
using UnityEngine;

public class CucumberManManager : MonoBehaviour {

    public static int currentCherryCount;
    public int tempCurrentCherryCount;
    public bool collectingCherries;
    public PointsManager _ptsManager;

    void Awake () {
        currentCherryCount = 0;
        tempCurrentCherryCount = 0;
        collectingCherries = false;
    }

    void Update () {
        if (collectingCherries) {
            if (tempCurrentCherryCount >= 60) {
                currentCherryCount = currentCherryCount + 1;
                tempCurrentCherryCount = 0;

                _ptsManager = GameObject.Find
    ("Score_Value").GetComponent<PointsManager> ();
                PointsManager.currentScore =
    PointsManager.currentScore + 5;

            } else {
                tempCurrentCherryCount = tempCurrentCherryCount + 1;
            }
        }
    }

    void OnTriggerEnter(Collider theObject) {
        if (theObject.gameObject.CompareTag ("CherryTree")) {

            collectingCherries = true;
            currentCherryCount = currentCherryCount + 1;
        }
    }

    void OnTriggerExit(Collider theObject) {
        if (theObject.gameObject.CompareTag ("CherryTree")) {
            collectingCherries = false;
```

```
            }
        }
    }
```

Adding points for hitting a beetle with a cherry

Our last points-related task is to update the BeetleNPC script so that appropriate points are added when a cherry hits a cucumber beetle. Here are the steps:

1. In the **Project** panel, select the **Custom Scripts | BeetleNPC**
2. Edit the script
3. Add the following class variable: `public PointsManager _ptsManager;`
4. Add the following lines of code inside the nested else if statement in the `OnTriggerEnter()` method:

```
_ptsManager = GameObject.Find ("Score_Value").GetComponent<PointsManager>
();
PointsManager.currentScore = PointsManager.currentScore + 10;
```

The two preceding lines of code create a reference to the `PointsManager` script and, on the second line, increment the `currentScore` by 10.

The updated `BeetleNPC` script's `OnTriggerEnter()` method should be as follows:

```
        void OnTriggerEnter(Collider theObject) {
            if (theObject.gameObject.CompareTag ("Cucumber")) {

                cucumberToDestroy = theObject.gameObject;
                BeetlePatrol.isEating = true;
                animator.Play ("Eating on Ground");
                StartCoroutine ("DestroyCucumber");
            } else if (theObject.gameObject.CompareTag ("Cherry")) {
                _ptsManager = GameObject.Find
    ("Score_Value").GetComponent<PointsManager> ();
                PointsManager.currentScore = PointsManager.currentScore + 10;
                BeetlePatrol.isAttacking = true;
                cherryHit = true;
                animator.Play ("Stand");
            }
        }
```

Summary

In this chapter, we designed, scripted, and implemented our game's point system. This included providing frame-by-frame updates to key on-screen components of the game's HUD. Our scripts enabled the collection of cherries from cherry trees, adding the cherry-throwing capability for our Cucumber Man. We also added points based on the collection of cherries and combat hits.

In Chapter 11, *Scripting Victory and Defeat*, we will design and script our game's victory and defeat conditions. This will include managing the Cucumber Man's health, lives remaining, and respawning the player character.

11
Scripting Victory and Defeat

In Chapter 10, *Scripting Our Points System*, we designed, scripted, and implemented our game's point system. We made changes to the appropriate GameObjects and wrote several scripts to manage the point system. We ensured the points were updated on our **Head's-Up Display (HUD)** for each frame of the game. In addition, we added the ability for the Cucumber Man to collect cherries from the cherry trees and use them as weapons against the Cucumber Beetles.

In this chapter, we will design and script our game's victory and defeat conditions. We will update the scripts we created in other chapters to manage the Cucumber Man's health, providing frame-by-frame onscreen updates and ensuring a player life is lost when the health runs out. We will manage, through scripts, the lives remaining. We will also design and script the respawning of our player character.

Specifically, we will cover the following in this chapter:

- Designing the defeat and victory conditions
- Updating the player's health
- Implementing the victory logic
- Implementing the end-of-game logic
- Updating the HUD with lives remaining
- Scripting the player character's respawning

Designing victory and defeat conditions

Currently, our game has no clear end and does not implement any reward for the player's actions. In this section, we will design our game's victory and defeat conditions so that there is a clear goal or way to win the game.

In Chapter 3, *Designing the Game*, we identified three end-of-game conditions: two ending in defeat for our Cucumber Man, and only one resulting in defeat for our Cucumber Beetles.

Here are the victory conditions for our game:

- The Cucumber Beetles win if:
    - There are no cucumbers left in the game
    - The Cucumber Man runs out of lives
- The Cucumber Man wins if:
    - There are no Cucumber Beetles left in the game

These victory and defeat conditions are pretty simple, and there can only be one winner. If the Cucumber Beetles win, the Cucumber Man loses.

In order to implement these conditions, we need to track the following with our scripts:

- Number of cucumbers
- Number of Cucumber Beetles
- Number of Cucumber Man lives remaining

In Chapter 10, *Scripting Our Points System*, we wrote the necessary scripts to keep track of cucumbers and Cucumber Beetles. We also ensured the HUD is continuously updated with those counts. It is important for the player to have a sense of how they are doing in the game. Beyond just points, the player will want to continually review how many cucumbers and Cucumber Beetles there are in the game. The player will also want to know how many Cucumber Man lives remain.

In the next section, we will update our game so the number of lives are updated and the player's health bar is put into use. These will provide the player with much-needed visual components of the HUD during gameplay.

Updating the player's health

In this section, we will fully implement our player's health. We will start the Cucumber Man with three lives, each with a full health value of 100. We will update our scripts so that the Cucumber Man loses health when a cucumber beetle attacks him. Our approach will be to deduct one point from the Cucumber Man's health for every second that it is colliding with a Cucumber Beetle. We will also script the HUD's health bar and start with that task in the next section.

Before we get started, you should open your Unity game project. Alternatively, you can download the *Starting-Chapter-11 Unity* project available from the publisher's companion site.

Scripting the health bar

In this section, we will create a new script and attach it to our HUD's health bar. We will edit the script and use it to manage our Cucumber Man's health and the visible status of the HUD's health bar.

Let's start by reviewing our health bar:

1. In the **Hierarchy** panel, select the `HUD_Canvas` | `Health_Slider`.

2. In the **Inspector** panel, review the **Slider (Script)** component. As you can see in the following screenshot, there is a **Value** component with a slider at the bottom of the interface:

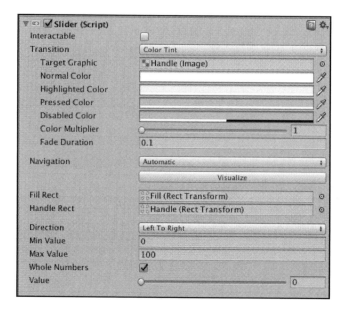

3. Click the **Game** view tab so you can see the HUD without being in game-mode.
4. In the **Inspector** panel, drag the **Value** slider and observe how the health bar functions.

You can see that the health bar already functions; we merely need to add a script to the slider so that it tracks the player's health and updates the HUD during game play. Here are those steps:

1. In the **Inspector** panel, click the **Add Component** button
2. Select **New Script** and name the script `HealthManager`
3. In the **Project** panel, click **Favorites** | **All Scripts**
4. Drag the `HealthManager` script to the `Assets` | `Custom Scripts` folder
5. Double-click the `HealthManager` script to open it in an editor

6. Edit the script so that it matches the following code, the first section of the code contains the namespace `import` statements and the `HealthManager` class declaration:

```
using System.Collections;
using System.Collections.Generic;
using UnityEngine;
using UnityEngine.UI;

public class HealthManager : MonoBehaviour {
```

The next section of code declares our class variables. We will use `currentHealth` to hold the value of the Cucumber Man's up-to-date health value. We will use `healthBar` as a reference to the slider:

```
public static int currentHealth;
public Slider healthBar;
```

Our `HealthManager` class has three methods; the first is the `Awake()` method. The first statement in this method gets a reference to the `Slider` component. The second statement sets the `currentHealth` to 100. This is our maximum health starting point for the Cucumber Man:

```
void Awake () {
healthBar = GetComponent&lt;Slider> ();
currentHealth = 100;
}
```

Our second method is the `ReduceHealth()` method. This will be used by other scripts to call for a health reduction. As you can see, the first statement simply decrements the `currentHealth` value by one. The second statement updates the slider on the screen:

```
void ReduceHealth () {
currentHealth = currentHealth - 1;
healthBar.value = currentHealth;
}
```

The last method for this class is the `Update()` method. We have one statement in that method to update the slider for each frame of the game. This results in the slider accurately depicting the player's health:

```
void Update () {
healthBar.value = currentHealth;
}
 }
```

In the next section, we will modify the appropriate script to call the `ReduceHealth()` method when the Cucumber Man is being bitten by a Cucumber Beetle.

Decrementing health

Our `BeetleNPC` script already detects collisions with the Cucumber Man, so we can simply update that script to deduct a point from the Cucumber Man's health when a collision is detected. We will do this by making a call to the `ReduceHealth()` method of the `HealthManager` script. Here are the steps:

1. In the **Project** panel, select **Assets | Custom Scripts** and double-click the `BeetleNPC` script.

2. Add the following statement in the class variables section of the script. This creates a variable we can use to reference the `HealthManager` class:

   ```
   public HealthManager _healthManager;
   ```

3. Add the following two statements in the `OnCollisionEnter()` method after the first `if` statement:

   ```
   _healthManager = GameObject.Find
   ("Health_Slider").GetComponent<HealthManager>();
   _healthManager.ReduceHealth();
   ```

With these two statements, we obtain a reference to the `HealthManager` script of `Health_Slider`, and then call the `ReduceHealth()` method.

You can now test your game and watch the health bar change as Cucumber Beetles start attacking the Cucumber Man.

Implementing victory

In this section, we will implement the victory condition for the Cucumber Man. The only victory condition for the Cucumber Man is when the number of Cucumber Beetles is zero. Our `BeetleManager` script already provides functionality for counting Cucumber Beetles. As you will recall, that is how we update our Cucumber Beetle count on our HUD. We will make some modifications to that script and create a new script in this section.

Let's start by creating an onscreen text component to display **You Won!** when the number of Cucumber Beetles reaches zero. Here are the steps:

1. Right-click an empty area of the **Hierarchy** panel.
2. Select **Create Empty**.
3. In the **Inspector** panel, rename the new GameObject to `EndofGame`. We will use this as a container for our victory and defeat text labels.
4. In the **Hierarchy** panel, drag the `EndofGame` GameObject to subordinate it to our `HUD_Canvas`.
5. With the `EndofGame` GameObject selected, in the **Inspector** panel, select the **Transform** dropdown and click **Reset**. This resets the transform of the object.
6. In the **Hierarchy** panel, right-click and select **UI | Text**.
7. Subordinate the new text object to the `EndofGame` GameObject.
8. Rename the new text object `Victory`.

The next four steps are used to configure the **Victory** text object in the **Inspector** panel:

1. Change the text property to `You Won!`
2. Set the **Font Style** to **Bold**
3. Increase the **Font Size** to **24**
4. Select a bright **Color** for the text

By clicking on the **Game** tab or putting the game into game mode, you can see the new victory text is displayed in the center of the screen. We only want that text displayed when the player has won the game. Let's tackle that task:

1. Ensure the **Victory** text component is selected
2. In the **Inspector** panel, click the **Add Component** button

3. Select **New Script** and name the script `VictoryManager`
4. In the **Project** panel, click **Favorites | All Scripts**
5. Drag the `VictoryManager` script to the `Assets | Custom Scripts` folder
6. Double-click the **VictoryManager** script to open it in an editor·
7. Edit the script so that it matches the following code, the first section of the code contains the namespace `import` statements and the `VictoryManager` class declaration:

```
using System.Collections;
 using System.Collections.Generic;
using UnityEngine;
using UnityEngine.UI;

public class VictoryManager : MonoBehaviour {
```

The next section of our script contains two class variable declarations and the `Awake()` method. In the `Awake()` method, we get the reference to the text component of our `Victory` UI object. We also set the initial text to null, so nothing will be displayed:

```
Text Victory;
int beetleCount;

void Awake () {

    Victory = GetComponent&lt;Text> ();
    Victory.text = "";
}
```

The last section of our script is the `Update()` method. Here we set the value of count to the current count of Cucumber Beetles, then test whether the count equals zero. If the `(count == 0)` condition is true, we display the victory text on the screen:

```
void Update () {

    beetleCount = BeetleManager.currentBeetleCount;

    if (beetleCount == 0) {
        Victory.text = ("You won!");
    }
}
}
```

Our next task is to update the `BeetleManager` script. We will make three changes to the script:

1. Add the `static` modifier to the `currentBeetleCount` class variable. The new line of code should be:

   ```
   public static int currentBeetleCount;
   ```

2. In the `Awake()` method, change `currentBeetleCount = 0;` to `currentBeetleCount =1;`. This will help ensure the game does not think there are no Cucumber Beetles when the game starts.

3. Add the following statement as the final statement in the `Update()` method: `currentBeetleCount = beetles.Length;`. This will update the `currentBeetleCount` variable for each frame.

You are now ready to test the game. Kill all your Cucumber Beetles to test the code changes you made. If something does not work correctly or you receive errors, please refer to the following updated `BeetleManager` script:

```
using System.Collections;
using System.Collections.Generic;
using UnityEngine;
using UnityEngine.UI;

public class BeetleManager : MonoBehaviour {

    public static int currentBeetleCount;
    Text Beetle_Count;
    public GameObject[] beetles;

    void Awake () {

        Beetle_Count = GetComponent<Text> ();
        currentBeetleCount = 1;
    }

    void Update () {

        beetles = GameObject.FindGameObjectsWithTag ("Beetle");
        Beetle_Count.text = beetles.Length.ToString();
        currentBeetleCount = beetles.Length;
    }
}
```

Now that the victory condition has been implemented, we are ready to implement our defeat conditions. We will do that in the next section.

Implementing defeat

There are two game conditions in which the player can lose the game. The first condition is if there are no cucumbers left in the game. The second condition is if all three lives are gone. Let's look at each of these defeat conditions separately.

Scripting defeat based on no cucumbers remaining

Our `CucumberManager` script already keeps track of the number of cucumbers in the game, so we merely need to give that script's `currentCucumberCount` class variable the static modifier and then update our `VictoryManager` script. Here are the steps.

1. Edit the `CucumberManager` script so the `currentCucumberCount` variable declaration is as follows:

   ```
   public static int currentCucumberCount;
   ```

2. In the `Awake()` method, change `currentCucumberCount = 0;` to `currentCucumberCount = 1;`. This will help ensure the game does not think there are no cucumbers when the game starts.

3. Add the following statement at the end of the `Update()` method, `currentCucumberCount = cucumbers.Length;`. This will keep the counter updated in each frame.

Those were the only changes needed for the `CucumberManager` script. Next, we will edit the `VictoryManager` script:

1. Edit the `VictoryManager` script by adding the `int cucumberCount;` class variable.

2. Add the following lines of code to the bottom of the `Update()` method. These lines will continually check to see whether there are no cucumbers remaining and display the **You Lost!** text when the count equals zero:

```
cucumberCount = CucumberManager.currentCucumberCount;

if (cucumberCount == 0) {
    Victory.text = ("You Lost!");
}
```

You are now ready to test this defeat condition.

You can speed up your testing by deleting cucumbers from the **Hierarchy** panel when in game mode. When you exit game mode, all deleted objects will be restored.

Scripting defeat for no lives remaining

We will use the `CucumberManManager` script to keep track of the number of lives the Cucumber Man has remaining. Edit that script and make the following changes:

1. Add the `public static int livesRemaining;` class variable. We will use this variable to track the number of remaining lives.
2. Add the `public Animator anim;` class variable. We will use this to play the Cucumber Man's death animation.
3. Add the `livesRemaining = 3;` statement to the bottom of the `Awake()` method.

4. Add the following `if` statement block to the bottom of the `Update()` method:

```
if (livesRemaining == 0) {
    anim = GetComponent&lt;Animator> ();
    anim.Play ("CM_Die");
}
```

As you can see in the changes to our `Update()` method, we are simply checking the value of `livesRemaining` and, when no lives remain, we play the appropriate death animation.

You can test this defeat condition by following these steps:

1. Remove the `static` modifier from the `public static int livesRemaining` statement
2. Put the game in game-mode
3. In the **Hierarchy** panel, click the `CucumberMan` GameObject
4. In the **Inspector** panel, scroll to the **Cucumber Man Manager (Script)** component
5. Change the **Lives Remaining** to 0 (zero). See the following screenshot for details:

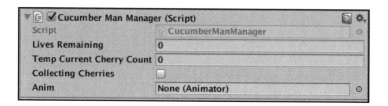

6. When your testing is complete, put the `static` modifier back into the statement from step 1

Updating the HUD with lives remaining

In the previous section, we modified the `CucumberManManager` script to track the number of lives our player has remaining and, when none were left, the appropriate animation was played. In this section, we will continue modifying the `CucumberManManager` script to update the HUD with the number of lives remaining.

We only need to modify the `CucumberManManager` script's `Update()` method. The completed `Update()` method is provided here with an explanation of the changes made:

```
void Update () {

    if (collectingCherries) {
        if (tempCurrentCherryCount ></span>= 60) {
            currentCherryCount = currentCherryCount + 1;
            tempCurrentCherryCount = 0;

            _ptsManager = GameObject.Find
            ("Score_Value").GetComponent&lt;PointsManager>();
            PointsManager.currentScore =
            PointsManager.currentScore + 5;
```

```
        } else {
            tempCurrentCherryCount = tempCurrentCherryCount + 1;
        }
    }

    if (livesRemaining == 2) {
        Destroy (GameObject.Find ("Life3"));
    }
    if (livesRemaining == 1) {
        Destroy (GameObject.Find ("Life2"));
    }
    if (livesRemaining == 0) {
        Destroy (GameObject.Find ("Life1"));
        anim = GetComponent&lt;Animator> ();
        anim.Play ("CM_Die");
    }
}
```

We added conditional statements to check for the number of lives remaining. When two are left, we destroy the third life image. We destroy the second one when only one life remains, and destroy the first life image when no life remains. We used the Destroy() method to accomplish this.

Scripting the player character's respawning

In the previous section, we modified the CucumberManManager script to track how many lives remain and to destroy the UI image elements as appropriate. In this section, we will modify that script to accomplish the following when a life is lost:

- Play the die animation
- Respawn the player on a respawn pad

Let's start by modifying the CucumberManManager script:

1. Add the following class variables:

    ```
    public Transform SpawnPad1;
    public Transform SpawnPad2;
    public Transform SpawnPad3;
    ```

2. In the **Hierarchy** panel, select the CucumberMan GameObject and, in the **Inspector** panel, scroll until you locate the **Cucumber Man Manager (Script)** component.

3. Drag SpawnPad1, SpawnPad2, and SpawnPad3 from the **Hierarchy** view to the designated spots in the **Inspector** panel. See the following for details:

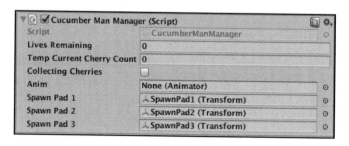

4. Modify the bottom section of the Update() method, as shown here:

```
if (livesRemaining == 2) {
    Destroy (GameObject.Find ("Life3"));
    anim = GetComponent&lt;Animator> ();
    anim.Play ("CM_Die");

    StartCoroutine ("ReSpawnCucumberMan");
}

if (livesRemaining == 1) {
    Destroy (GameObject.Find ("Life2"));
    anim = GetComponent&lt;Animator> ();
    anim.Play ("CM_Die");

    StartCoroutine ("ReSpawnCucumberMan");
}

if (livesRemaining == 0) {
    Destroy (GameObject.Find ("Life1"));
    anim = GetComponent&lt;Animator> ();
    anim.Play ("CM_Die");
}
```

Reviewing the preceding code reveals that there are three conditions being checked based on the value of the `livesRemaining` variable. In each case, the appropriate UI image component is removed from the HUD, and we play the `CM_Die` animation. For the first two cases (`livesRemaining` equals two or one), we have a `StartCoroutine("RespawnCucumberMan");` method call. We will write that method next:

1. Write the `ReSpawnCucumberMan()` method. Enter the following code after the `OnTriggerEnter()` methods in the `CucumberManManager` class:

```
IEnumerator ReSpawnCucumberMan () {

    int randomNumber = Random.Range (1, 4);

    if (randomNumber == 1) {
        yield return new WaitForSecondsRealtime (4);
        this.transform.position = SpawnPad1.transform.position;
    } else if (randomNumber == 2) {
        yield return new WaitForSecondsRealtime (4);
        this.transform.position = SpawnPad2.transform.position;
    } else {
        yield return new WaitForSecondsRealtime (4);
        this.transform.position = SpawnPad3.transform.position;
    }

    anim.Play ("CM_Idle");
}
```

Our `ReSpawnCucumberMan()` method starts by obtaining a random number of 1, 2, or 3. We then check to see which random number was generated, and branch appropriately. We have a four-second delay in order for the die animation to complete. We then respawn the Cucumber Man to the spawn pad corresponding with the randomly generated number. Lastly, we play the idle animation.

Summary

In this chapter, we designed and scripted our game's victory and defeat conditions. We updated our game's scripts to manage the Cucumber Man's health, including updating the HUD's health bar. We implemented our victory and end-of-game logic through scripting. We also implemented the lives remaining and the onscreen indicators of those lives. Lastly, we scripted the respawning of our player character.

In the next chapter, we will plan and implement audio and visual effects in our game to help enhance overall game play. Specifically, we will add audio to key events in our combat system and add several special effects using Unity's particle system to add to the game's visual appeal.

12

Adding Audio and Visual Effects to Our Game

In Chapter 11, *Scripting Victory and Defeat*, we designed and scripted our game's victory and defeat conditions. We updated our game's scripts to manage the Cucumber Man's health, including updating the HUD's health bar. We implemented our victory and end-of-game logic through scripting. We also implemented the lives remaining and enabled dynamic on-screen indicators of those lives. Lastly, we scripted the random respawning of our player character.

In this chapter, we will plan and implement audio and visual effects to help enhance overall gameplay. Specifically, we will add audio to key events in our combat system and add several special effects using Unity's Particle System to enhance the game's visual appeal.

Specifically, we will cover the following in this chapter:

- An overview of Unity's audio system
- Planning our game's audio
- Implementing our game's audio
- An introduction to Unity's lights and shadows
- An overview of Unity's special effects
- Adding visual effects to our game

Discovering Unity's audio system

Unity has an impressive array of audio capabilities. It supports 3D spatial sound, which provides a surround-sound effect. This gives our audio source a point and dimension. There are also extensive mixing and mastering capabilities in Unity.

In this section, we will explore the basics of audio in Unity and take a look at the Audio Mixer.

Unity audio basics

Unity supports several audio effects, including the **Duck Volume Audio Effect**, which allows us to manipulate an audio signal's volume.

 The term duck refers to making the audio signal quieter.

We can use a variety of audio formats in Unity. You can see the four formats listed here:

- **Audio Interchange File Format (AIFF)**
- MP3
- **Ogg Vorbis (OGG)**
- WAV

If you have audio assets that are in a file format different from these four, you can probably use a free audio conversion tool to change the file format.

When we import an audio file into a Unity game, the file becomes an audio clip. Audio clips can also be created from within Unity by using your computer's microphone. You can even create audio clips via scripts during your game.

In Unity, audio sources are attached to objects. These audio sources emit, or play, sound and audio listener components do receive the sound emitted by audio sources. You can think of audio listeners as the player's ears inside the game world, hearing what's near them. Usually, one audio listener component is attached to the main camera so that the sounds it picks up on align well with what is displayed in the game view. Listeners are also attached to objects. Let's look at an example to see how a GameObject, an audio source, and listeners are related.

Let's say we are creating a zoo simulation and are working on the bovine section. There is a holding area for cows. Cows are generally quiet, but might be noisy eaters. The cow would be our GameObject and it would emit a *chewing* audio clip. The audio clip's RAW file (that is, `chewing.aiff`) would be identified as an audio source component attached to the cow GameObject. Now, let's say there is a farmer character. We can attach a listener to the farmer, which is also an object. That listener is a script that performs certain actions if it hears the sound from the cow. Perhaps, if the listener picks up the *chewing* sound, they will know that more hay is needed.

The following diagram illustrates the relationships between the various components:

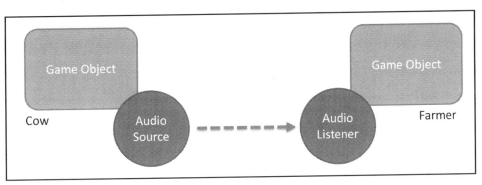

You will learn how to use these components later in this chapter.

Unity's Audio Mixer

Unity's **Audio Mixer** gives you the ability to mix and master audio sources and effects. To access the **Audio Mixer**, you select **Window** from the pull-down menu, and then select **Audio Mixer**.

When you first open the **Audio Mixer** window, you will see that there are no mixers in your project. As you can see in the following screenshot, there is a + icon on the far-right side of that window:

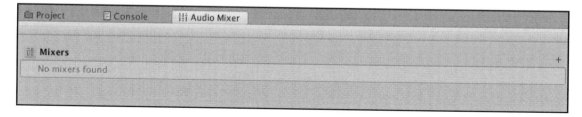

Clicking that icon enables you to create a mixer.

When you have a mixer in your project, the **Audio Mixer** window reveals four sections on the left. As shown in the following screenshot, these are **Mixers**, **Snapshots**, **Groups**, and **Views**. All the mixers in your project will be listed here. The **Snapshots** are a collection of parameters that you can use in your mixer. An **Audio Mixer Group** can be used to modify audio source sounds prior to them reaching the listeners. The final section is **Views**. A **View** is just a saved state of the mixer groups:

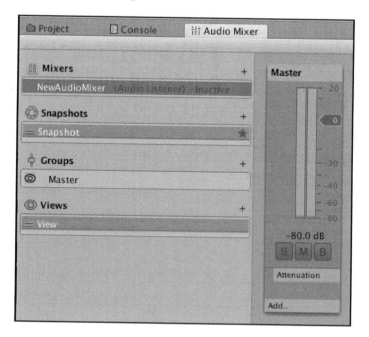

To the right of the **Audio Mixer** window, you see a single mixer in our project. When you click the **Add** button, you will see a popup, shown here, that reveals several options:

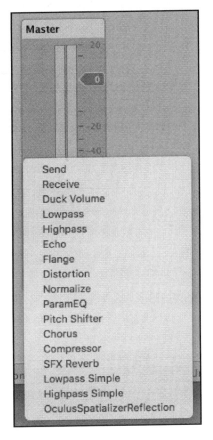

We will not use these options in our game, but they are worth exploring if you intend to implement advanced audio effects in your game.

Planning our game's audio

Planning a game's audio is an important part of game design. Just because we can do something with regards to audio, does not mean we should. Too much audio can be as off-putting as not enough.

The audio selected for the Cucumber Man game is intended to provide sufficient demonstration of how to import, configure, and script a game for various audio effects. To that end, the following audio will be implemented in our Cucumber Man game:

- Animations that require sounds:
  - Cucumber Man
    - Jump
    - Throw
    - Die
    - Respawn
  - Cucumber Beetles
    - Eat
    - Standing Run
    - Die

- Events that require sounds:
  - Player Defeat
  - Player Victory

We will perform the implementation in the next section.

Implementing our game's audio

In this section, we will implement the audio requirements listed in the previous section. We will import, configure, and script our game to complete the implementation. Before we get started, you should open your Unity game project. Alternatively, you can download the **Starting-Chapter-12** Unity project available from the publisher's companion site.

We will implement our game's audio in three steps, each handled in subsequent sections:

- Importing audio assets
- Implementing Cucumber Beetle audio
- Implementing Cucumber Man audio

Importing audio assets

Our first task is to import the audio assets into our game project. Here are the steps:

1. Open the game project.
2. In the **Project** panel, right-click **Assets** and select **Create | Folder**.
3. Name the new folder `Audio`.
4. Right-click the `Audio` folder and select **Import Package | Custom Package**.
5. Navigate to the `cucumber_man_audio.unitypackage` file available from the publisher's site for this book. You should see the following screenshot pop up in your Unity interface:

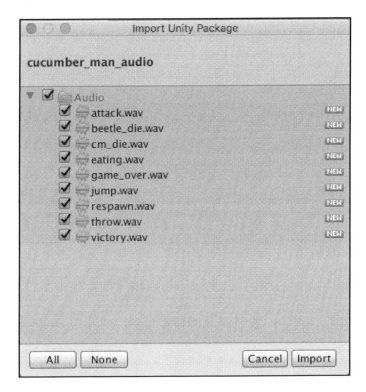

6. In the **Import Unity Package** dialog window, ensure all audio files are selected and click the **Import** button.
7. In the **Project** panel, select the first audio file. Then, in the **Inspector** panel, use the interface to play the audio clip.

8. Repeat step 7 for each of the nine audio clips. This will familiarize you with each sound and ensure they can play on your computer.

Now that we have our audio assets in our game project, let's review how each of them will be used. The following table maps each audio file to the appropriate in-game animation or event:

In-Game animation/Event	Related GameObject	Audio asset
Jump animation	Cucumber Man	`jump.wav`
Throw animation	Cucumber Man	`throw.wav`
Die animation	Cucumber Man	`cm_die.wav`
Respawn event	Cucumber Man	`respawn.wav`
Eat animation	Cucumber Beetle	`eating.wav`
Standing Run animation	Cucumber Beetle	`attack.wav`
Die on Ground animation	Cucumber Beetle	`beetle_die.wav`
Die Standing animation	Cucumber Beetle	`beetle_die.wav`
Player Defeat event	Cucumber Man	`game_over.wav`
Player Victory event	Cucumber Man	`victory.wav`

Implementing the Cucumber Beetle audio

In this section, we will configure the Cucumber Beetle prefab so that it supports audio when the Cucumber Beetles eat, when they run while standing, and when they die. Here are the steps:

1. Select the beetle prefab in the **Project** panel's `Assets | Prefabs` folder. If you have more than one prefab, be sure to use the one that is used in your game.
2. In the **Inspector** panel, scroll to the bottom and click the **Add Component** button.
3. Select **Audio | Audio Source**.
4. Uncheck the **Play On Awake** box.

Normally, we would assign an `AudioClip` to our **Audio Source** component. Since our Cucumber Beetles will have more than one audio clip, we will not assign one here.

Our next step is to edit the `BeetleNPC` script. Open that script file and make the following modifications:

5. Add the following member variables:

```
public AudioSource audioSource;
public AudioClip eating;
public AudioClip attack;
public AudioClip die;
```

6. Add the following statement to the `Start()` method:

```
audioSource = GetComponent<AudioSource> ();
```

7. Edit the `OnTriggerEnter()` method as shown here. You will see two `audioSource.PlayOneShot()` statements, one each for the `eating` and `attack` audio clips:

```
void OnTriggerEnter(Collider theObject) {
    if (theObject.gameObject.CompareTag ("Cucumber")) {
        cucumberToDestroy = theObject.gameObject;
        BeetlePatrol.isEating = true;
        animator.Play ("Eating on Ground");
        audioSource.PlayOneShot (eating);
        StartCoroutine ("DestroyCucumber");
    } else if (theObject.gameObject.CompareTag ("Cherry")) {
        _ptsManager = GameObject.Find
        ("Score_Value").GetComponent<PointsManager>();
        PointsManager.currentScore = PointsManager.currentScore + 10;
        BeetlePatrol.isAttacking = true;
        cherryHit = true;
        animator.Play ("Stand");
        audioSource.PlayOneShot (attack);
    }
}
```

8. Edit the `DestroySelfOnGround()` method, shown as follows. Here you can see that we added the `audioSource.PlayOneShot(die)` statement:

```
IEnumerator DestroySelfOnGround() {
    yield return new WaitForSecondsRealtime (4);
    animator.Play ("Die on Ground");
    audioSource.PlayOneShot (die);
    Destroy (this.gameObject, 4);
}
```

9. Edit the `DestroySelfStanding()` method as shown in the following code block. Here, you can see we added the `audioSource.PlayOneShot(die)` statement:

```
IEnumerator DestroySelfStanding() {
    yield return new WaitForSecondsRealtime (4);
    animator.Play ("Die Standing");
    audioSource.PlayOneShot (die);
    Destroy (this.gameObject, 4);
    cherryHit = false;
}
```

Now that the scripting task is complete, we need to assign the designated audio clips to the variables we created:

10. In the **Inspector** panel, scroll until you see the **Beetle NPC (Script)** component.
11. Drag the `eating` audio clip from the **Project** panel's `Assets | Audio` folder to the appropriate spot in the **Beetle NPC (Script)** component.
12. Repeat step 11 for the `attack` and `beetle_die` audio clips. Your **Beetle NPC (Script)** component should look like the following:

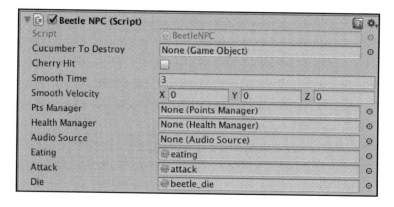

All that's left is for you to test this new functionality by playing the game.

Implementing the Cucumber Man audio

In this section, we will configure the Cucumber Man prefab so that it supports audio when the Cucumber Beetles eat, when they run while standing, and when they die. Here are the steps:

1. Select the Cucumber Man in the **Hierarchy** panel.
2. In the **Inspector** panel, scroll to the bottom and click the **Add Component** button.
3. Select **Audio | Audio Source**.
4. Uncheck the **Play On Awake** box.

> Normally, we would assign an `AudioClip` to our **Audio Source** component. Since our Cucumber Man will have more than one audio clip, we will not assign one here.
>
> Our next step is to edit the `BeetleNPC` script. Open that script file and make the following modifications:

5. Add the following member variables:

```
public AudioSource audioSource;
public AudioClip dying;
public AudioClip respawning;
public AudioClip gameOver;
```

6. Create a `Start()` method, shown as follows:

```
void Start () {
    audioSource = GetComponent<AudioSource> ();
}
```

7. Edit the `Update()` method, as shown here, so that it includes the three `audioSource.PlayOneShot()` statements:

```
if (livesRemaining == 2) {
    Destroy (GameObject.Find ("Life3"));
    anim = GetComponent<Animator> ();
    anim.Play ("CM_Die");
    audioSource.PlayOneShot (dying);
    StartCoroutine ("ReSpawnCucumberMan");
}
if (livesRemaining == 1) {
    Destroy (GameObject.Find ("Life2"));
    anim = GetComponent<Animator> ();
```

```
        anim.Play ("CM_Die");
        audioSource.PlayOneShot (dying);
        StartCoroutine ("ReSpawnCucumberMan");
    }
    if (livesRemaining == 0) {
        Destroy (GameObject.Find ("Life1"));
        anim = GetComponent<Animator> ();
        anim.Play ("CM_Die");
        audioSource.PlayOneShot (gameOver);
    }
```

8. Edit the `ReSpawnCucumberMan ()` method as shown here. You can see that we added the `audioSource.PlayOneShot ()` statement:

```
IEnumerator ReSpawnCucumberMan () {
    int randomNumber = Random.Range (1, 4);
    if (randomNumber == 1) {
        yield return new WaitForSecondsRealtime (4);
        this.transform.position = SpawnPad1.transform.position;
    } else if (randomNumber == 2) {
        yield return new WaitForSecondsRealtime (4);
        this.transform.position = SpawnPad2.transform.position;
    } else {
        yield return new WaitForSecondsRealtime (4);
        this.transform.position = SpawnPad3.transform.position;
    }
    audioSource.PlayOneShot (respawning);
    anim.Play ("CM_Idle");
}
```

Now that our script changes for the `CucumberManManager` script file are complete, we need to assign the designated audio clips to the variables we created. Here are the steps:

9. In the **Inspector** panel, scroll until you see the **Cucumber Man Manager (Script)** component.

10. Drag the `cm_die` audio clip from the **Project** panel's `Assets | Audio` folder to the appropriate spot in the **Cucumber Man Manager (Script)** component.

11. Repeat step 10 for the `respawn` and `game_over` audio clips. Your **Cucumber Man Manager (Script)** component should look like this:

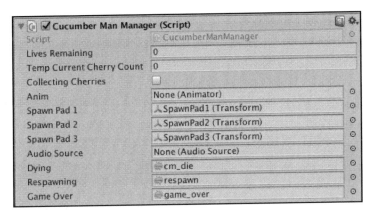

So far, we have taking care of the dying, respawning, and game over audio clips. Next, we will handle the jumping and throwing audio clips:

12. Open the `PlayerController` script for editing.

13. Add the following member variables:

```
public AudioSource audioSource;
public AudioClip jumping;
public AudioClip throwing;
```

14. Add the following statement to the `Start ()` method:

```
audioSource = GetComponent<AudioSource> ();
```

15. Add the following statement to the beginning of the `Jump ()` method:

```
audioSource.PlayOneShot (jumping);
```

16. Add the following statement to the beginning of the `Throw ()` method:

```
audioSource.PlayOneShot (throwing);
```

Now that our script changes for the `PlayerController` script file are complete, we need to assign the designated audio clips to the variables we created. Here are the steps:

17. In the **Inspector** panel, scroll until you see the **Player Controller (Script)** component.

18. Drag the `jump` audio clip from the **Project** panel's `Assets | Audio` folder to the appropriate spot in the **Player Controller (Script)** component.

19. Drag the `throw` audio clip from the Project pane's `Assets | Audio` folder to the appropriate spot in the **Player Controller (Script)** component. Your **Player Controller (Script)** component should look like the following:

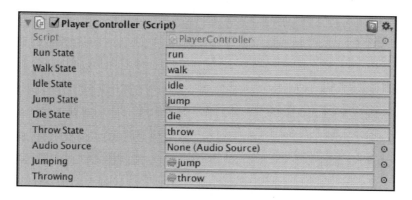

The last audio clip for us to implement is the victory clip. We will start by editing the `VictoryManager` script. Open that script file and make the following modifications:

20. Add the following member variables:

```
public AudioSource audioSource;
public AudioClip victory;
```

21. Create a `Start ()` method, as shown here:

```
void Start () {
    audioSource = GetComponent<AudioSource> ();
}
```

22. Edit the `Update ()` method, shown as follows. You will notice that we only added an audio clip playback for the victory condition, as we've already taken care of the defeat condition:

```
void Update () {
    beetleCount = BeetleManager.currentBeetleCount;
    if (beetleCount == 0) {
        Victory.text = ("You won!");
        audioSource.PlayOneShot (victory);
    }

    cucumberCount = CucumberManager.currentCucumberCount;
```

```
if (cucumberCount == 0) {
    Victory.text = ("You Lost!");
}
}
```

Now that our script changes for the `VictoryManager` script file are completed, we need to assign the victory audio clip to the variable we created. Here are the steps:

23. In the **Hierarchy** panel, select `HUD_Canvas` | `EndOfGame` | **Victory**.
24. In the **Inspector** panel, scroll until you see the **Victory Manager (Script)** component.
25. Drag the `victory` audio clip from the **Project** panel's `Assets` | `Audio` folder to the appropriate spot in the **Victory Manager (Script)** component. Your **Victory Manager (Script)** component should look like the following screenshot:

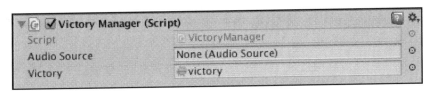

You are now ready to test this new functionality by playing the game.

This is an excellent time to save both your scene and your project.

Introduction to Unity's lights and shadows

Lighting in games is important as it is what allows GameObjects to be seen. If we did not have lights in our game, the game screen would be completely black. In Unity, it is easy to take lighting for granted because, when we create a new scene, there is a default **Main Camera** and a **Directional Light**.

Shadows in game worlds are another component that can be taken for granted because Unity's default settings regarding shadows is often sufficient for games.

In this section, we will look at light sources and shadows.

Adding light sources

In Unity, lights are GameObjects and are available in several different types. Here are the most common types of light sources:

- Directional light
- Point light
- Spot light
- Area light

Let's look at each of these lights.

Directional light

The Directional light is like the sun. As you can see from the following **Inspector** panel, there are several settings that can be adjusted for Directional lights beyond the Transform's **Position**, **Rotation**, and **Scale**:

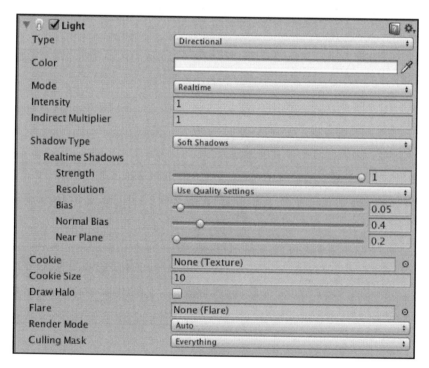

The following table provides information about key settings for Directional lights.

Setting	Details
Color	You can select a color for the light to emit. For realistic outdoor scenes, you would probably use a light yellow color.
Mode	You can select from **Realtime**, **Baked**, or **Mixed** lighting modes. When **Realtime** is selected, the direct light is computed each frame during the game. This provides a realistic game experience and is the default mode.
Intensity	Adjust this to control brightness.
Shadow Type	There are three options here: **Soft Shadows**, **Hard Shadows**, and **No Shadows**. **Soft Shadows** cast soft edges and avoid the sharp-edged shadows that are cast using **Hard Shadows**. As you would expect, **Soft Shadows** is more processor-intensive than **Hard Shadows**.
Realtime Shadows	This area provides additional control over your shadows.

Point light

Point lights are like light bulbs without lampshades. In fact, they are the ideal type of light to use to simulate a small, local source of light such as a table lamp, wall sconce, or chandelier. As you can see in the following screenshot of the **Inspector** panel, you can modify the **Range**, **Color**, and **Intensity**. You can also select from **Realtime**, **Baked**, or **Mixed** render modes:

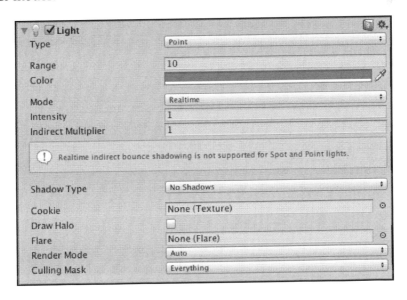

Spot light

A **Spot** light is like a flashlight and provides cone-shaped illumination. This type of light is ideal for simulating flashlights, automobile headlights, plane lights, search lights, and Spot lights. As you can see in the following **Inspector** panel screenshot, there is a **Spot Angle** property. Spot lights also have properties in common with other types of lights.

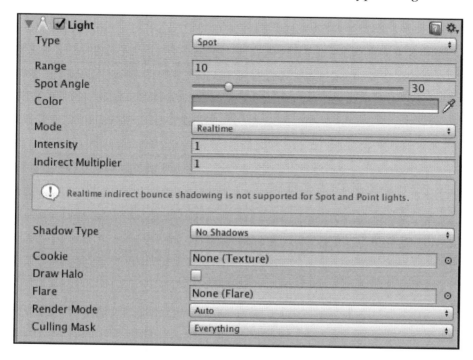

Area light

An **Area (baked only)** light is something that is used when you bake images into textures. This type of light is great for simulating light coming out of a building, such as from a window. Area lights are also good for LED stadium lighting. The properties Width and Height, shown in the following screenshot, are not present in **Directional**, **Point**, and **Spot** lights:

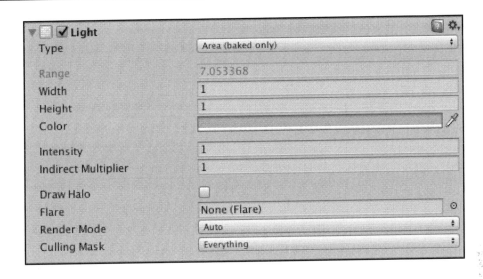

Shadows

Unity affords us great control over shadows in our game scenes. We can control which objects cast shadows, which objects can receive shadows, and various properties of the shadows. Shadows in Unity closely replicate the way shadows exist in the real world. As discussed earlier in this chapter, there are soft shadows and hard shadows.

Soft shadows result in greater realism, but at the cost of additional computations and processing. Hard shadows provide less realistic, but often acceptable, shadows during a game and are less processor intensive. Hard shadows are easy to identify in a game because the shadows cast will have sharp, blocky shadow edges.

Discovering Unity's special effects

Unity has a great capabilities for special effects in three categories: **Particle System**, **Trail Renderer**, and **Line Renderer**. These are available via the **GameObject** | **Effects** top menu.

Adding an **Effects** component to a GameObject is accomplished by using the **Add Component | Effects** option in the **Inspector** panel. As you can see in the following screenshot, the **Particle System**, **Trail Renderer**, and **Line Renderer** options are available via this method. There are also additional options, such as **Lens Flare** and **Halo**:

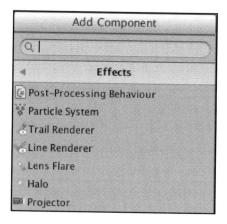

In this section, we will discuss the **Particle System** and **Trail Renderer** effects.

Particle System

Particle Systems use a vast number of tiny 2D images or meshes in a scene to simulate effects such as liquids, smoke, flames, pixie dust, fireworks, and clouds. The basic concept is that one simple 2D image or mesh can be used in large quantities to create a robust and dense visual effect. These 2D images or meshes are the particle, and they collectively form the Particle System.

Each particle in a Particle System is rendered from a specific point and has a limited lifespan. How long this lifespan lasts depends on your implementation, but it typically only lasts a few seconds.

As you can see from the following **Inspector** panel screenshot, there are several parameters that allow us to customize the behavior of Particle Systems. We will add a **Particle System** to our game later in this chapter:

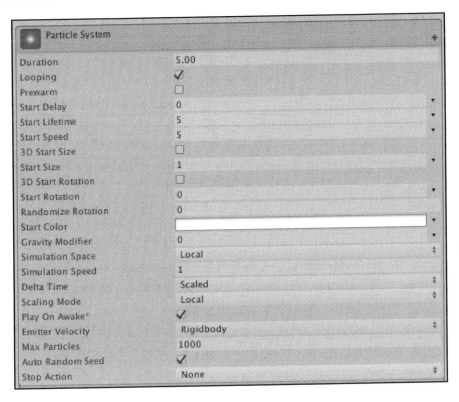

When we add a **Particle System** to our scene, Unity presents us with an interface, the
Particle Effect panel, in the lower-right corner of the **Scene** view. This interface allows us to
play, pause, and stop the Particle simulation, as well as adding additional parameter
settings while observing the changes to the simulation:

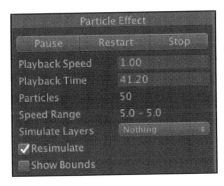

Unity 2018, in beta at the time of this book's publication, has support for GPU instancing of Particle System mesh rendering, support for Orbital Velocity, and enables particle emitter shapes, which permits texture reading for masking and color tinting.

Trail Renderer

A **Trail Renderer** is a visual effect that creates a trail behind a GameObject as it moves. Classic examples of this are a jet's afterburner, a car's exhaust, and the Tasmanian Devil's visual swoosh (dust cloud). The following **Inspector** panel screenshot illustrates the parameters that can be manipulated to customize a **Trail Renderer**:

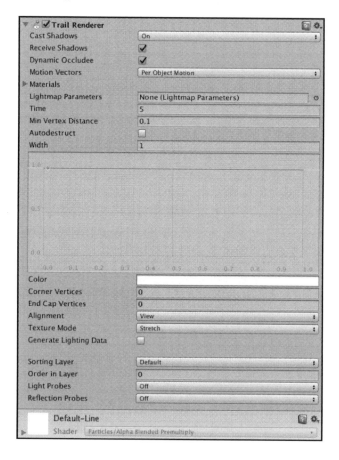

The primary **Trail Renderer** settings are described here:

Setting	Description
Cast Shadows	There are four options here: **On, Off, Two-Sided**, and **Shadows Only**. The default setting is **On**.
Receive Shadows	This is an on/off toggle.
Materials	You can select a particle shader for the material and adjust the size.
Time	This setting defines the length of the trail.
Autodestruct	You can select this option to have the trail GameObject destroyed once it has been idle for the number of seconds set in the **Time** setting.

Adding visual effects to our game

Our game already has a **Directional** light and, as discussed earlier in this chapter, it acts like the sun—shining light from high above our terrain. The shadows from our Cucumber Man, Cucumber Beetles, cherries, cherry trees, and cucumber patches can be seen on the grass. We do not need to make any changes to them.

The visual effects changes we will make in this section are:

- Adding a Point light to our cherry trees
- Adding a special effect using the Particle System

Adding a Point light to our cherry trees

Currently, the Cucumber Man can walk up to and under the cherry trees in our sandbox area. Those trees are very dense and, because the only source of light comes from our directional light, it is too dark for the Cucumber Man to see the cherries he is picking from the tree. This is just simulated for the sake of adding a point light. So, we will use the following steps to add a point light to our cherry trees in the sandbox area of our scene:

1. In **Scene** view, navigate to a cherry tree and zoom in so that you can see the base of the tree
2. Using the top menu, select **GameObject | Light | Point Light**
3. Relocate the **Point Light** so that it is at the center of the tree trunk

4. In the **Inspector** panel, select a **Color** such as a light red
5. In the **Inspector** panel, change the **Range** to 11
6. In the **Inspector** panel, increase the **Intensity** to 30
7. Reposition the point light so that it looks similar to the following image:

Repeat steps 1 through 7 for each cherry tree in your sandbox area. Test your game in game mode to see the results.

Add a special effect using the Particle System

In this section, we will add a particle system to our spawn pads so that a special effect is attached to them. Here are the steps:

1. In **Scene** view, navigate to a spawn pad and zoom in so you can see the pad clearly.
2. Using the top menu, select **GameObject | Effects | Particle System**.
3. Relocate the **Particle System** so that it is at the center and base of the spawn pad.

4. In the **Hierarchy** panel, drag the **Particle System** so that it is subordinate to a spawn pad.

5. In the **Inspector** panel, click the settings cog in the **Transform** component and select **Reset**. This resets the position of the **Particle System** to the **Transform** of the spawn pad.

6. In the **Inspector** panel, select a **Color** that contrasts with the red of the spawn pad and the green of the terrain and cherry tree, such as blue.

7. In the **Inspector** panel, change the **Max Particles** to 10,000.

8. In the **Inspector** panel, increase the **Shape | Shape** to **Edge**.

9. In the **Inspector** panel, increase the **Shape | Radius** to **1.5**.

When completed, your Particle System should look similar to the following screenshot:

Repeat steps 1 through 9 for each spawn pad in your sandbox area.

Summary

In this chapter, we planned and implemented audio and visual effects to enhance the overall gameplay. Specifically, we added audio to key events in our combat system and added lighting and particle special effects. We started with an overview of Unity's Audio System, then planned and implemented our game's audio. We then shifted to an introduction to lights and shadows in Unity and covered selected special effects. We concluded by adding a **Point** light to our cherry trees and a special effect to our spawn pads.

In Chapter 13, *Optimizing Our Game for Deployment*, you will learn how to diagnose performance problems and how to optimize scripts and graphic rendering. You will also learn how to deploy your game to multiple platforms.

13
Optimizing Our Game for Deployment

In the last chapter, we planned and implemented audio and visual effects into our game to enhance overall gameplay. Specifically, we added audio to key events in our combat system and added lighting and particle special effects. We started with an overview of Unity's audio system, then planned and implemented our game's audio. We then shifted to an introduction to lights and shadows in Unity and covered select special effects in Unity. We concluded by adding a point light to our cherry trees and a special effect to our spawn pads.

This chapter has two areas of focus: optimization and deployment. In the optimization sections, you will learn how to diagnose your Unity game for performance problems and how to optimize scripts and graphics rendering. In the deployment section, you will learn about the Unity build process, how to create a standalone player, and how to deploy your game to multiple platforms.

Specifically, in this chapter, we will cover the following topics:

- Using the Profiler window
- Optimizing scripts
- Optimizing graphics rendering
- Additional optimizations
- Creating builds

Using the Profiler window

Unity has a native tool that helps us to examine how our game performs. This is a Profiler tool and is accessible via the **Window** | **Profiler** top menu option. As you can see in the following illustration, there are 13 components available in the **Profiler** window:

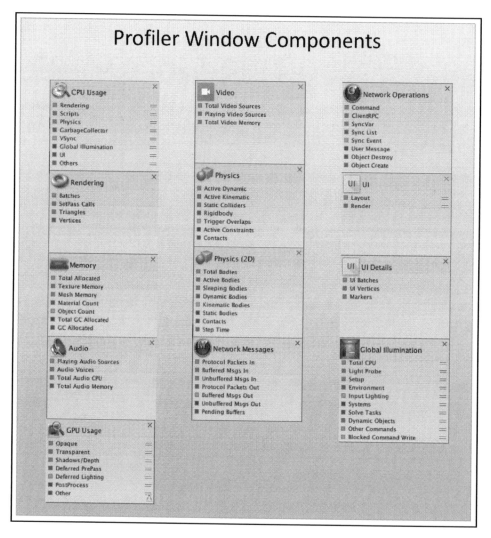

Profiler Components

The individual Profiler names provide a clear indication of what performance measure is being analyzed. In order to fully explore the **Profiler** window, let's get it up and running with the following steps:

1. Open your Unity game project. Alternatively, you can download the **Starting-Chapter-13** Unity project available from the publisher's companion site.

2. Using the top menu, select **Window** | **Profiler**. Depending on your system, this can open the **Profiler** in a new window or as a tab.

3. In the **Profiler** window or tab, use the **Add Profiler** button to add any Profilers not loaded by default. The Profilers that are already loaded will appear in gray and the unloaded Profilers will appear in black.

4. Put your game in game mode.

5. Scroll through the Profilers and, using the *x* in the top-right corner of the Profiler box, close the Profilers that provide little or no data on your game. For example, the **Network Operations** and **Network Messages** Profilers are not applicable to the Cucumber Man game. You might leave the following Profilers in your **Profiler** window:

   - **CPU Usage**
   - **GPU Usage**
   - **Rendering**
   - **Memory**
   - **Audio**
   - **Physics**
   - **UI**
   - **Global Illumination**

6. Let your game run for at least a minute or more, then exit the game. It does not matter whether you play the game while it is running or just sit back and watch the cucumber beetles search for and eat cucumbers. You will have the Profiler data available to you even after the game stops.

We can examine each Profiler to help determine how our game is performing and identify any performance problems. Let's look at the **GPU Usage** Profiler by clicking on it in the **Profiler** window. When we select a Profiler, detailed information is provided in the bottom section of the **Profiler** window.

By reviewing the detailed information provided, such as the GPU Usage information shown here, we can determine component-level performance. In the following example, we can see that our `Camera.Renderer` takes the greatest draw on the GPU. We can also drill down to greater fidelity by clicking the gray triangles to the left of each component:

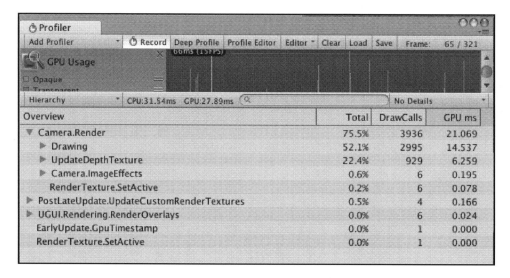

Getting more out of the Profilers

The **Profiler** window has several controls, segmented into left, center, and right sections of the interface. As you can see from the following screenshot, the **Add Profiler** drop-down button consumes the left-most section of the **Profiler** window's tool bar. We can use that button to add additional Profilers to the window:

Profiler Toolbar

The center section of the interface contains four functions, detailed here:

- Record: This button is enabled by default and is used to record or not record the active game's Profile information. When troubleshooting a specific section of your game, this button makes it easy to start and stop recording.
- **Deep Profile**: This function, when enabled, will Profile all script usage including function calls.

- **Profile Editor**: This function allows you to toggle the profiling of the Profiler.
- **Editor**: You can use this function to designate an IP address for the Profiler and log data to be sent. The default is for it to be sent to the editor.

The right-most section of the **Profiler** window's tool bar includes controls to **Clear**, **Load**, and **Save** the Profiler information. If you selected a frame, the frame information will be displayed. You also have the ability to step through the frames using navigational buttons in this section.

 Don't be surprised if your game performance is noticeably impacted when using the profiling tools.

Optimizing scripts

Unity games run several frames per second and many of our scripts are executed each frame. Even uncomplicated games, such as the Cucumber Man, can have several scripts running every frame, causing the computer's CPU to stay very busy. The goal is to ensure our scripts are not causing any unnecessary CPU load.

Our game has 145 scripts, but most of them are part of the standard asset package and are not assigned to any game objects. The scripts we want to review are the ones we put in the Assets | Custom Scripts folder. Reviewing that folder reveals that there are only 14 scripts:

- BeetleManager
- BeetleNPC
- BeetlePatrol
- CameraFollower
- CherryControl
- CherryManager
- CucumberManager
- CucumberManManager
- HealthManager
- PlayerController
- PlayerMotor
- PointsManager

- ThrowCherry
- VictoryManager

Our goal is to reduce the number of instructions the CPU has to execute, especially when we are dealing with several executions per frame and multiple frames per second. Here are some things to check when reviewing your Unity scripts:

- Ensure all function calls are necessary.
- As appropriate, move function calls out of the `Update()` method.
- As appropriate, move statements out of loops to limit the number of times they are executed.
- Use NPCs only as needed. Our game is relatively simple and we do not have hoards of cucumber beetles. You might try an experiment where there are 10,000 cucumber beetles in your game. Since each one of them has AI-associated code, the CPU will be very busy.

Optimized code example

The following script is not optimized. Review the script to see what can be done to optimize it. Then, review the information provided after the script:

```
public class CucumberManager : MonoBehavior {
    public static int currentCucumberCount;
    Text Cucumber_Count;
    public GameObject[] cucumbers;

    void Update() {
        Cucumber_Count = GetComponent<Text>();
        currentCucumberCount = 1;
        cucumbers = GameObject.FindGameObjectsWithTag("Cucumber");
        Cucumber_Count.text = cucumbers.Length.ToString();
        currentCucumberCount = cucumbers.Length;
    }
}
```

Hopefully you were able to spot the inefficient, unoptimized component of the script. In the preceding example, all the statements other than the variable declarations occur in the `Update()` method. Consider the optimized version of the following script:

```
public class CucumberManager : MonoBehavior {
    public static int currentCucumberCount;
    Text Cucumber_Count;
```

```
public GameObject[] cucumbers;

void Awake() {
    Cucumber_Count = GetComponent<Text>();
    currentCucumberCount = 1;
}

  void Update() {
      cucumbers = GameObject.FindGameObjectsWithTag("Cucumber");
      Cucumber_Count.text = cucumbers.Length.ToString();
      currentCucumberCount = cucumbers.Length;
  }
}
```

In the optimized version of this script, the `GetComponent()` method call and the `currentCucumberCount` variable initialization are moved over to the `Awake()` method. Those statements only need to run once. Putting them inside the `Update()` method would have caused undue strain on the CPU.

It is important for a game's overall performance to have optimized scripts. Checking for script optimization at the end of a project is a good idea. Ideally, you will ensure your scripts are optimized as your write, as opposed to reviewing them later.

Optimizing graphics rendering

Three graphics rendering concepts that should be explored when aiming to enhance game performance are occlusion culling, lighting, and mesh renderers. Each of these concepts are covered in the following sections.

Occlusion culling

Cameras are a critical game object in our Unity games. They allow the player to see the game environment. Unity works diligently during gameplay to render objects within a camera's frustum. Graphics rendering can represent a tremendous performance issue. It is therefore important that we pay special attention to our camera's occlusion culling parameter. When enabled, Unity will not render objects that are occluded, or not seen by the camera. An example would be objects inside a building. If the camera can currently only see the external walls of the building, then none of the objects inside those walls can be seen. So, it makes sense to not render those. We only want to render what is absolutely necessary to help ensure our game has smooth gameplay and no lag.

Lighting

When we create our scenes in Unity, we have three options for lighting. We can use real-time dynamic light, the baked lighting approach, or a mixture of real-time and baked. Our games perform more efficiently with baked lighting compared to real-time dynamic lighting, so if performance is a concern, try using baked lighting where you can.

Area lights are distinct from the other types of light in that they can only be baked. This means that real-time rendering will not take place during gameplay. The reason for this is to conduct all the processing regarding area lights prior to gameplay. This processing, if accomplished in a game in real time, would likely result in sufficient lag.

Mesh renderer

The mesh renderer component of a game object can be viewed in the Inspector panel. There are multiple settings that can be adjusted to enhance performance.

The Cast Shadows setting can be set to On, Off, Two-Sided, or Shadows Only. The default is On, so you should disable this for all objects that do not need to cast shadows.

The receive shadows is a toggle that tells Unity whether you want that object to receive shadows or not. As you would expect, this takes extra processing to display during the game. So, if you do not need an object to receive shadows, deselect this for greater performance.

Additional optimizations

Two additional areas where you can optimize your game is with level of detail and using static colliders. Both of these concepts are discussed in the sections that follow.

Level of detail

Level of detail refers to how much detail is rendered on any given game object. The greater the number of polygons, the greater the level of detail your game objects will have. In order to reduce render times, you should consider what elements of detail need to be part of the 3D model and which ones can simply be included in the texture.

There are also **level of detail (LOD)** models. This is when you use multiple models of the same object in a game, each with a different level of detail. Think about a game where the player stands on the coast, looking at the horizon. A ship that is 12 miles away does not need the same level of detail as when it is just a few yards away.

Static colliders

Static colliders are game objects with a collider but without a rigidbody. As the name suggests, these game objects do not move. Because the physics engine knows these objects will not move, pre-calculations can be made to make the game more efficient.

So, to increase efficiency, you should strive to use static colliders when possible.

Creating builds

Creating a build for your game is not complicated when you are working on your own projects. You essentially ensure your assets (for example, 3D models, textures, animations, and scripts) are on your computer and you use Unity to create the build. This process is much more complicated when you are working on large and distributed teams. This section covers the individual developer where all assets are on a single computer.

Understanding the Unity build process

The Unity build process seems pretty easy. We can simply select **File | Build & Run** from the top menu and get great results. Unity actually does a lot of work to create a build. Here are the basic steps the Unity game engine takes to create a build of your game:

1. Generates a blank build copy of your game
2. Sequences through the scene list, optimizing them before integrating them with the build
3. Calculates and stores data regarding what assets are needed for each scene

There are additional aspects of the build process that we should be aware of. For example, if we assign the EditorOnly tag to a game object, it will not be integrated into the build.

Once you have completed your game, you can select the **Build & Run** or **Build Settings** options from the **File** pull-down menu:

Build settings

We access the **Build Settings** dialog window via the **File | Build & Run** top menu option. With that interface open, displayed as follows, we can make several decisions regarding our build:

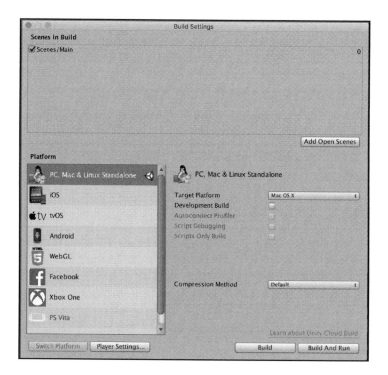

The top section of the **Build Settings** interface lists the Scenes that will be included in the build. You can use the **Add Open Scenes** button to quickly add those scenes to the build. You can also select and deselect scenes to ensure you only include the scenes needed for the build.

In the next section of the **Build Settings** interface, you'll select a platform. Each of the platform options is covered in the next few sections.

PC, Mac, and Linux standalone

For this platform group, you will need to select **Mac OS X**, **Windows**, or **Linux**. As you can see from the following screenshot, each operating system selection has its own set of options:

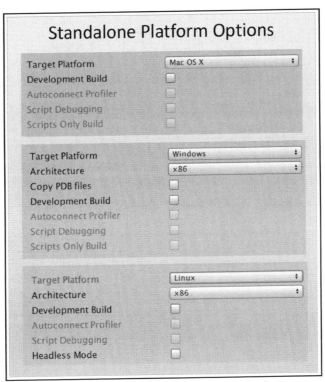

For **Mac OS X**, you will decide whether this is a development build or not. If it is, you will have the additional options of **Autoconnect Profiler**, **Script Debugging**, and **Scripts Only Build**.

For **Windows**, you will select whether it is a 32-bit or 64-bit build and select whether you want to copy the PDB files. You will also decide whether this is a development build or not. If it is, you will have the additional options of **Autoconnect Profiler**, **Script Debugging**, and **Scripts Only Build**.

For Linux, you will select whether it is a 32-bit, 64-bit, or Universal build. You will also decide whether this is a development build or not. If it is, you will have the additional options of **Autoconnect Profiler**, **Script Debugging**, and **Scripts Only Build**. Lastly, you will select whether your build will support **Headless Mode**.

> Headless mode refers to a server-based game that does not contain visual elements.

iOS

When developing for iOS devices (iPad, iPad Pro, iPad Mini, iPhone, iPod Touch) you need to have Xcode installed on your computer. Xcode is also required for developing for macOS devices.

> You can obtain the latest version of Xcode here: `https://developer.apple.com/develop/`.

Using the **Build Settings** interface, you can identify your version of Xcode and decide whether you want to run it as a release or in debug mode. You can decide whether you want your Xcode project to directly reference the Unity iOS runtime library from the Unity Editor's install location. This is accomplished by selecting the **Symlink Unity libraries** checkbox. You should not use this for your final build:

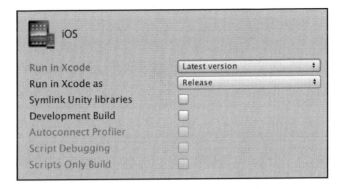

You will also decide whether this is a development build or not. If it is, you will have the additional options of **Autoconnect Profiler**, **Script Debugging**, and **Scripts Only Build**.

tvOS

As you can see here, the options for tvOS are the same as iOS:

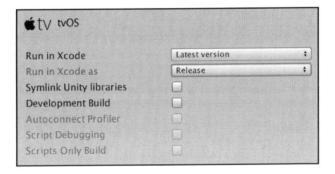

Android

When developing for Android devices, you have several **Texture Compression** options to choose from. You can also identify **16-bit**, **32-bit**, or 32-bit half resolution as the **ETC2 fallback**. You can use the internal **Build System** or Gradle, which is a build tool used in Android Studio and elsewhere:

You will also decide whether this is a development build or not. If it is, you will have the additional options of **Autoconnect Profiler**, **Script Debugging**, and **Scripts Only Build**.

You can learn more about developing for Android devices here: `https://developer.android.com/`.

HTML 5/WebGL

When developing for HTML 5/Web GL, you will decide whether this is a **Development Build** or not. If it is, you will have the additional options of **Autoconnect Profiler** and **Scripts Only Build**:

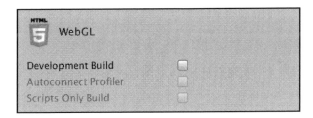

Facebook

When developing a Unity game that will be published on Facebook, you will need the Facebook SDK and an App ID. For Target Platform, you can select Gameroom (Windows) or WebGL:

You will also decide whether this is a development build or not. If it is, you will have the additional options of **Autoconnect Profiler** and **Scripts Only Build**.

Consult the following URL for instructions on how to register and configure a Facebook app: `https://developers.facebook.com/docs/apps/register`.

Xbox One

Access to the Xbox One player is handled through the Microsoft ID@Xbox program.

 Visit the following link to learn how to develop games for Xbox One: `https://www.xbox.com/en-US/developers`.

PlayStation 4 and PlayStation Vita

Access to PlayStation 4 and PlayStation Vita players is handled through Dev NET and requires a Unity Plus or Unity Pro license.

Player Settings

Using the **Edit** | **Project Settings** | **Player** menu option, you have access to the Unity **Player Settings** in the **Inspector** panel. In this context, the term player does not refer to the person playing the game, but to the software that runs the game.

As you can see in the following screenshot, there are data fields for the name of the company and the game's title. Icons and cursors are also uploaded here:

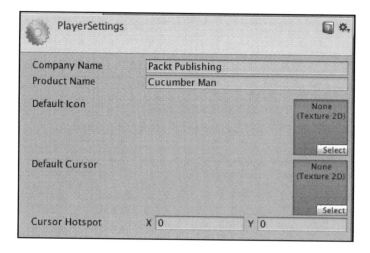

Beneath the general settings area of the **PlayerSettings** interface are six buttons. As you can see in the following image, there is one button for each of the platforms that Unity can generate a player for. This does not include Xbox or PlayStation players:

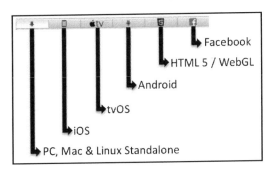

For each of the platforms, there is a set of player configuration settings sections. This includes the following:

- **Resolution and Presentation**
- **Icon**
- **Splash Image**
- **Debugging and crash reporting**
- **Other Settings**

Not every settings section will be applicable to all platform types. Also, the Other Settings content varies based on the platform you are developing for.

If you are developing for multiple platforms, you will need to review the settings for each platform type.

Summary

In this chapter, we focused on optimization and deployment. We learned how to diagnose Unity games for performance problems and how to optimize scripts and graphic rendering. We also explored how to deploy our Unity games, including learning about the Unity build process, how to create a standalone player, and how to deploy games to multiple platforms.

In Chapter 14, *Virtual Reality*, we will examine Unity's capabilities with regards to virtual reality. We will start with a quick introduction to virtual reality including hardware requirements, and then look at how to create a virtual reality game using the Unity game engine. We will also look at the available starter content from the Unity Asset Store.

14
Virtual Reality

In the previous chapter, we explored several processes and techniques to diagnose our Unity games to help improve performance. We did this by optimizing scripts, garbage collection, and graphic rendering. We also looked at how to deploy our Unity game for multiple distribution platforms.

In this chapter, we are going to examine Unity's capabilities in regards to virtual reality. We will start with a quick introduction to virtual reality, including hardware requirements, and then look at how to create a virtual reality game using the Unity game engine. This is a bonus chapter and does not require you to own expensive virtual reality hardware. The purpose of the chapter is to give you an introduction to virtual reality and its possibilities with the Unity game engine.

Specifically, we will cover the following content in this chapter:

- Welcome to virtual reality
- Enabling virtual reality in Unity
- Starter content

Welcome to virtual reality

Virtual reality is not a new term, but it has gained tremendous attention lately. The advent of 3D graphics and stereoscopes contributed to the state of virtual reality as it exists today. The following diagram illustrates the basic concept of stereoscopes and how they create virtual 3D images:

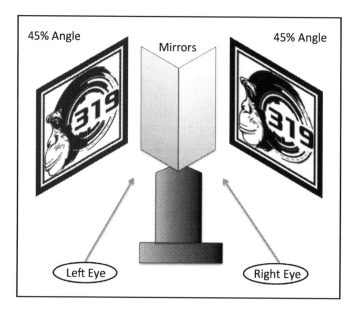

As you can see, the same image is presented twice from different angles. This results in a virtual 3D image. The same concept exists for videos.

Conceptually, virtual reality is fairly simple. It is the creation of a synthetic and believable virtual environment or world. There are two basic components: hardware and software. The hardware components typically involve a headset that has an individual lens for each eye and one or more display panels behind each lens. Most often, we are inserting our mobile phone into the headset, instead of having the display panels. Specialized lenses are used to focus the light from the mobile phone surface onto your eye's retina.

To see the value of the specialized lenses, hold your mobile phone up to your eyes at a distance of approximately 2 inches. Your eyes are not able to focus on the screen—it is too close. Specialized lenses allow us to see the screen that close.

Some advanced headsets include movement and positional tracking hardware, such as the following examples:

- **Inertial Measurement Units (IMUs)** for high-speed motion tracking
- Various techniques for positional tracking such as with cameras, lasers, and magnetic fields

The software component consists of the game or simulation software the user interacts with. Creating that content and instantiating it in a virtual reality game or simulation is where the heavy lifting is for virtual reality.

Development tools

There is an increasing number of virtual reality hardware and software solutions available. At the time of this book's publication, Unity had native support for Oculus, Gear VR, OpenVR, and PlayStation VR. What follows are some brief descriptions of each of them.

Oculus

Oculus is the umbrella term that incorporates Oculus VR, a division of Facebook, and Oculus Rift, the virtual reality headset.

You can learn more about Oculus at the following official websites:

- **Hardware site**: `https://www.oculus.com/`
- **Developer site**: `https://developer.oculus.com/`

GearVR

GearVR is a headset that a mobile phone is inserted into. It requires one of the following:

- Samsung Galaxy S6
- Samsung Galaxy S6 Edge
- Samsung Galaxy S6 Edge+
- Samsung Galaxy S7

- Samsung Galaxy S7 Edge
- Samsung Galaxy S8
- Samsung Galaxy S8+

You can learn more about GearVR at the official website, `http://www.samsung.com/global/galaxy/gear-vr/`.

OpenVR

OpenVR is a **Software Development Kit (SDK)** containing a runtime and an **Application Programing Interface (API)**. OpenVR supports generic access to multiple VR hardware. This type of access negates the need to develop for specific virtual reality hardware.

You can learn more about OpenVR at the GitHub website, `https://github.com/ValveSoftware/openvr`.

PlayStation VR

PlayStation virtual reality, formally referred to as Project Morpheus, is Sony Interactive Entertainment's VR solution for the PlayStation hardware platforms.

You can learn more about PlayStation VR at the following official websites:

- **Hardware**: `https://www.playstation.com/en-us/explore/playstation-vr/`
- **Development**: `https://www.playstation.com/en-us/develop/`

Enabling virtual reality in Unity

Enabling virtual reality in Unity consists of two basic steps. The process begins with ensuring you have the requisite SDK or runtime environment installed, with the next step being the configuration of the Unity project. We will look at both of these steps in this section, followed by hardware and software recommendations from Unity technologies.

Requisite SDKs

As an example, if you are developing a virtual reality game for the Oculus Rift device, you will have the following packages available to you at the Oculus developers, site (`https://developer.oculus.com/downloads/`):

- **Oculus Utilities for Unity**: This is the core package for developing virtual reality games. Since Unity supports Oculus Rift natively, this package is optional. In addition to containing the Oculus `OVRPlugin`, this package includes prefabs, scripts, sample scenes, and other assets to help get you started.
- **Oculus Avatar SDK**: This SDK is helpful if you are implementing a hand presence or make use of touch controllers in your virtual reality game. You can also use this package to incorporate avatars created in Oculus Home.
- **Oculus Platform SDK**: The platform SDK is used for incorporating the following components into your virtual reality game: Achievements, cloud storage, in-app purchases, matchmaking, and voice chat. This SDK contains a sample app, which can help you get started a lot faster than developing any of these functionalities from scratch.
- **Oculus Sample Framework for Unity 5 Project**: This sample project lets you learn by seeing working scenes. It also demonstrates virtual reality functionalities, such as crosshairs, driving, first-person movement, and hand presence.
- **Cubemap Viewer**: This tool provides a virtual reality cubemap viewing application. You can use this to preview cubemap snapshots before submitting them as part of the app store submission process.
- **Oculus Remote Monitor for OS X**: This client tool connects to mobile virtual reality applications that are running on remote devices for the purposes of capturing data, displaying data, and storing data. The reported purpose of this data capturing, displaying, and storing is for performance evaluation and testing.
- **Oculus Remote Monitor for Windows**: This tool is similar to the Oculus Remote Monitor for OS X.

There are also several audio packages available to you. These packages are:

- Oculus Ambisonics Starter Pack
- Oculus Audio Loudness Meter
- Oculus Audio Pack 1
- Oculus Audio Profiler for Windows
- Oculus Lipsync Unity

- Oculus OVRVoiceMod for Unity 5
- Oculus Spatializer DAW Mac
- Oculus Spatializer DAW Windows
- Oculus Spatializer FMOD
- Oculus Spatializer Native
- Oculus Spatializer Unity
- Oculus Spatializer Wwise

Configuring your Unity project

Once all the necessary SDKs are installed, you are ready to create a new Unity project. You do this the same way you would with any other Unity project. With the new project open, you will select **Edit** | **Project Settings** | **Player**. That will expose the **PlayerSettings** in the **Inspector** panel. As you can see in the following screenshot, there is an **Other Settings** option:

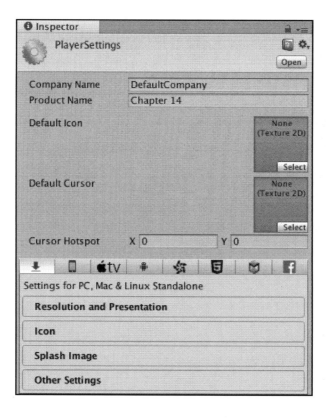

Clicking on the **Other Settings** button displays several options that can be toggled. To enable virtual reality, you will need to select the **Virtual Reality Supported** checkbox. As illustrated in the following screenshot, toggling that option on reveals the virtual reality SDKs:

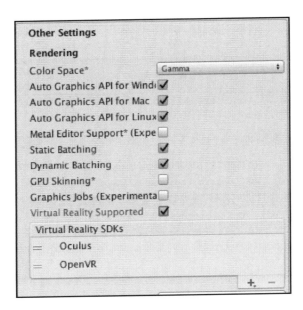

Recommendations from Unity technologies

Having capable hardware and up-to-date software are key components of ensuring a good gameplay experience in virtual reality games. There are a few key considerations to make that can greatly impact the user experience. These include:

- Ensuring graphics drivers are up to date
- Ensuring the frame rate matches the head-mounted display's refresh rate
- Having updated core processors
- Having updated graphics cards
- Ensuring you have sufficient volatile memory

The operating system on the playback device is also important. With Oculus as an example, the following are supported:

- Windows 7, 8, 8.1, and 10
- Android OS Lollipop 5.1 and later

You have probably noticed that Mac OS was not listed. At the time of writing, Oculus no longer supports OS X. This means that you will need to use Unity on a Windows PC to develop natively supported virtual reality games for Oculus.

Starter content

In the game industry, hardware manufacturers want you to buy their products and software toolmakers want you to use their software. And, with both hardware and software, their creators want you to develop games so people can play them. To be more specific, VR headset manufacturers would like to sell as many headsets as possible, so they encourage developers by providing them with free tools and assets. This is not an evil plan, rather a symbiotic relationship between hardware manufacturers and game developers.

Any look at the Unity Asset Store is a snapshot in time because of the dynamic nature of the store. At the time of writing, there were several free VR-related assets from various hardware manufacturers. This section reviews those assets.

Oculus VR

Oculus VR provides several free assets in the Unity Asset Store to support your development for Oculus Rift and Samsung Gear VR.

Oculus Sample Framework

The first pack is the Oculus Sample Framework. It contains three sample scenes as well as guidelines on how to accomplish fundamental VR-related functionality. This partial list of scripts gives you an idea of the types of functionality that you can discover using this free asset package:

- Boundary
- Camera rig
- Debug head controller

- Display
- Grabbable
- Grabber
- Haptics
- Haptics Clip
- Input
- On Complete Listener
- Overlay
- Platform Menu
- Reset Orientation
- Touch Pad
- Tracker

There are also animations, materials, meshes, prefabs, scenes, shaders, and textures as part of this asset package. In addition, there are also help text files.

Using this asset package is a great way to kick-start your virtual reality exploration.

Oculus Stereo Shading Re-Projection Sample

In August 2017, Oculus released the Oculus Stereo Shading Re-Projection Sample asset package to the Unity Asset Store. This package provided an innovative technique to optimize VR rendering. The technique uses a two-pass approach. In the first pass, rendered pixels from one eye are re-projected to the other eye. Then, in a second rendering pass, the gaps are filled in.

The Oculus Stereo Shading Re-Projection Sample asset package contains an instructional text file and all necessary content, such as materials, prefabs, shaders, scripts, textures, and a scene.

Oculus VR reports that this re-projection approach saves over 20% GPU cost per frame. Your results might vary, but the sheer possibility of optimization on this scale makes checking this asset package out a must.

Oculus Integration

The Oculus Integration asset package provides scripting examples for the Oculus Rift, Gear VR, and Touch. These examples include:

- Input and haptics
- Layered rendering
- Platform:
    - Achievements
    - Cloud Storage
    - Entitlement Check
    - Identities
    - In-App Purchases
    - Keys
    - Leaderboards
    - Matchmaking
    - Peer-to-Peer Networking
    - Rooms
    - Voice over IP (VoIP)
- Rendering Audio:
    - Room Model Settings for Reverb
    - Room Model Settings for Early Reflections
    - Spatializer Fine-Tuning
- Rendering Avatars:
    - Personalized Appearances
    - Social Presence
    - Touch and Hand Modeling
- Rendering Social
- Room Scale
- Tracking

This is a tremendous list of samples provided by Oculus, making our entry into virtual reality game development much easier and helping to ensure our success.

Vive software

Vive software provides several free assets in the **Unity Asset Store** to support your development for the HTC Vive.

Vive Stereo Rendering Toolkit

The Vive Stereo Rendering Toolkit includes a set of reusable game assets that can be used to create stereoscopic rendering effects. This toolkit is compatible with Unity's native VR rendering.

The stereoscopic rendering effects include the following:

- Basic example
- Callbacks example
- Mirror example
- Portal door example
- Renderer creation example

The meshes, materials, textures, shaders, and scripts associated with the stereoscopic rendering effects are included in the asset package.

Vive Input Utility

The Vive Input Utility is a plugin that gives you access to the Vive device status, including the Vive Tracker. The plugin has the following features:

- Collider event
- Pointer 3D
- Pose tracker
- Vive input utility
    - 2D drag and drop
    - 3D drag and drop
    - Teleport

The plugin also contains materials, prefabs, scripts, animations, models, sprites, and shaders to support the examples in the asset package. This package also includes several tutorials.

Vive Media Decoder

The Vive Media Decoder plugin can be used to support streaming on Windows. The plugin provides support for Windows 7 and DirectX 11. The two primary features of this plugin are:

- High-performance decoding
- Video streaming

NVIDIA

NVIDIA is the leading manufacturer of the GPUs that we use in our gaming computers. They have several free assets in the Unity Asset Store to help showcase the power of their GPUs. Two of these free assets are specific to VR and are covered in this section.

NVIDIA VRWorks

This asset package contains a text-based guide and scripts and shaders for creating the following:

- Lens-Matched Shading
- Multi-Res Shading
- Single-Pass Stereo
- VR SLI

To use this package, you must have the following:

- Windows PC
- DX11
- NVIDA Geforce 9 or higher
- VS 2015 redistribution
- Unity 2017.1.0b6 or higher

NVIDIA VR Samples

This package helps showcase the capabilities of modern GPUs and has the VRWorks package integrated. Samples included in this asset package include:

- Anti-aliasing
- Bloom and flares
- Blur
- Camera motion
- Color correction
- Contrast
- Cease shading
- Depth of field
- Edge detection
- Fish eye
- Global fog
- Grayscale
- Image effects
- Motion blur
- Noise and grain
- Noise and scratches
- Post effects
- Quads
- Screen overlay
- Screen space ambient obscurance and occlusion
- Sepia tone
- Sun shafts
- Tilt shift
- Tone mapping
- Triangles
- Twirl
- Vignette and chromatic aberration
- Vortex

The shaders, textures, models, scenes, animations, controllers, meshes, audio, fonts, materials, prefabs, and scripts supporting the examples are all included in the asset package.

Unity Technologies

Unity Technologies, the company that makes Unity and owns the Asset Store, has a robust VR Samples asset package. It contains a menu and four mini-games that can be used to help you get started in creating virtual reality games for Oculus DK2 and GearVR.

Here are the basics included in the asset package:

- Floating World-Space GUI
- Static World-Space GUI
- Flyer
- Maze
- Shooter

As you would expect, all the related shaders, audio, fonts, materials, textures, animations, controllers, mixers, meshes, models, prefabs, scenes, and scripts are included.

Summary

In this chapter, we examined Unity's capabilities in regard to virtual reality. We started with a quick introduction to virtual reality, including hardware requirements, and then looked at how to create a virtual reality game using the Unity game engine. We also took a look at the available starter content from the Unity Asset Store.

Having read this book, you will have the ability to create your own dynamic games using Unity and you will have an idea of what is required to start making virtual reality games. You are getting started at a good time: virtual reality is still a very young technology. For example, the human eye requires approximately 16,000 x 16,000 pixels per eye for a photographic-quality virtual reality experience, but best current VR displays provide up to 1080 x 780. So we have a long way to go with this technology, and its future is promising.

Other Books You May Enjoy

If you enjoyed this book, you may be interested in these other books by Packt:

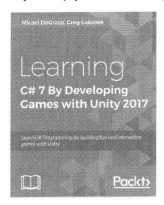

Learning C# 7 By Developing Games with Unity 2017 - Third Edition
Micael DaGraca, Greg Lukosek

ISBN: 978-1-78847-892-2

- Create your first 2D and 3D games in Unity
- Understand the fundamentals of variables, methods, and code syntax in C#
- Use loops and collections efficiently in Unity to reduce the amount of code
- Develop a game using object-oriented programming principles
- Implement simple enemy characters into the game to learn point-to-point movement and Tree behaviors
- Avoid performance mistakes by implementing different optimization techniques
- Export 3D models and animations and import them inside a Unity project

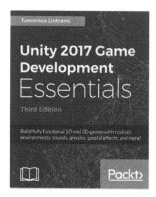

Unity 2017 Game Development Essentials - Third Edition

Tommaso Lintrami

ISBN: 978-1-78646-939-7

- Script games using C#
- Build your very first 2D and 3D games
- Work through the key concepts in game development such as animations, physics, and scripting
- Test and optimize your games to attain great performance
- Create fully functional menus, HUDs, and UI
- Create player character interactions with AI and NPC

Leave a review - let other readers know what you think

Please share your thoughts on this book with others by leaving a review on the site that you bought it from. If you purchased the book from Amazon, please leave us an honest review on this book's Amazon page. This is vital so that other potential readers can see and use your unbiased opinion to make purchasing decisions, we can understand what our customers think about our products, and our authors can see your feedback on the title that they have worked with Packt to create. It will only take a few minutes of your time, but is valuable to other potential customers, our authors, and Packt. Thank you!

Index

3

3D game engines
  about 12
  CryENGINE 12
  Lumberyard 13
  Microsoft's XNA Game Studio 13
  Unreal game engine 14
3D objects
  creating 128
  creating, in Unity 124
  creating, with prefabs 126

A

Account button 53
additional optimizations
  about 286
  level of detail (LOD) 286
  static colliders 287
Amazon Web Services (AWS) 13
Android developing
  reference link 292
animation controller
  working 171, 175, 176, 178
animations
  previewing 163
Animator component
  reviewing 160, 162
Application Programing Interface (API) 300
Area light 270
Artificial Intelligence (AI) 21
assets menu 35
assets
  about 120
  acquiring, from Unity Asset Store 130
  packages 121

B

Beetle Count
  scripting 219

C

camera projections
  orthographic projection 105
  perspective projection 105
cameras
  working 102
canvas
  adding 205
  working 205
Capsule Collider
  component parameters 153
  fine-tuning 153
character
  fine-tuning 148
cherry collection
  points, adding 231
cherry picked
  points, adding 232
Cherry Trees
  planting 134, 136
Cherry UI components
  adding 211
cherry-throwing capability
  adding 227
  creating 227
CherryControl script
  writing 229
Cloud button 53
combat hits
  points, adding 231
component menu 37
Cucumber Beetle game

idea 62
input controls 63
winning and losing 64
Cucumber Beetle UI components
adding 213
cucumber beetle
points, adding with cherry 234
Cucumber Count
scripting 218
cucumber patch area
creating, in sandbox 182
cucumber patches
adding, to terrain 181
planting 137, 140, 183
prefabs, preparing 137
Cucumber UI components
adding 213
custom assets
incorporating, in game 131

D

defeat based
scripting, for no lives remaining 247
scripting, on no cucumbers 246
development tools, virtual reality
GearVR 299
Oculus 299
OpenVR 300
PlayStation VR 300
Directional light 268
directional lighting 110
dynamic content
scripting 217

E

edit menu 33

F

Facebook, configuring
reference link 293
features, Unity
editor 21
graphics 21
file menu 33

first-person shooter (FPS) 14
frustum
orientating 105

G

game character
about 64
Cucumber Beetle 66
Cucumber Man 65
importing 144
game concept 61
game engine
first-person shooters (FPS) 9
for game genres 9
massively multiplayer online game (MMOG) 12
overview 8
third-person shooters (TPS) 10
Game View 43
game's audio
audio assets, importing 259
Cucumber Beetle audio, implementing 260
Cucumber Man audio, implementing 263, 266
implementing 258
planning 257
game's defeat conditions
designing 238
implementing 246
game's victory conditions
designing 238
implementing 243
game
considerations 74
plan, implementing 76
GameObject menu 36
GameObjects 120, 122
Gameplay
cherry trees, collisions detecting 222
collection of cherries, simulating 223
condition 70
creating 221
Cucumber Man, collisions detecting 222
Heads-Up Display (HUD) 72
Heads-Up Display (HUD), updating with cherry
count 225
inventory, updating 225

layout 68
point system 71
GearVR
  reference link 300
Gizmo Toggles 52
graphics processing unit (GPU) 12
Graphics Processing Unit (GPU) 23
graphics rendering
  lighting 286
  mesh renderer 286
  occlusion culling 285
  optimizing 285

H

Heads-Up Display (HUD)
  about 72, 203, 221, 237
  components 204
  designing 204
  updating, with lives remaining 248
Health Bar UI components
  adding 206, 208
health bar
  scripting 239
health
  decrementing 242
help menu 41
Hierarchy Window 47
High Dynamic Range (HDR) 104

I

imported assets
  Cherry Trees, planting 134, 136
  cucumber patches, planting 137, 140
  working with 133
Inertial Measurement Units (IMUs) 299
input controls
  changing 154, 156
  refining 154, 156
Inspector Window 48

L

layers 53
layouts 53, 54
Layouts option 38

Learning AWS Lumberyard Game Development
  reference link 13
level of detail (LOD) 286
light sources
  adding 268
  Area light 270
  Directional light 268
  Point light 269
  Spot light 270
lighting
  area lights 113
  directional lighting 110
  point lighting 111
  Spot light 112
  working with 109
Lives Remaining UI components
  creating 209
Lumberyard 13

M

massively multiplayer online game (MMOG) 12
Mastering CryENGINE
  reference link 13
menu 31
Mesh Renderer, components
  cast shadows 117
  Light Probes 117
  receive shadows 117
  Reflection Probes 117
Microsoft XNA 4.0 Game Development
  reference link 14
mini-map
  creating 215
motor controls
  fine-tuning 148, 150
multiple cameras
  using 108
Multisample Anti-Aliasing (MSAA) 105

N

non-player characters (NPCs)
  about 10, 166
  animating 168
  animation controller, working 171, 175, 176, 178

importing, into game 167
incorporating, into game 169
scripting 188, 189, 193, 195, 196
scripts, organized 188
NVIDIA 308
NVIDIA VR Samples 309
NVIDIA VRWorks 308

O

Oculus Integration 306
Oculus Sample Framework 304
Oculus Stereo Shading Re-Projection Sample 305
Oculus VR 304
Oculus
  references 299
OpenVR
  reference link 300

P

Paint Height tool 88
Paint Texture tool 90
player character's respawning
  scripting 249
player character
  about 65
  animating 157
player controller
  configuring 145
  script, reviewing 157, 160
player settings 294
player's health
  updating 239
PlayStation VR
  references 300
Point light 269
point lighting 111
points manager script
  creating 231
prefabs
  used, for 3D objects creating 126
Profiler window
  about 282
  using 280
project organization

about 77, 80
  custom assets 78
  standard assets 80
Project Window 45

R

real-time-strategy (RTS) 8
Reflection Probes
  implementing 114

S

scale
  fine-tuning 151, 152
Scene View 42
scoring UI components
  adding 210
Screen Real Estate 30
Scriptable Rendering Pipelines (SRP) 19
scripts
  code optimized, example 284
  optimizing 283
SDKs packages
  reference link 301
SDKs
  audio packages 301
  Cubemap Viewer 301
  Oculus Avatar SDK 301
  Oculus Platform SDK 301
  Oculus Remote Monitor, for OS X 301
  Oculus Remote Monitor, for Windows 301
  Oculus Sample Framework, for Unity 5 project
    301
  Oculus Utilities, for Unity 301
  requisites 301
shadows 116, 267, 271
Skybox
  creating 106
Software Development Kit (SDK) 300
Spot light 112, 270
system requisites
  about 22
  developing 23
  playback 24

T

terrain
  cherry trees, planting 179
  creating 83
  cucumber patches, adding 181
  cucumbers, adding 185
  height maps, working 84
  importing 84
  painting 90
  sandbox area, designating 178
  shaping 86
  smoothing 86
  spawn points, creating 88
  spawning sites, creating 180
  terraforming, for Cucumber Beetles 178
  terraforming, for Cucumber Man 164
third-person shooters (TPS) 10
toolbar
  about 49
  Account button 53
  Cloud button 53
  Gizmo Toggles 52
  layers 53
  layouts 53
  transform tools 50
Transform Gizmo Toggles 52
transform tools 50

U

Unite events
  reference link 22
Unity Asset Store
  using 128
Unity build
  Android 292
  creating 287
  Facebook 293
  HTML 5/WebGL 292
  iOS 290
  Linux standalone 289
  Mac 289
  PC 289
  PlayStation 4 294
  PlayStation Vita 294

  process 287
  settings 288
  tvOS 291
  Xbox One 294
Unity menu 32
Unity project
  configuring 302
Unity standard asset package
  working 142
Unity technologies
  about 310
  recommendations 303
Unity's audio system
  audio basics 254
  Audio Mixer 255
  discovering 254
Unity's lights
  about 267
  light sources, adding 268
Unity's special effects
  discovering 271
  Particle System 272
  Trail Renderer 274
Unity
  about 15, 20
  community 22
  downloading 25
  features 20
  installing 25
  Version 1.0 - 2005 15
  Version 2.0 - 2007 16
  Version 2017 - 2017 18
  Version 2018 span class= 19
  Version 3.0 - 2010 17
  Version 4.0 - 2012 17
  Version 5.0 - 2015 18
Unreal Engine, Game Development
  reference link 15
user interface (UI) 205

V

vegetation
  adding 95, 100
virtual reality
  about 298

development tools 299
  enabling, in Unity 300
  Requisite SDKs 301
visual effects
  adding 275
  point light, adding 275
  special effect adding, particle system used 276
Vive Input Utility 307
Vive Media Decoder 308
Vive software 307
Vive Stereo Rendering Toolkit 307

W

water plane
  adding 92
  saving 95
Window menu 38

X

Xbox One
  reference link 294
Xcode
  reference link 290

Made in the USA
Lexington, KY
06 July 2018